YESTERDAY ONCE MORE

YESTERDAY ONCE MORE

The Carpenters Reader

Edited by RANDY L. SCHMIDT

Foreword by Daniel J. Levitin

REVISED AND EXPANDED EDITION

CHICAGO
REVIEW
PRESS

An A Cappella Book

Published by Chicago Review Press, Incorporated
814 North Franklin Street
Chicago, Illinois 60610

ISBN 978-1-61374-414-7

A list of credits and copyright notices for the individual pieces in this collection
can be found on pages 351–54.

Cover design: Monica Baziuk
Cover photograph: The Carpenters, shot by Annie Leibovitz for *Rolling Stone*,
Downey, California, May 1974 (Michael Ochs Archives/Getty Images)
Interior design: PerfecType, Nashville, TN

Library of Congress Cataloging-in-Publication Data
Yesterday once more : the Carpenters reader / edited by Randy L. Schmidt ;
foreword by Daniel J. Levitin. — 2nd ed.
    p. cm.
 Articles, interviews, essays, and reviews originally published 1971–2000.
 Discography: p.
 Videography: p.
 Includes index.
 ISBN 978-1-61374-414-7 (pbk.)
 1. Carpenters (Musical group) 2. Singers—United States—Biography. I. Schmidt,
Randy (Randy L.)

ML421.C28Y47 2012
782.42164092'2—dc23

                          2012019681

Printed in the United States of America
5 4 3 2 1

To Frank Bonito, my new friend, trusted advisor, and advocate.

◆

To Frank Pooler, the "multitalented choir genius" and man I greatly admire as a fellow music educator, mentor, and friend.

◆

To Evelyn L. Wallace, longtime Carpenters secretary, on behalf of many who cherish the years of correspondence and friendship.

CONTENTS

PART V   A SONG FOR YOU

FOREWORD

In the summer of 1970, as the Beatles' "The Long and Winding Road" (backed with "For You Blue") tumbled from the top five, and just two months after the Kent State murders, "Close to You" reached number one on the American charts. The Carpenters sprang up in an era of protest songs and antiwar demonstrations with a repertoire composed primarily of love songs. (Were they the only ones heeding the musical advice of the newly disbanded Beatles, that "all you need is love"?) Though many songs from that time now sound dated because of their political messages or gimmicky use of instruments, the Carpenters' songs still sound fresh today.

Between 1969 and 1982, the Carpenters released an average of one album per year. With over 100 million records sold worldwide, they are among the top-selling musical groups of all time. In the summer of 1971, Karen and Richard hosted their own variety series on NBC, *Make Your Own Kind of Music*. They toured internationally throughout the '70s, and their 1976 tour of Japan was the largest-grossing tour in the country up to that point. The rapid and vast commercial success of the Carpenters catapulted A&M Records from a small middle-of-the-road label to a major radio force, ushered in a new era of signings at A&M, and bankrolled a number of artists, including the Police, Bryan Adams, and Supertramp.

"When Supertramp first went out on the road," Richard Carpenter recalled, "the head of marketing for A&M UK said to them, 'Whatever god you believe in, bow down to him before your shows and thank him for the Carpenters—because, without them, you wouldn't be here.'"

The Carpenters were an anomaly—at once anachronistic, hearkening back to the golden age of Tin Pan Alley, and also ahead of their time. Richard has been credited with inventing the power rock ballad

("Goodbye to Love"), and their music has influenced generations of artists from Madonna and k. d. lang to Sonic Youth and Chrissie Hynde
of the Pretenders. Their songs are considered true pop standards—I'd
be willing to wager that "(They Long to Be) Close to You" and "We've
Only Just Begun" have been performed at more weddings than any other
songs. More recently, the two songs were inducted into the Grammy
Hall of Fame.

One reason the music of the Carpenters has endured is because it was
never trendy, never tried to be anything it wasn't, and ultimately because
it strikes the right balance between immediate familiarity (it draws you
in) and rich complexity (it keeps you coming back for more). Then there
are Karen and Richard themselves. Karen had one of the purest and most
perfect voices in the history of recorded popular music; Richard's soaring talent as an arranger and producer places him among the most highly
respected musicians in recording history.

The first thing one hears is the Voice. It's instantly recognizable.
Karen possessed that rare quality shared by great singers. Consider
Frank Sinatra, Ella Fitzgerald, Perry Como—within hearing one note,
you can make no mistake about who is singing nor confuse the voice
with that of anyone else. And, like Perry Como, Karen sings with a clar-
ity so free from artifice or affectation that no one can imitate it. I think
that one of the reasons they've endured for so many decades is because
of the emotional depth and complexity that Karen brings to the songs.
With just a few words, she can eloquently capture the contradictions
of human emotional life. There's a world-weariness in her voice when
she sings "hangin' around" in the opening verse of "Rainy Days and
Mondays." You believe that she really has nothing to do, nowhere to
go, and no one to be with. But there is no sense of self-pity in Karen,
no stark depression lingering beneath the words—we understand that
the state is temporary. The gift of her singing is that she can sing about
being sad and make us feel uplifted. We're not happy that the singer was
jilted in "Superstar" ("Don't you remember you told me you loved me,
baby"), but the performance of the song is so beautiful that it makes us
feel happy.

Even with a great voice, a singer goes nowhere without the right
song and the right arrangement of that song. What has been well-known

throughout the music industry for four decades, yet generally unknown to the public, is the real secret of the Carpenters' career: Richard Carpenter. Richard worked tirelessly behind the scenes to select the material for the group, often recording songs that other industry pundits had turned down or ignored and bringing those songs to the top of the charts. When he couldn't find suitable material for his sister, Richard wrote songs for her that ended up becoming some of the group's biggest hits, including "Only Yesterday," "Yesterday Once More," and "Top of the World." On more than one occasion, he butted heads with record-company executives, insisting that he knew how to make a hit record and choose hit singles. In these disagreements, Richard was always right. Always. In recognition of his arranging skills, he has been nominated for a Grammy five times.

Richard is pleased with, and perhaps a bit surprised by, their longevity. "Our music seems to hold up very well—we're at 100 million units worldwide—and they're still selling in large numbers. The critics who dismiss us must not be getting it. Someone is buying those albums."

Since Karen's unexpected death in 1983, Richard has remained relatively active, releasing a solo album—*Time*—in 1987 on A&M and another in 1996, *Richard Carpenter: Pianist, Arranger, Composer, Conductor*. He served as executive producer for the 1989 television movie *The Karen Carpenter Story*, which painted a stark and honest picture of the siblings' personal lives, the often strained relationship with their parents, and Karen's struggle with anorexia.

The Carpenters have remained one of the most popular bands in Japan across the last two decades. "In 1995, we did a Japanese release, *Twenty-Two Hits of the Carpenters*, which was enormously successful," Richard explained. "It became the biggest-selling international album of 1996, and we sold 3.2 million units of these things. I received the Japanese equivalent of a Grammy for it and, of course, the rest of our catalog went well, too."

Richard has gone back into the studio to remix (and sometimes rerecord parts of) the Carpenters' repertoire for compilations such as 1991's boxed set *From the Top*. He oversaw the assembly and digital remastering of several new collections, including *Interpretations*, *As Time Goes By*, and *Carpenters Perform Carpenter*, a compilation of songs written by Richard. A Carpenters biography, painstakingly researched by Ray Coleman (who also wrote biographies of John Lennon and Eric Clapton), was released in 1994, followed by Randy Schmidt's critically acclaimed *Little Girl Blue: The Life of Karen Carpenter*, published in 2010.

This collection of essays, reviews, and interviews that Randy has lovingly collected make for the definitive Carpenters resource. Some of music's finest writers are represented here, expressing reactions ranging from adoration and intrigue to skepticism and outright dislike. This wide range of perspectives makes for fascinating and illuminating reading. Most of all, it gives us a chance to spend more time with Karen and Richard and with the dozens of great writers who were moved by them.

—Daniel J. Levitin

INTRODUCTION

B e it a TV biopic, a greatest-hits repackaging, a tribute album, or a string of documentaries, something comes along from time to time that fuels a resurgence of interest in the lives and music of Karen and Richard Carpenter. Whatever the catalyst for revival, it's nice to see their classic recordings celebrated by nostalgia buffs. But it is especially pleasing to see them shared with new generations of ardent music lovers. A new wave of appreciation surfaced in 2010 with the release of my book *Little Girl Blue: The Life of Karen Carpenter*. Not only did this new biography spark the curiosity of faithful diehards, but it brought a number of dormant admirers out of the woodwork.

As the author of *Little Girl Blue*, I have recently had the pleasure of meeting Carpenters enthusiasts—young and old—across the country at various book-related events. Some recall having "We've Only Just Begun" in their wedding. Others have fond memories of attending a Carpenters concert as adolescents. Longtime fans are dusting off their old Carpenters LPs, and new devotees are cranking playlists of the duo's hits on their iPods. The letters, e-mails, and interview requests I receive have no apparent geographic constraints. No matter the story, the sentiment is the same—fans share a warmth and affection for the Carpenters and their recordings. The music is timeless; its appeal universal.

More than a decade ago, I compiled and edited what was (and still is) the first Carpenters book of its kind: *Yesterday Once More*. Well, it's back again, just like a long-lost friend. But this time, it's revised and expanded—a history book of sorts, in the making for more than forty years.

Featuring the thoughts and words of journalists and critics, as well as Karen and Richard themselves, this collection holds more than fifty articles, essays, interviews, press releases, and reviews. The Carpenters are well suited to this pointillism-style biography. Their happiness and heartbreak, their triumphs and tragedies, were all recorded on the pages of magazines and newspapers all around the world.

Varying perspectives and opinions on the group were intentionally included to convey a sense of how the Carpenters were viewed during their heyday—and how they have been continually rediscovered in the years since Karen's untimely death in 1983. Through the years, the Carpenters had cynics questioning (and even occasionally attacking) them, but they had some eloquent defenders, too. Writers such as Tom Nolan, Ray Coleman, John Tobler, and Robert Hilburn explore the artistry of the Carpenters in critical assessments. Scholarly essays from music authorities, such as Frank Pooler and Daniel Levitin, analyze the technical elements of the group's innovative vocal and instrumental arrangements. Extensive interviews with Karen and Richard provide the duo's own assessment of their music, their goals, and their image. Reviews from *Variety* and other sources trace the Carpenters' concerts from their early Vegas shows to their concert-hall triumphs, such as their 1976 London Palladium engagement, and all the way through to some of Richard's more recent solo performances.

In addition to analyses from respected music-industry publications such as *Billboard*, *Blender*, *Rolling Stone*, and *Melody Maker*, this book includes some rather lightweight articles from entertainment- and teen-oriented magazines, such as *Rona Barrett's Hollywood*, *'Teen*, and *TV Radio Mirror*, as well as press releases from A&M Records. Also included are a number of articles from the *Southeast News* and other publications from Downey, California—they offer a unique "hometown" perspective on the Carpenters.

For me, researching and collecting published material on the Carpenters became an ongoing pursuit that began in 1989. Most of the groundwork was done before the Internet became a commonplace research tool. I visited public and college libraries, rummaging through dusty shelves and scrolling through what had to be miles of microfilm in hopes of finding even one more piece of the puzzle. At some point, I realized that some of the best and most insightful articles on the Carpenters had been out of widespread circulation for years (and some never received wide circulation in the first place).

The first edition of *Yesterday Once More* contained several pieces that were extensively edited or truncated for a variety of reasons. Almost all have been restored to their original form for this revised and expanded edition, though misspellings, style inconsistencies, and factual errors have been silently corrected.

This archival history of Karen and Richard Carpenter is intended to entertain and inform both the Carpenters neophyte and the die-hard Carpentersphile. I hope that, collectively, these articles will provide insight as to why the Carpenters continue to garner new fans and why their music seems to gain more respect the more it is reexamined.

—Randy L. Schmidt

Part I

WE'VE ONLY
JUST BEGUN

THE CARPENTERS

THEY'VE ONLY JUST BEGUN

Dean Gautschy

TV Radio Mirror, 1971

W hat a super trip! Initially they took a "Ticket to Ride" (the Beatle classic), and the Carpenters, handsome six-foot Richard and his pretty brown-eyed sister Karen, rode nonstop to fame and fortune in the spinning of this 45-rpm disc on airwaves around the world. Their second record release, "Close to You," proved an even bigger hit and the new sound introduced by the pair was sweeping the music industry—the same industry that had previously rejected their talents.

"We were under contract to RCA Victor," recalls Richard with a catlike grin. "But they wanted us to do instrumentals. We cut two records although I told them they would never sell. They were never even released as it turned out.

"But we don't feel so badly. RCA once rejected Herb Alpert."

Actually, it was Alpert who later became aware of their commercial potential. He flipped when he heard a "homemade" tape of their blended voices, and immediately signed them to a lucrative contract to record for his A&M label. It turned out to be one of the best talent deals the trumpet-playing executive has ever made.

"We've Only Just Begun" was another hit single on their road to success. But the Carpenters are continually bettering their efforts. With the smash success of Oscar-winner "For All We Know," it looks as if they will be around for a very long time, much to everyone's delight. They've already proved they're no flash in the pan—they're loaded with talent . . . talent that they have been nurturing for years, which has now blossomed into stardom.

This summer proved a lot cooler because the Carpenters are such a refreshing welcome to off-season weekly television. Their Tuesday night show on NBC is called *Make Your Own [Kind of] Music*. The popular Doodletown Pipers and Mark Lindsay, the hip songster, also are regulars on the one-hour musical.

Already the Carpenters' success has been chronicled by music journals such as *Cashbox*. Recently, they were honored by their peers, receiving Grammy Awards as the best new artists and vocal group of 1970. But behind the statistics of record charts and phenomenal sales is a beautiful, warm story of two beautiful and warm people.

The only children of Harold and Agnes Carpenter, Richard and Karen were born in New Haven, Connecticut. Richard on October 15, 1946, and Karen on March 2, 1950. Their father worked for a printing firm. The three-bedroom house in a middle-class neighborhood was small in size but the atmosphere was a loving one.

Both Richard and Karen attended the neighborhood grammar school, Nathan Hale Elementary. But child prodigies they were not; they did the usual childhood things.

Karen has a marvelous sense of humor, and Richard, though more serious in nature, also has an upbeat personality.

"Mom has a nice voice," Rich says admiringly, "but she never sang professionally. Dad has a fantastic love for all music. They were very instrumental in helping us get where we are today.

"When I was nine, I started taking piano lessons. The book type of lessons where the teacher comes to your home. I disliked this, and finally convinced my parents they were wasting money.

"Not until I was about thirteen did I really get into music. This time it was my idea to take lessons again, and by the time I got into high school (Wilbur Cross in New Haven) I was really hooked. In fact, I learned everything the music books could teach me and so I enrolled for more courses at the nearby Yale Music School."

Meantime, Karen played at being Richard's cute kid sister.

"I idolized Richard," recalls Karen, "and would tag along with him. You might say I was a tomboy. I loved playing baseball."

Rich interrupts with, "It was slightly embarrassing. Karen was a better ballplayer than I was, and when choosing sides for sandlot games, she'd be picked first."

TV Radio Mirror recently interviewed brother and sister in their suite at the Sands Hotel in Las Vegas. After two weeks singing at the gambling spa, Karen had developed "Vegas throat" (the most common malady singers suffer from in the dryness of the desert).

"It's amazing," Karen says as she clears her sore throat with a cough. "I always figured 'Vegas throat' was some kind of a put-on. But for the past few days I have been losing my voice during the day and luckily finding it before show time."

Both performances each night on a co-bill with comic Don Adams were sold out. Not only is their music pleasant to the ears, they give the audience the impression, honestly so, that they are indeed beautiful people.

Barely over twenty-one, Karen in many ways has remained a wholesome sweet sixteen. Not that she's un-hip, either. She's very hip. But she has never lost a youthful innocence, and we hope she never does. All five feet, four inches of her frame, from her flowing brown hair to her tiny feet, bubbles with gaiety, although she is very aware of a troubled world.

"The situation of the whole world is a drag," she says. "Everybody fighting everybody. Through our music, Richard and I try to do our best to pull people together—not apart."

Whereas Richard's talent was quite apparent by the time he was in his early teens, Karen didn't test her musical ability until she was in high school: ironically, not as a vocalist either, but on the drums. The 120-pounder became a heavyweight drummer without taking a lesson.

When Richard was sixteen, the Carpenter family was faced with a major decision. For several years Harold Carpenter had been offered another position by a former boss. But it would mean a move to Southern California.

By now most everyone in the New Haven area who knew anything about music realized that Rich was destined for bigger things.

"My parents are very hip," Rich smiles. "They didn't have to be told that Los Angeles was where music was happening. So mainly for my future, we moved."

Actually, the Carpenters at first got only a brief glimpse of Los Angeles as they passed through the city and settled off the Santa Ana Freeway in Downey. Harold's job was at the Container Corp. of America in nearby Vernon.

Richard finished his senior year at Downey High School and then enrolled at Long Beach State College. Karen entered South Junior High and soon the Carpenters had adjusted to their new home.

Still Karen was not aware of her musical talents.

"Junior high was a waste," she says, "and I didn't do much of anything in music until I was sixteen. This was really the turning point in my career.

"At Downey High I became a member of the band, but I really couldn't play any instrument. It all came about because both Richard and I hated gym.

"If you took band you didn't have to take gym and run around and do all those weird things. Richard took band and got to know the band director very well.

"When Richard was at Downey High, he marched in and said he wanted to be in the band. They asked him what instrument. He said 'Piano,' and they laughed. 'Baby or grand?' Of course everyone knows nobody plays a piano in a marching band, and Richard ended up playing a trumpet, although he knew little about the instrument.

"But after the band director heard him play the piano, he was so impressed he didn't care if Richard never tooted a note. Sometimes the whole band would just gather around and listen to Richard play.

"So I went to the band director when I was a sophomore—Richard was going to Long Beach State—and I told him I was Richard's kid sister and wanted to be in the band. I couldn't play anything. Well, I ended up with a mallet playing the glockenspiel.

"This wasn't what you would call playing heavy music. Still I didn't care because I got out of taking gym. Later I became interested in the drums when I started to listen to Frankie Chavez, a neighborhood school pal who had been playing the drums since he was three.

"At first I was just fooling around on the drums and then my parents started to encourage me. They even bought me a set of drums for Christmas. Actually, I taught myself and did most of the things that experienced drummers could do.

"To teach me what I didn't know, Frankie recommended some lessons at Drum City."

However, Richard points out there was very little about percussion that Karen hadn't learned naturally. The Carpenter kids formed a trio with tuba-bass player Wes Jacobs and started playing sophisticated jazz. Richard did all the arranging and in the summer of 1966 they rehearsed daily from dawn to well into the night.

That same year they entered the Battle of the Bands at the Hollywood Bowl. Competition was fierce; dozens of other groups were entered. Richard had had experience before a live audience. As he says, "My hair was longer and I wore glasses, making me look older, so I was able to pick up club dates while at college."

But little Karen had never been exposed to such a spotlight. She always felt "safe and lost" while performing on a football field with the band. "I thought I'd be scared, but I was too involved in the music to worry about it," she says.

"Well, it was sort of unbelievable," Richard admits. "Karen was the only girl drummer in the contest, and the audience would stare at first in disbelief when she sat down behind the drums . . . like is this for real? . . . this pretty little girl behind a massive set of drums.'

"When she started playing, though, they believed. She's fantastic. She'd whiz through press rolls, and speedily maneuver the sticks as if she had been born in a drum factory. It was really groovy."

The judges thought so, too. For the finale Wes switched from the bass to the tuba, and the solo, says Richard, "blew everybody's minds." The trio won nine trophies that included the sweepstakes award. An RCA talent scout signed the three to a contract practically before the applause had died down.

"What a letdown," Rich remembers. "I wanted to record some new arrangements, adding vocals to make us sound more commercial. RCA said 'no,' and we cut two jazz numbers, including the tuba solo, that I knew would never sell."

By now the tumultuous sounds of hard rock were sweeping the country. RCA finally realized that Richard was right. The records went unreleased, and RCA decided not to pick up the option on the trio's contract. For a time the threesome worked local gigs, but could not play the bigtime clubs since Karen was a minor.

Meantime, Karen continued to learn. Following graduation from high school, she joined big brother as a music major at Long Beach State. Richard was in the choir. "I thought the group was really groovy," she says, "so I tried out, although I never had done any singing before."

It was the school's choir director, Frank Pooler, who amazed Karen by telling her that she had a good voice.

"Mr. Pooler," Karen said admiringly, "is a multi-talented choir genius. We picked up a lot from him."

Later, when Wes Jacobs decided to play classical tuba (he's currently a member of the Detroit Symphony Orchestra), the award-winning trio was "retired." Undaunted, Richard formed Spectrum, a harmony group featuring Karen as lead singer and backed by Cal State pals Leslie Johnston, Danny Woodhams, Gary Sims, and John Bettis.

This time both Richard and Karen felt that their soft-rock sound would make it. Spectrum played such choice dates in the Los Angeles area as the Troubadour, Disneyland, and the Whisky A Go-Go. But they were only a supporting act, and while appearing at the Whisky, a top hard rock spot, the management became annoyed because the dancers stopped to listen to the Carpenters sing.

Apparently the boss figured the club's reputation of presenting only hard rock acts was in jeopardy, because he terminated Spectrum's engagement.

"We really hadn't made a dime," says Richard, "and we were very discouraged. We were determined, though . . . determined to stick it out, but Spectrum gradually broke up."

THEN CAME THE BIG BREAK

Around 1966, through their music contacts, the two had met electric bass man Joe Osborn. Joe is originally from Shreveport, Louisiana, and had played in back-up groups for Ricky Nelson, Glen Campbell, and many other top recording stars. Joe tinkered around with electronics and began collecting recording equipment he installed in the garage of his home.

More or less as an experiment, Richard and Karen started recording in multitrack, blending their voices into four, six, or more parts by overdubbing as Joe worked the controls at his mini-studio. The resulting tape was aired for several record producers. Each one claimed it would never sell.

Finally, as a last resort, Richard talked his way into A&M Studios and got [Herb Alpert to listen. Alpert was impressed with the multi-voices and signed them to the label.]

Soon, under Alpert's personal supervision, the Carpenters cut an album, *Offering*. One of the cuts, "Ticket to Ride," took off as a top-100 single. Alpert then had the pair record [Burt] Bacharach's "[(They Long to Be)] Close to You," a song that other singers had recorded with only moderate success. It was used as the title song of the Carpenters' second LP, and became a number one single on the charts.

From there the Carpenters started recording hit after hit. The most recent is a ballad by Karen, "Rainy Days and Mondays." Two former members of Spectrum, bassist Dan Woodhams and guitarist Gary Sims, rejoined the Carpenters for the success trip, although Sims is now away on military service. Doug Strawn, reed player and former barbershop [quartet member], and Bob Messenger, versatile musician on reeds and guitar, are also group regulars.

Rich and Karen recently bought a modern home for their parents in Downey. Harold Carpenter is retired. His now-famous children continue to live at home—when they're in town, that is.

"We haven't had a day off in a year," Karen points out. "Most of the time we've been on the road. But I love living at home—our parents are the greatest."

Neither Karen nor Richard has any steady romantic entanglements. They're both very eligible, although both claim they don't have the time to date very often. Drag-racing is their main offstage interest. Richard and a pal own a souped-up Barracuda dragster.

"I would like to drive it in competition myself," he says. "I just don't have any spare time."

Someday Karen feels she'll make a good wife for the right man. She digs cooking when she has time, fixing dishes like veal parmesan, eggplant, and a specialty, shrimp [suiza]. She neither drinks hard liquor nor smokes. "I'm hooked on iced tea," she says. "I drink gallons a day."

Today religion no longer plays the part it once did in the pair's life. They were reared as Methodists and now "believe what we want to believe."

One of the things Richard most admires about his sister is that she has a good head on her shoulders.

"Most girls want to get married to the first cat they feel is all right, and sometimes, before they know it, they are divorced. Not Karen. Especially now that she has her career."

Karen agrees with her brother. "As long as we're on the road most of the time, I will never marry. I've seen how marriages have broken up because a wife or husband isn't understanding of the other's career."

Ask Karen what she admires about Richard, she'll tell you, "He has a rich, inborn talent for anything pertaining to music. He's damn good. He's all together."

Along with their success there has been at least one big disappointment. The Academy did not invite them to sing the nominated "For All We Know" at this year's award telecast. The song won an Oscar, as predicted by most people, and the Carpenters' hit recording had undoubtedly been a factor in its success.

One music critic told us, "The record was sweeping the country and Academy voters probably heard it every time they turned on the radio. Because of the Carpenters, it was the most publicized nominated song ever."

Petula Clark sang it on the show. To add insult to injury, only one of the three songwriters who composed the number for the movie *Lovers and Other Strangers* acknowledged the Carpenters when they accepted their Oscars.

However, the Carpenters realize there will be other Oscar shows. We know, too, that Richard and Karen launched a new kind of music for the 1970s and the decade is relatively a baby. Yes, the Carpenters have "only just begun" and what a wonderful beginning, too, for such beautiful people.

MOONDUST
AND STARLIGHT

THE *CLOSE TO YOU* ALBUM

John Tobler

2000

B y all accounts, Herb Alpert, hit-making founder of the desperately hip A&M Records, was felt by some (including his employees) to have lost his mind when he persevered with the Carpenters after the desultory chart performance of *Offering*, the duo's debut album. His staff may have thought he was hanging around too much with Gram Parsons of the Flying Burrito Brothers, who wore Nudie suits with embroidered designs of tablets and drug paraphernalia.

In fact, what apparently happened was that Alpert had just heard Richard and Karen's newly-recorded cover version of "Close to You," a Burt Bacharach/Hal David composition which had previously been recorded by Dionne Warwick, but had only been the B-side of a minor hit. In fact, the original recording of the song was released as the B-side of a 1963 US Top 50 hit by Richard "Dr. Kildare" Chamberlain titled "Blue Guitar." (Incidentally, both the Chamberlain and Warwick versions listed the song's title as "They Long to Be Close to You," while the Carpenters' rendition put the first four words in parentheses.)

Alpert played the Carpenters' recording to Bacharach over the phone, and Bacharach loved it, although it was arranged quite differently from Warwick's 1965 reading. Released as a single, it became the first number one hit for the Carpenters, as well as the title track of their second album.

The title track wasn't the only huge hit single on the *Close to You* album. Almost as massive was the enduring and romantic "We've Only Just Begun," written by Paul Williams and Roger Nichols, which became [the Carpenters'] second million seller in three months. This song had started life as a TV commercial for the Crocker Citizens Bank of California, and its tunefully romantic sentiments captivated Richard Carpenter when he heard the brief commercial. Richard asked if there was a complete song, [and fortunately there was.]

Williams and Nichols [staff writers at A&M Records] also wrote "I Kept On Loving You," which appeared on the album, as well as being the B-side of the "Close to You" single. [Williams described this situation as "the traditional free ride that every songwriter dreams of—'Close to You' was the A-side, and 'I Kept On Loving You' was the B-side. We were getting paid anyway!"]

There were a number of other above-average tracks on *Close to You*, including the duo's second Beatles cover. *Offering* had featured "Ticket to Ride," while *Close to You* included "Help!" Similarly, just as *Offering* had included covers of two folk rock standards (the Youngbloods' "Get Together" and Buffalo Springfield's "Nowadays Clancy Can't Even Sing"), *Close to You* featured a cover of Tim Hardin's "Reason to Believe." In addition, *Close to You* contained two more Bacharach songs in "Baby It's You" (a hit for the Shirelles which was also covered by the Beatles), and the under-rated "I'll Never Fall in Love Again" (originally by Dionne Warwick, but a bigger hit in the UK for Bobbie Gentry).

Where *Offering* had included a preponderance of original material written by Richard Carpenter (with lyrics by John Bettis), this time there were only four such songs, all dating from the pre-fame period when Richard, Karen and Bettis were members of Spectrum, a close harmony group. In comparison with their later efforts (such as "Goodbye to Love," "Top of the World," etc.), the Carpenter/Bettis songs here are mostly of minor significance. The exception is "Mr. Guder," which was written about a supervisor at Disneyland, whom Richard and Bettis (who once worked there as a musical duo) found officious. This song was featured in the Carpenters' live shows during the early '70s, and it possesses a curious non-mainstream appeal.

Also of note on *Close to You* is the delightfully bouncy "Love Is Surrender," an "outside" song (penned by Ralph Carmichael) which must rank as one of the great undiscovered gems of the Carpenters' recorded catalog.

Overall, *Close to You* was a huge step forward from *Offering*, and it became the first of a succession of gold albums for the Carpenters. It included two signature songs ("We've Only Just Begun" and the title track), which the siblings almost certainly felt obliged to perform at every subsequent live show until Karen's tragically early death. Many years later, this album remains one of the duo's finest achievements, and in many ways, it became the blueprint for subsequent collections.

THE CARPENTERS
AND THE CREEPS

Lester Bangs

Rolling Stone, 1971

S AN DIEGO—Where there's lots of money being made, as any hack journalist will tell you, there's probably some kind of story; and when a once-floundering group has two giant hits in a row, some psychological transaction must be taking place between them and the public. Success stories like Melanie and Grand Funk [Railroad] are obvious; but what about a group like the Carpenters, who are at present riding high even though they don't seem to have any particular image, concept, much material or anything definite except a pleasant-voiced girl and a facile arranger? Is there some subtle catalytic ingredient hiding somewhere beneath that too-clear surface? Or is their whole phenomenon just blind coincidence?

Thus it was that I took my musical sensibilities in my hands and attended a Carpenters concert. Oh, I had really liked "We've Only Just Begun"—[it was,] in fact, the reason why I'd just re-fallen in love with a childhood sweetheart at the time it was riding the radio, and it was, well, it was Our Song. Even if it did originate in a bank commercial. Karen Carpenter had a full, warm voice, and her brother Richard's musical settings were deft and to the point. The LP cover and promo pix showed 'em side by side, identical, interchangeable boy-girl faces grinning out at you with all the cheery innocence of some years-past dream of California youth. Almost like a better-scrubbed reincarnation of Sonny & Cher.

What also sparked your curiosity was the question of audience: who pays five bucks for a Carpenters concert? Somehow you couldn't see the usual rock show crowd of army-fatigued truckers and seconaled stooges. But they must have found a major following *somewhere* because, in San Diego at least, the show was totally sold out.

We got there late and, indeed, the first thing you noticed was the audience, and what was striking was its diversity: little tots, Bobby Sherman nymphets, college couples (rather sedately straight for the most part), Mom and Pop and a smattering of grandparents. And all of them sitting there open-mouthed, staring solemnly at the stage where a rather delicate looking fellow named Jake Holmes was hunching his shoulders intensely and singing in a broken near-whisper a song about alienation and "people whose elbows touch but never their eyes."

So spellbound was the audience with this emotional indictment, in fact, that the usher told us to wait till it was over before taking our seats, then turned her attention back to Mr. Holmes, gaping as raptly as the rest of them.

The crowd flipped for Holmes, brought him back for an encore, and then we all settled back to pleasant anticipation of what the Carpenters, minor mystery that they were, could have for a stage act. But nothing— *nothing* that we might ever dreamed of could have prepared us for what we saw when those curtains parted.

In the first place, there is no balance, no center of attention. Here are six people on a stage singing and playing various instruments, and your eye just keeps shifting from one to another without ever finding a nexus to focus on. They are an odd and disjunct congregation. My girl said they made her nervous; I would say that they have the most disconcerting collective stage presence of any band I have ever seen.

Besides being a motley crew, they are individually peculiar-looking. Here it almost becomes cruel to go on, but there is no getting around it, especially since most of the music was so bland, and their demeanor so remarkable, that you could spend the entire concert wondering at the latter without once getting bored. I found the Band almost like tintypes of themselves, and Van Morrison, so visually static himself, had me laid back dreaming; but I couldn't take my eyes off the Carpenters. I'll never again be able to hear "We've Only Just Begun" without thinking, not of a certain sentimental autumn as I used to, but inevitably of that disgruntled collection of faces.

The first thing is that Karen Carpenter not only sings lead but also plays drums—she's pretty damn good, too, seldom falters—but singing from behind that massive set she just doesn't give you much to look at, lovely and outgoing as she is. This band should invest in a drummer.

Brother Richard plays piano, and he's excellent technically, if not emotionally, ripping out crisp though somewhat stereotyped demi-jazz lines that even managed to save an otherwise awkward version of "Nowadays Clancy Can't Even Sing." But watching him . . . he was a chubby, rather nervous little fellow with a round face, pudding-bowl hair and a white suit with vast lapels that only served to accentuate that odd combination of qualities, giving him a strong resemblance to the cloven-hoofed conductor of a barnyard symphony in an old cartoon. And in quiet numbers, when the lighting was subdued and he was tinkling out pearly arpeggios, he would stare up and off into space with mournful almost-crossed eyes as passionate as Chopin in the throes of creation.

Or the others, guitarist Gary Sims and Doug Strawn, who plays electric clarinet and tambourine and sings a couple of numbers in a fine voice that they should utilize more (the promo sheet says he's "a former Barbershop Quartetist"), are pretty ordinary-looking cats. Bassist Bob Messenger, who doubles on tenor [sax] and flute, looks vaguely like a Walt Kelley caricature of Joe McCarthy as a badger (it says here, "When not playing good music for the Carpenters, his job is to keep the kids out of trouble—he's the oldest member of the band"), and Danny Woodhams, who does backup vocals and plays tambourine and "assorted junk," as Richard said, is absolutely incredible. He looks about like your average bushy-headed L.A. Whisky scene-maker, with his Edwardian velour jacket and Maltese Cross earring, but he is the most outrageous ham I've ever seen in a professional group. Maybe it's because he doesn't really *have* anything to do but sing once in a while and bash the tambourine with all the pyrotechnic intensity of an Elvin Jones.

The music itself was entirely predictable, a pleasant and mildly bracing flow: ice-cream music. Their few originals, like "Mr. Guder" (cute moralizing about a tight-assed Disneyland [talent supervisor] are never going to be their hits, and like their albums their show depends on bright, cream-puffy arrangements of 1965 Beatle songs, old Burt Bacharach hits, and innocuous "hip" standards like "Reason to Believe" and ["Get Together."] Strawn sang a couple of rather weird ragtime-hoedown "novelty" numbers, with lyrics like "There went Granmaw / Swingin' on the outhouse door," and breaks right in the middle for short spoken *Laugh-In* trade-offs between band members. They also did one bit where Strawn asked for a volunteer from the audience for a "magic trick," selected a little girl from the first row and when he got her on stage he asked how old she was.

"Seventeen." The girl, naturally, is giggling and blushing and Strawn does a broad double-take when she tells her age and makes her stand a few inches away. Howls from the audience. Now he closes his eyes and says that she should think of a number and he will guess it. "Go ahead," he says, "pick a number, any number—*between three and five!*" Dynamite. Strawn sends the girl back to her seat and they're off into another old Dionne Warwick hit.

As we oozed out of the theater I looked around me and speculated that this must have been a sort of diplomatic project in many homes: Mom and Dad would come and learn to Dig the Kids' Music. I was still dazed from the absolute incongruity of those faces, and I *had* to ask some of the people around me what they'd thought. I really wanted to ask them what in the hell had ever brought them to this oddball event in the first place, but a lot of them looked pretty odd themselves, in a self-consciously middle-class sort of way, so I just turned towards a well-dressed, rather cold-looking blonde girl about 20 and said: "I'm doing a piece on this show for a magazine. What'd you think of it?"

She just stood there staring at me in an incredulous, slightly hostile way: "What?"

I repeated myself, and still she stood there and just stared at me, her mouth open, her boyfriend behind her eyeing me suspiciously. They simply could not believe that someone could be asking such a thing of them; they looked at me as if I were insane, or had sidled up and asked for a handout. And me with a suit on and everything! I gave up; we glumly found the way to our car and got in feeling curiously numb, just as the whole evening had been mildly unsettling on some peculiar level. I was not acclimated only to long-haired audiences, but something about band and audience both at this one just gave me the creeps. All around us on the tiers of the 11-story parking lot, kids were gunning their engines, screeching out, laying rubber. I reflected that you seldom heard that when the cars were filled with stoners leaving rock concerts; but what that and all the rest ultimately signified I never will fathom.

KAREN IN THE KITCHEN

WHO SAYS A YOUNG FEMALE SUPERSTAR CAN'T BE A TOP-NOTCH COOK?

A&M Records Press Release, 1971

They say that if you're a jack-of-all-trades, you're master of none. Or, conversely, if you're a master of one trade, you don't have the time, energy or talent to master another. But for some special people, it just t'aint so. Karen Carpenter—who, with her brother Richard, form possibly the most celebrated sibling duo since Jack and Jill—is, indeed, a Jill of several trades. At the mere age of 21, she is—aside from being one solid half of the nation's number one singing group—a whiz in the kitchen. Now what's all this stuff about the incompatibility of a hectic career and the cultivation of domestic arts? Karen quickly dispels this: "I've always loved to cook, ever since I was a child. I've been a musician since I was 16, a singer since a few years after that, but it's never stopped me from inventing new recipes or perfecting them." What does she like to cook? "Oh, lots of things: pies, cookies, shrimp dishes, veal and eggplant concoctions. . . ." Speaking of which, she's consented to supply a recipe for one of her specialties—a treat that the whole Carpenter family and lucky friends feast on from time to time. It's called "Far-Out Eggplant" and much of its success hinges on her "Stupendous Carpenter Tomato Sauce." Okay, ladies, get your pencils:

I.   **Stupendous Carpenter Tomato Sauce**
     1 big can tomato puree
     2 small cans tomato paste
     ½ bag [Parmesan] cheese
     1 medium onion
     2 buds garlic
     Garlic salt to taste

     Mix ingredients together over stove, let reach boil, lower heat to simmer for several hours.
     Now . . .

II. Take 1 medium eggplant; peel and slice it thin. Dip the pieces into an egg and milk mixture. Flour it. Fry it in oil.
III. In a casserole dish, alternate layers of eggplant with sauce, parsley sprigs, [and] strips of mozzarella cheese. Top with a sprinkling of [Parmesan] cheese. Bake at moderate [heat] till bubbly.
IV. Cool . . . and enjoy!

     The Carpenters will be cooking—musically, that is—at _____ from _____ to _____ . Don't miss them!

THEY PUT ROMANCE INTO ROCK

ON THE ROAD WITH THE CARPENTERS, WHO STILL BELIEVE MOTHER KNOWS BEST

Digby Diehl

TV Guide, 1971

EDITOR'S NOTE: Digby Diehl interviewed the Carpenters three or four times over a period of a month in 1971. His work on this *TV Guide* feature led to an invitation from the duo's manager, Sherwin Bash, to write a stage act for the Carpenters, who would soon be performing in Las Vegas for the first time. Accompanying Karen and Richard on tour that summer, Diehl was informed by Bash (in no uncertain terms) that his "real job" was to get Karen out from behind the drums. It wasn't an easy assignment, but within several months, she hesitantly drifted toward center stage, and the Carpenters hired another drummer. Although Karen became a confident front for the group, Diehl later recalled that Richard remained rigid and uptight onstage: "I never got him out from behind the piano."

◆

When you're on tour, the whole world looks Motel Green. The Cincinnati motel room that houses Richard Carpenter, one half of the hot new singing team that has dared to put romance back into Pop, is no exception. The sun beats down at a muggy, unrelenting 90 degrees. The air-conditioner is stuck on fast-freeze. The ever-present TV set, its big eye blank now, stares out over a roomful of depressing furniture and obscenely oversized beds.

Richard sips iced tea and takes a tranquilizer. His sister Karen just grouses. They are feeling travel-worn, homesick and apprehensive about tonight's concert, one of 15 one-nighters in the last three weeks.

The motel-green telephone rings, and Richard trips over his half-opened suitcase to grab it. This time it is not an irate conductor in Minneapolis or a booking agent in Kansas City; it's Agnes, the *original* Carpenter, calling from the family home in Downey, Cal. Only the news is not sunshine. Her voice crackles over the phone. Ma Carpenter is giving her now-famous offspring a motherly piece of her mind.

Richard wilts into the motel-green bedspread as Ma Carpenter reads an angry letter from a fan who had brought her family to a concert in Hershey, Pa., last week and was dismayed that the Carpenters did not sign autographs after the show. Richard is sputtering, "But Mom . . . but Mom . . ." What Mom doesn't know is that it was pouring rain in Hershey, a thousand kids were about to rush the car, and they're lucky they weren't run over. Karen is just plain furious: "We're practically the only group in America that signs autographs, and we nearly get killed every time we do it."

Minutes later, an anguished and dutiful Richard is calling Hershey, apologizing and promising to send autographed copies of the three Carpenter albums. The woman, only slightly mollified, lays it right out there. "Richard," she says, "we were very disappointed with you in Hershey." Karen is wild: "This is incredible! Could you just see Mick Jagger apologizing for not giving an autograph?"

In fact, there's probably no one else in the whole hard-nosed world of pop music who would have made that phone call except the Carpenters. But it is this honest, eager-to-please folksiness that separates the Carpenters from the Jaggers. They want everybody to love them. It is their richly harmonied, romantic music that makes them as sweetly unique in the world of rock as [*Love Story*] in the world of contemporary literature. Arriving just last year in the Top 10 with "Close to You" and "We've Only Just Begun," the Carpenters have already collected Grammy Awards as the best new artists and as best contemporary performance by a vocal group of 1970. Their success has also won them another kind of accolade: their own summer TV show, *Make Your Own Kind of Music.*

The telephone call over, the Carpenters manage to get it together, hop in a rented car and head for the bowling alley. As we walk in, a few of the Ohio Mayflower set give Richard's long Prince Valiant haircut a hostile look. Karen laughs, "Why don't they understand that we're just two kids from Downey who like to take showers?"

We settle down in Alley 19 and the kids start chuckling. Also talking. To hear them tell it, life is one long series of comic chases through motel corridors, practical jokes, and the general stuff of a college spree amongst the entourage of 15 musicians and equipment. In Lansing, Mich., for instance, the horseplay climaxed in a dressing-room water-balloon fight that left the entire group soaking wet minutes before curtain time.

HERE IN CINCINNATI, the game has been to elude three teen-age girls who have been following them cross-country ever since they played Carnegie Hall a week previously. Richard, hardly a lady-killer, is befuddled by the relentless fans: "Everybody else in the music business meets a chick for one night and she's happy, they're happy. But me, I've got this whole troop that won't go home. What am I supposed to do?"

Unlike many of their middle-America counterparts, Karen and Richard are so immersed in their music that they are socially and politically uninvolved. "Sure, we think the world's a big mess," says Richard, laying down a sharply breaking hook. "But we couldn't get seriously into politics now because we're too busy."

It may be part of the secret of the Carpenters' success that many listeners are taking refuge in nostalgia for better days gone by, love stories, and love songs. "For the kids to make number-one records with their romantic sound, when the rest of the music scene is still heavy rock, amazes even me," Sherwin Bash, their unflappable veteran manager, told me later. "A song like 'Rainy Days and Mondays' is the kind of thing

Sinatra might have done when he was doing songs like 'Violets for Your Furs'! It's instant nostalgia. The Carpenters' music may never be put in a time capsule, but the people certainly love it now. There's a young pretty girl and a young bright-eyed boy doing pretty things they love and that's all we're talking about." [. . .]

"The television show is very exciting for us," says Karen, "but introductions and comedy bits aren't really our thing; basically we're musicians." Richard would like to experiment more with musical innovations eventually. "There's so much you can do with the voice that I don't think would be commercially cool to do just yet," he says. "I'd like to do a choral album like that vocal segment of [*2001: A Space Odyssey*], tone clusters and radical harmonics."

But it's time to go. Richard underlines his point by throwing three straight strikes and, in high spirits, heads the rental car toward the Cincinnati Gardens.

The concert is a plague. They've been booked into this hockey rink where the stage is too high and there is a seven-second echo delay bouncing off the walls. Promotion has been weak, the dressing room smells like old ice skates, and everyone is feeling low. But it's all part of life on the road. Once on stage, the Carpenters start singing, and suddenly that hockey rink is the most romantic place in the world. Afterwards, they sign autographs, just like Mom told 'em.

THE CARPENTERS

NAILING DOWN SUCCESS

Fiona MacDougall

'Teen, 1971

'TEEN recently dropped in to chat with Karen and Richard Carpenter at their plush home in Downey, California. Care to join in on the fun?

When we arrive, Karen and Richard are busy on the telephone, so Mrs. Carpenter, their mother, gives us a guided tour of their home.

"We just had the whole house redecorated," she informs us proudly.

The living room is beautifully done in soft blues and greens with lots of plants and fresh flowers adorning the coffee tables. A grand piano stands in the corner of the room. A crystal chandelier hangs overhead.

"We're having another room added to the house this year so that Richard can have someplace to write and not be disturbed. He wants to get another grand piano—a larger one," Mrs. Carpenter says.

We find Mr. Carpenter reading the morning paper in the den, a comfortable room complete with bar, color television, pool table and a leopard skin couch! Karen and Richard's Grammy Awards sit impressively on the bookshelves.

We begin rapping about their children's success. "Well, naturally we're both very proud parents," exclaims Mr. Carpenter. "We didn't have much money when they were young but we always tried to give them everything they wanted. Richard has been interested in music since he was knee high! In fact we moved out to Los Angeles because we knew that this was the best place for him to start a music career."

Richard arrives on the scene, casually dressed in a light blue ribbed sweater and dark blue slacks.

"There's always something to take care of," he mutters. "What I wouldn't give for ONE day with no interruptions!"

If Richard's wish came true, he told us that he'd probably spend the day doing practically nothing!

"First of all, I'd sleep in," he laughs. "That to me is a luxury. When I got up, I'd eat a huge breakfast and read the paper. Then I'd disappear upstairs to my music room and listen to records until my ears started buzzing!! Do you want to see the music room?" he asks humbly. He runs upstairs and opens one of the many doors leading off the hallway.

The music room is small and cozy. Stacks of albums line the room wall-to-wall. The only piece of furniture besides the stereo record player and speakers is a large black leather swivel chair in the center of the room.

"I have tons of albums," Richard explains, "but no time to listen to them. Half of them haven't even been opened!"

The door opens and Karen bursts in. She's much prettier and more feminine in person than her pictures show her. Dressed in a black midi pinafore dress with a white lace blouse, she looks lovely!

"What's going on?" she asks. Then in the same breath, "Do you want some iced tea? Mom makes the best iced tea in Downey," she jokes.

Karen seems more lively and outgoing than Richard. She constantly jokes and clowns during the entire interview. She leads the way to her bedroom to show 'TEEN her stuffed animal collection. "They all have names," she tells us solemnly. "That's Gru-pig and there's Marshfield," she says, pointing to a checkered pig and huge pink dog.

Karen's bedroom is decorated in yellow and black. A black fur bedspread with yellow trim covers her king-size bed and suitcases are scattered all around the room.

"You must excuse the mess," she apologizes, "but we're leaving on tour again tomorrow and I'm in the middle of packing."

Is it fun traveling with 10 guys or does Karen ever wish she weren't the only girl?

"It's amusing. Sometimes I feel as if I've got to have another girl to talk to, but that's only natural. Being the only girl makes you the center of attraction, and let's face it, any girl likes to get attention. The guys are all very protective toward me. It's wild. I tell you, I can't make a move. They're always watching out for me."

Karen and Richard have always been very close but "I think the older we got, the closer we got because we had the ability to understand one another more. Also, as I got older I started getting into music, which has always been Richard's thing," Karen sums up.

Karen started playing the drums in the summer of 1966. Richard found a bass player at his school and because they had nothing else to do, they decided to form a jazz trio.

Since then there's been no looking back for the Carpenter family. Karen and Richard have brought romance back to rock music with their beautiful renditions of "Close to You," "We've Only Just Begun" and "Rainy Days and Mondays."

In fact, they are both so busy these days that they hardly ever get any time to date!

"We just don't get a chance to meet anyone in Los Angeles," Richard says, "because we're never here. Most of the girls I knew from here are all married now. I see one girl quite a bit—Leana. But quite a bit these days means about once a month!"

However, Richard admits to being terribly shy with girls. "I'm terrible. I probably have an inferiority complex. I used to get turned down by girls quite a bit. I probably still would if I had the time to ask more, so somehow the feeling's still in me that I should offer something appealing to the girl, like an expensive meal or a good show. I'm so shy with girls. I watch the guys in our group operate and I couldn't do it in a million years, but I'd love to. It's sort of like a dream to me."

Karen likes her dates to "have a good sense of humor, dress well in modern gear and have long hair. Nine chances out of nine he'll be a musician, because I probably couldn't live with anyone else."

Richard, on the other hand, likes the quiet, sincere, girl-next-door type. "I don't like overbearing girls who talk too much. I love a feminine girl. I can't stand to hear a girl swearing," he tells us.

We wander downstairs, pick up our iced teas and make our way outside to sit by the pool. Karen looks at her watch and says she'll have to leave soon to go into Hollywood for a dress fitting.

Are they thinking about doing solo albums, since everyone these days seems to be doing likewise?

"I doubt it," says Karen, "but you never can tell. However, if I came out with an album by myself, all my charts would be done by Richard anyway, so it would probably still sound like a Carpenters LP. Richard could do a piano album, though. He's a great pianist! Our main thing right now is what we've got in our laps at the moment." They both agree that it's easier to work together because they *are* related.

"You can take a lot more," Karen explains. "We're a lot more tolerant of each other. The brother and sister thing has developed a relationship in our group where everyone is like one big family. We're all very, very close. We've been on the road together for one and a half years and none of us has ever had a fight!"

"It's true," adds Richard. "We never fight at all. On our music we agree—what songs we like, what songs we should put out. We have exactly the same opinions! It never ceases to amaze us how much alike we are!"

"I've got to go," announces Karen, "I can't be late for this fitting. I'll be back in a couple of seconds," she says as she whisks upstairs to her room.

She returns in a moment, her arms laden with clothes. "Now, how much do you want taken in on these pants?" she asks Richard as she hands him a pin and a pair of dark grey slacks. "Is there anything else you want me to drop off at the tailor's for you?" Karen calls as she heads towards the front door. But before Richard can answer, she disappears into her car and is off.

"Karen loves to drive fast!" he declares. "We're all car maniacs in our family. I just bought a Maserati, which I'm going to race at Ontario Speedway as soon as I get a chance." He pauses briefly, then says, "I think I'll wash one of the cars."

And so we leave the Carpenter household. Mr. Carpenter has returned to his newspaper; Mrs. Carpenter is busy fixing lunch. Karen is off buying and fitting clothes and Richard is washing his car. Sounds like the all-American family, doesn't it? But how many American families have a wall filled with gold records? And they've only just begun!

CONCERT REVIEW

SANDS, LAS VEGAS, MARCH 24, 1971

Variety, 1971

The news this three-framer is Vegas debut of the Carpenters, Karen & Richard, with their musicians, and the extraordinary age longitude and latitude the pop warblers excite sharing the bill with many-timer Don Adams, whose "Get Smart" image is still intact. [. . .]

The turn to mellowness in pop tunes and presentation was given a tremendous boost by Karen & Richard Carpenter in their immensely successful second album, *Close to You*. What makes the pair even more intriguing is the exact sound re-created for bounds outside of a recording studio. Banks of electronic gear, extra speakers spaced about the room and a precise balance bring the spinning disk to life. Richard, at the electric piano, handles all the narrative well, coloring the group as "a road version of the Partridge Family." Karen, ensconced behind a battery of drums, manages to be seen very often and heard to very good advantage, her clear voice calmly picking its graceful way among the lyrics.

A couple of doubtful inclusions are a Christmas song ["Merry Christmas, Darling"] and a rather pointless and callow break in the song action when musician Doug Strawn brings up a girl from the audience for a [pointless] five minutes or so. Otherwise the logging is very good, ranging from their very best known lacquerings to novelties such as a raucous throwback to the mid '20s and a Mason Williams antic tune ["Cinderella Rockefella"].

Helping to achieve the Carpenter blend are sidearm Strawn on reeds and rhythm noisemakers; Bob Messenger, electric bass, tenor sax and flute; Gary Sims, electric bass and guitar; and Danny Woodhams, electric bass. [. . .]

"SUPERSTAR"

THE CARPENTERS' SURPRISINGLY DIRTY DITTY

Johnny Black

Blender, 2002

Richard Carpenter has a very clear memory of the first time he heard "Superstar." "I'd come home from recording one night and turned on *The Tonight Show*. Johnny Carson had Bette Midler as a guest, before she was a household name, and she sang 'Superstar.' She sang it more as a modern-day torch song, but the song really caught my ear."

Why he immediately decided it was perfect for the Carpenters is just one mystery surrounding "Superstar," given that its central theme—a groupie yearning for one more tryst with a rock star who's left town— would have been considered exceedingly risqué in those days, especially when sung by an artist as apple-pie wholesome as Karen Carpenter.

However, with the passage of time and the tragic circumstances of Karen's 1983 death from anorexia, it's become apparent that the Carpenters' appeal was no simple thing, and certainly not limited to mainstream America. Acoustic slowcore guru Mark Eitzel [American Music Club], one of many alternative rockers who contributed a track ["Goodbye to Love"] to the 1994 tribute album *If I Were a Carpenter*, observes that the

Carpenters' "pastel, chicks-and-puppies aspect is undercut with a trau-
matic kind of thing."

Although the song is credited as a collaboration between Leon
Russell and Bonnie Bramlett, "Superstar" actually began with Rita
Coolidge. Russell has acknowledged that Coolidge gave him the title
and the basic idea for a groupie/rock star lyric. Which rock star? Eric
Clapton, Coolidge has said: "He was the only guitar player we knew at
the time."

Coolidge knew Clapton from having sung backup vocals on his 1970
solo debut, and shortly after, she played with Bramlett and Russell on Joe
Cocker's *Mad Dogs and Englishmen* tour, a legendarily debauched U.S.
jaunt whose backstage amusements have been described by the drummer
Jim Keltner: "Sharing girls. Screwing every chick in sight. Most were
there for that purpose. The drugs were just as easy to get."

It was in this period that Coolidge's idea found its way to Russell and
Bramlett, who turned the initial concept into a finished song. "Although
Rita did not write on the song," Bramlett says, "without her help, it
would not have gotten done. She sat and sang harmony so I could build
parts. I can't tell you what the other writers were thinking of, but as far
as I was concerned, it was the lament of a groupie. Hence its co-title,
'Groupie Song.' Now, it's about whomever the listener wants it to be
about. The point is, he's not there and he probably will never come back
for her. But because she's still singing it, she still has hope."

It was during the *Mad Dogs* mayhem that Coolidge first performed
the song before an audience, and her soulful version appears on *Mad
Dogs and Englishmen*, the tour's live album.

Richard Carpenter didn't see the Joe Cocker tour, but when he heard
"Superstar" on *The Tonight Show*, he loved it: "I thought it was a hit, no
two ways about it." He immediately presented the song to Karen, whose
initial resistance to recording it surprised him. "It was one of the very
few tunes that Karen ever questioned me on," Richard has said. "Usually
our tastes were the same, and I thought she'd just go crazy over this, but
she didn't. So I asked her to indulge me and sing it and listen to it as it
was being put together."

It would have been hard for Karen to find much fault with the track,
given that it employed the talents of veteran players from the Wrecking

Crew, the West Coast's top session pool, whose credits ran from Elvis Presley through the Beach Boys and virtually every hit ever produced by Phil Spector. As Karen listened, Richard has said, "She changed her mind. It became one of her favorites." Still, its origins with the Carpenters were inauspicious. Legend holds that the vocal take on the finished record was Karen's first run-through, and that she was reading the words off a napkin on which Richard had hastily scrawled them.

Given the prevailing societal attitudes of the day, Richard had felt it was necessary to make a slight alteration to the lyrics Bramlett and Russell had written. "We had to change only one word in the whole song," he said. "At that time, Top 40 radio in America would not have played something that said 'can hardly wait to sleep with you again.' So I changed it to 'be with you again.'"

By the time "Superstar" was released as a single, the album it appears on, *Carpenters*, had sold a million copies in the U.S. The song became the Carpenters' fifth gold single, and Richard's backing-vocal arrangement soon scored him a Grammy nomination.

"Superstar" was neither the Carpenters' biggest hit nor their best-loved song. But although it's been covered many times—by artists as diverse as Luther Vandross, Cher and Sonic Youth—it has become indelibly associated with the Carpenters' myth, turning up on the soundtrack of the 1995 Chris Farley movie *Tommy Boy*, and in the title of *Superstar—The Karen Carpenter Story*, a 1987 biopic filmed by Todd Haynes with Barbie dolls instead of live actors. (Karen's estate successfully sued to prevent the film's release and distribution; it is almost never seen.)

"Songs like 'Superstar' have a very melancholy way of hanging this message on you," says Redd Kross's Steve McDonald, another contributor to *If I Were a Carpenter*. "[Karen] had a warm voice with an androgynous quality."

RAINY DAYS AND CARPENTERS ALWAYS GET ME DOWN

Ken Michaels

Chicago Tribune Magazine, 1971

W here *are* they? Are they here? Wait—here they come now. Outside, everybody. Hurry up! The *kids* are here!

A red Maserati zooms off La Brea, dips under the 8-by-24-foot CARPENTERS sign, zips thru the tunnel entrance of Charlie Chaplin's old studio, past the obsequious guard, and scoots into a parking slot stenciled "Daugherty."

Casually, out of the Maserati climbs one of the kids, Karen, looking Blasé about the Whole World, looking like an Unhappy Jane Wyman.

Her Act: custom-job Maserati, sunglasses atop the hair like song writer Burt Bacharach wears his, sloppy saffron sweater drooping over slacks. Go in, get this Act over and get on to the next. . . .

From the Maserati's driver's side tumbles the other kid, Richard, his All-American shoulders tossing under a worried, boyish face. Big Hard Work Day Coming Up. Where *is* everybody?

The sound stage is like a junior high school gym. Basketball court, with boards and hoops; overhead, vari-colored streamers and pompons. Bleachers filled with boppers.

An orchestra, a chorus, four supporting singers and musicians, and in the center the kids themselves: Richard at the Electrapiano Rock-si-Chord, Karen at drums, holding a mic. Bored. Been thru this a jillion times. Let's get on with it, what do you say, hey?

Karen's a good singer. She knows what she's doing, what the market wants. Soft rock, they call it; low-key stuff with wide appeal. For a while, as she sings "For All We Know," the Oscar-winning song from *Lovers and Other Strangers*, Karen makes us *believe* it. She feels it, the sound system issues it superbly, everything is right. A mood is created, everybody forgets everything except the singer and the song. But then— between phrases—Karen drinks from a paper cup, yawns ho hum, is this putting me to sleep. She frowns at another phrase, sticks her tongue out at it. Done it so many times it's a drag.

When the ensemble does Richard's composition "Benediction," Richard's blue eyes keep asking, Where the hell did they get this chorus from? And this director? Every bar or so Richard leaps from his stool to the orchestra and chorus, and makes them hop. "Nope. Not right. Like *this*." He takes over from the director, hisses shhhh! to violins, shoots a dirty look toward the brass section. The chorus? Forget it.

Everybody's talking. Talking when Richard solos on Electrapiano Rock-si-Chord, talking when Karen sings. Producer-talk, manager-talk, agent-talk, PR man–talk, gofer-talk, bopper-talk. And everybody has his own camera: director, orchestra members, chorus, the bleacher kids. Everybody is taking everybody's picture. It's an Instamatic orgy.

During a break, the whole cast does the Break Act. Take five, gang. Exaggeratedly they stagger from the studio, wilted. Whew! The heat! Where're the *Cokes*? Too much! Whew! Outasight!

"YOU CAN MEET them now," a publicist whispers. "Just for a minute tho, they said."

From a dull passage the kids emerge, with downer faces. Don't feel like the Greeting Bit again. Uptight today.

Led by the publicist, Richard bounds over, dumps the annoyance look, spreads a capped smile, offers a strong handshake and says, "Hi, how are you, nice to see you." Then he darts past, to the Maserati.

As Karen approaches, her frown deepens. You touch her hand hello and she frowns more, then smiles while she's frowning and says, "Glad to meet you." She goes silent, looking trapped. Disgusted that she had to come out here at all.

What do you break ice with?

You tell Karen you notice she's working with a big chorus today.

"We've worked with choruses before."

Nice full orchestra, too. Where are they from, anyway?

"Have no idea." Karen tosses a hand. "All I know is they send us the best. They get the best singers and best musicians and send them to us." Karen leans tight against the bricks, maintains the frown. She's 21.

The publicist presses in. "The minute is up," he grins sheepishly at Karen.

"Good," she says, and stalks away. At the Maserati the boppers take her picture. Karen smile-frowns for them.

"Big day today," says the publicist. "Lot of pressure. They got the [Hollywood] Bowl tonight. It'll be their largest appearance ever. Maybe catch them this aft during Bowl rehearsal, talk then. Good dealie-doo?"

Meet the Carpenters—A&M Records' young brother-sister hit-makers whose gentle harmony, wholesome image and natural, unpretentious personalities have virtually crashed thru to make them the nation's No. 1 recording team. Their sonorous magic has endeared them to music fans of every age and taste, and may be marking the beginning of a new musical mood for the '70s; bringing back the three H's—hope, happiness, harmony. With soft-pedaled persistence and talent galore, these melodic siblings have revolutionized the music industry.

—A&M Records Publicity Sheet

[. . .] "You meet Jack Daugherty? He discovered them. Was working at North American Aviation, see, a regular job. One night he heard the kids' tape, took them to Herb Alpert, who flipped. Jack Daugherty's their producer now, has a big office at A&M Records, has nothing to worry about. Meet him at the Bowl. If not, get talking to him at the cocktail party Stanley Kramer's throwing afterward. You can talk with the kids then, too. Good dealie-doo?"

AFTERNOON AT HOLLYWOOD Bowl. Where *are* they? Are they here?

From between massive pillars you look out and up forever past green-canvased box seats and hundreds of rows of brown chairs to the top, to the sky, where benches and seats up there under the trees look like dollhouse furniture. Enough to scare the hell out of any performer.

"How many expected tonight?"

"We'll fill it. Over 16,000. Lots of folks, and"—the agent rubs together money thumb and fingers—"lots of money."

A roar of Maserati in the lot, a clomp upstairs, a squeeze between pillars, and the kids trot casually to stage center.

One number later, Richard sweats at the Electrapiano Rock-si-Chord. A gofer dashes to him with Coke. Richard guzzles, blows Whew!, wipes his sweat-wet hair, rips off his polo shirt.

Mic in hand, Karen slumps, buried in the drum set. "*Wah*" mouths Karen into her mic, testing sound. And the *wah* booms out over 10 acres.

Doing "Ticket to Ride," they get in trouble. Richard stops the sound. "Not right. Too boxy. Unbalanced."

A bearded engineer hotfoots it backstage to bawl the hell out of an assistant. Richard says, "Start." A second later he orders, "Stop." He shakes his head: "Still not it. Less Danny—more Karen." Assistants fly, adjust the eight front mics and five back. You wonder why the kids couldn't skip the rehearsal and lip-synch the program.

Trouble breaks during "Do You Know the Way to San Jose?"

"More bottom. Terribly boxy. More Karen."

Richard hops on the stool, pounds the Electrapiano Rock-si-Chord. His drawers keep drooping, he keeps yanking them up. His body is wet and red. He shouts damn and hell. He swigs voraciously. Looks for hope from Daugherty, high in the control booth. Daugherty's face is gray; Daugherty says nothing. Karen says, "*Wah.*"

"She's really nice—and loves how I do her hair. She sits back in the chair and hums all the pop songs." Karen's hairdresser—in her twenties but looking like a bopper—perches at the reflector pool by the stage apron. "Karen never thought she could sing. All thru high school she wanted to, but couldn't. One day somebody told her to sing everything an octave lower. She did and it was like a fairy tale, it was beautiful. Isn't her hair nice? It's nice to work with, too."

The orchestra is rushing things, the director's hair is funny, uptight. The choir's voices are gone—no matter how many mics they can't be heard past the apron—except for one frog in the bass section whom Richard keeps trying to find, in his constant trips to the podium. So he can kick the guy out. Richard looks familiarly at Karen: Geez, if I could only find Frog-voice, if I could only run this myself, get rid of all these cretins, get it right!

Karen nods familiarly: I know what you mean.

Wah. Boxy. Crap. Hell. Wah.

THEY WRAP IT up. Daugherty and Richard have a summit meeting among scattered music stands. Karen feigns exhaustion: Whew! Too much! Agents and gofers scamper to her rescue, to hug and soothe, to whisper Hollywood nothings in Karen's ear.

"Bad time to talk to them now," the publicist says. "You can catch them tonight."

> Hi, everybody, we're the Carpenters. It's really great to be in ———,
> and it's great to be listening to ——— [D.J.], one of the hippest
> music-masters on the air. We're glad you're tuned in . . . and we hope
> you drop in at the ———, where we'll be playing until ———. It'd
> be really great to see you all in person.
>
> —A&M Records Radio Spot Sheet

Hollywood at night: Where *are* they? Are they here?

A lousy rock group with two drummers yeah-yeahing each other to death is trying to turn the crowd on. Not 16, but 18,000 tonight, it's SRO at $7.50 top. Boppers, Mom and Dad, Uncle Ray and Aunt Flossie, all nice and clean and pressed.

Down front in boxes sit 42 members of the Carpenter clan. Mom Carpenter, in pink, is up and around, making pantomime greetings as the amplifiers scream and the drummers freak, go native on the stage.

Then a 45-minute sound setup, electricians all over the place.

Then a rustling of granny-dress, and from behind the Samson pillars—backed by dawn-pink afterglow—lilt two silhouettes: one moving to the silhouetted Electrapiano Rock-si-Chord, the other to silhouetted drums.

Sidemen take places by silhouetted mics, violin bow silhouettes are poised. A down beat, a drum roll: LADIES AND GENTLEMEN—THE CARPENTERS!

The boppers freak.

Richard smiles. The sidemen smile. Karen smiles. It's total metamorphosis. No slumping, no glumness tonight; as Karen sings, she toddles like a bopper, rolls her eyes like dolly. Wonderful! How did we ever make it so quickly to the top? Hollywood Bowl sellout? Don't ask me. I can't believe it, either, but here we are!

The music is pretty eclectic: pop and rock, surf and jazz, Bacharach, Beatles and Beach Boys. They do "Help!" and "Superstar" and "Baby It's You." Finishing a Bacharach medley with "Do You Know the Way to San Jose?" they rush to a snap-off ending with computer-like precision. The crowd goes ape. Karen wipes mock-sweat from mock-brow: Wow! She rolls dolly eyes: Ooooogh! Whew! Hard song? How did we ever get thru it without flaw? Whew! Boy!

Richard shouts Hi! to the kids in the trees. He gets a roaring Hi! back. He tells how just a year ago, before they made it big with "Ticket to Ride" and "Close to You" he and Karen were just like you guys up there, sitting up there in the cheap seats, too. And now look at us. Eighteen thousand people, and *we're* down here! Is that beautiful?

Richard plays one of his compositions, then tells the audience about the latest gold album, *Carpenters*, and about an appearance on an upcoming TV show, and about how Stanley Kramer personally called them up to do the sound track for his movie *Bless the Beasts and Children*.

They play the soundtrack number, then Karen talks to the audience about the career, introduces Herb Alpert Tijuana Brass—who smiles and nods out in the 10th row. Then the group does two more songs which sound like the last ones they did.

The audience response is polite applause. They clap more at the beginnings, like a contest: Who can recognize the song first? That's all that seems to matter.

With a tiny spotlight on her face, Karen—not quite like Judy Garland—tiptoes to the apron and whispers how swell it is to be up from those humble beginnings, how she and Richard walked the streets of L.A. with only that little tape recording in their pocket, how they'd like to say to you people out there a simple—thanks.

When Karen finishes, the Carpenters bow offstage and the audience—politely applauding—starts getting up to leave.

It's an embarrassment. Will the Carpenters be allowed to stay off? Won't they be brought back?

From nowhere they reappear, sprinting forward like middle-distance runners, bowing profusely. The audience sits, claps to a mild plateau, then cools it fast. The Carpenters run backstage, pivot, and like fire-horses race on again, bowing. The audience sits down. Then they get up. Then they sit down again. The audience doesn't know what to do.

What's the matter with you people, don't you know *talent*? With *that* kind of angry face, who rises from an apron-side box, clapping her curls off? Karen's hairdresser. Like a shill, she's up tall, pounding her palms together, her curls jumping like Shirley Temple's, giving filthy, resentful looks to anybody who dares remain seated, which is everybody.

But the hairdresser accomplishes Mission Impossible. First the familial cluster stands—the aunts, uncles and cousins—then the rest of the boxes, then it spreads thru the intermediate prices and up into the cheap seats under the trees. In a sweep of seconds, all 18,000 are on their feet, clapping away, and the Carpenters are smiling and bowing and that's the show.

◆

THE RECEPTION. WHERE *are* they? Are they here?

Midnight, everybody downing free cocktails at Bistro's bar—a nice, rosy room with flowered-glass ceilings.

Where are they?

Herb Alpert Tijuana Brass, at the center with a knot of seekers around him, looks at his watch, worried the kids aren't here.

The drinks are fine, but the smell of *chiles rellenos* and *enchiladas* wafting from the buffet draws a lot of the bar crowd in to dine. The rest wait drinking for the Arrival.

The publicist, who's racing around both rooms like Speedy Gonzales, gives you a quick aside on the way by: "Kids won't be able to talk to you much, big night tonight, pooped. Big success, too, notice? How many acts pull a standing ovation from 18 thou at the Bowl? Tell you what: Call the kids long distance, chat long distance with them next month when they come back from tour. Good dealie-doo?"

You head for the *enchiladas*.

Most dining room people haven't heard of the Carpenters. They got an invitation from Stanley Kramer to hear about his new picture, and came over, is all. Is that who it's for, the Carpenters? Who are they?

In the middle of your second helping of food there's great tumult and shouting and popping of bulbs. The kids!

Three couples knock over a table getting up, and streak from dining to the bar. The rest—including Stanley Kramer and his party and Arte Johnson and his—keep eating and telling stories.

In rushes the publicist, with red face, bulls across the dining room snorting. "Been looking for you. You should be out there. Get *near* them. The kids are really popping off, adlibbing about the concert and the career. Go on"—he pushes your coat shoulder padding—"Go out there right *now!*"

You tell him you can't, you've got to finish your chocolate mousse.

A half-hour later, as Karen enters thru one dining room door you exit thru the other. In the bar Richard is still holding forth for a following of five, describing how terrific, how outasight it went over tonight before the 18,000. The rest have backed off and are at side tables pouring down free Drambuies. When the inner circle diminishes to two, Richard bows out to dining, to a table of relatives, where Karen slumps in the head chair, frowning.

Arte Johnson and his wife leave. Stanley Kramer and his party leave. Herb Alpert Tijuana Brass leaves. Some gofers and back-up men stay boozing at the bar, pub-talking with agents, managers, PR men and wives.

The lights lower, and next everybody's down Bistro's stairs and onto Cañon Drive where it's a soft moonlit night in Beverly Hills.

Parked illegally in the lot next to Bistro crouches the Maserati. Almost dawn, the ritual begins anew. A residue of crowd collects around the kids' red car, all getting in the last word, the last shake, the last touch, before the kids finally break away, climb into the bucket seats and, with a mechanized roar, leave all the ordinary folks behind.

WHY THEY'RE ON TOP?

Dan Armstrong

Southeast News, 1971

H ow well performers do their thing under pressure is often the difference between success and failure. Karen and Richard Carpenter
will have a new single on the radio Friday morning called "Hurting Each
Other." They'll be finishing it tonight, Richard says. "Thursday morning," Karen corrects.

What the Downey pair will do tonight is put the finishing touches
to the songs, adding things none but the best-trained ears will even hear.
But Richard hears, and Karen hears, and they are perfectionists.

Monday night they put in an evening session at A&M Studios, Herb
Alpert's fantastically successful operation. To the average listener the
song was already completed, and even those of us watching and listening
were unable to perceive why the Carpenters would suddenly stop, say
"no, that's not right," and start over again.

It went something like this . . .

KAREN: I want to make the "We ares" huge.
RICHARD: They are huge.
KAREN: I want to make them huger.

Karen won.

With a technician standing by, the Carpenters entered the sound booth and the 16-track tape containing their latest release was started. It will sound like 12 to 15 voices on the radio Friday, and all of them are Richard's and Karen's.

At the appropriate spot, the Carpenters each added a "we are" to the umpteen that were already there.

RICHARD: No!
KAREN: What do you mean, no?
RICHARD: Just what I said, no.

There was no anger, no exasperation. Richard had said it wasn't quite right and that was it.

The tape started again, again they sang, again not quite right. Richard said no. Finally he was satisfied, and they decided to work on a single word, "stop."

The phone rang. Richard answered.

RICHARD: The organ's ready? What are we going to do with it? There's no room in here. Okay, bring it down and leave it in the hall.

Again the Carpenters adjusted themselves behind a pair of microphones, the music started, and just as they started to sing, Richard suddenly stopped.

"Hold it. Somebody's moving an organ out there."

There were chuckles all around, and then back to work.

"Stop" got the same treatment "we are" had before.

After about three repetitions, none of them exactly right, Karen smiled.

"It's a good omen," she said. "When it takes so long to get one right, watch out. Smash City."

When you hear "Hurting Each Other" Friday, it will last approximately three minutes. If you like easy listening, you'll probably like it.

Richard Carpenter probably won't, though. Undoubtedly he will find some little thing that "isn't quite right." That's very likely what put the Carpenters where they are.

CONCERT REVIEW

RIVIERA, LAS VEGAS, SEPTEMBER 22, 1972

Variety, 1972

When handsome brother-sis team of Richard & Karen Carpenter was warming up on the tune scene about 18 months ago, it was as opening act for Don Adams at the Sands; now that it's hot, it's top-lining at the Riv.

Carpenters' looks, sound, chatter and attitude are highly refreshing. Whether their primarily youthful fans will pause at the gaming tables remains to be seen.

Richard maneuvers in an ingratiating manner; he organs, duets with his younger (22) distaff partner, but wisely spotlights her role as lead singer. She's a charmer, has a fine, identifiable sound, and invariably wins over both youngsters and oldsters who are seeing her for the first time. One of their most ardent fans is in the latter category—their conductor Ray Bloch.

Carpenters do their trademarks, of course ("Close to You," "We've Only Just Begun") and offer such oldies as "Jambalaya" and freshies as "Top of the World" (their latest single). If trimming is in order, the medley of 1957–64 hit tunes could be chopped perhaps in half for good effect. They're backed by six of their own sidemen (Miss Carpenter's vocals are gracefully blended with her cocktail drumming) plus 19 members of the Jack Cathcart house orchestra. [. . .]

KAREN CARPENTER

A DRUMMER WHO SANG

Rod Fogarty

Modern Drummer, 2001

To say that Karen Carpenter was one of the finest female vocalists of her generation is nothing new. Songs like "We've Only Just Begun," "Superstar," "Rainy Days and Mondays," and "Top of the World" weren't just radio staples in the '70s, but have withstood the test of time. And a whole new generation, inspired by a fondness of all things groovy and smiley-faced, has embraced Karen's amazing singing and her brother Richard's wonderful songs and arrangements. In fact, the 1994 album *If I Were a Carpenter* featured a stellar cast of alternative artists like Sheryl Crow, Cracker, Sonic Youth, the Cranberries, and Redd Kross interpreting the duo's hits in a whole new way.

Yet many have failed to recognize just how good a *drummer* Karen Carpenter was. This can probably be attributed to the fact that many of the better-known Carpenters recordings featured studio drummers like Hal Blaine, Cubby O'Brien, Jim Gordon, and Ronnie Tutt. Fortunately, in recent years we've seen the release or reissue of many recordings where we can hear Karen playing. These bring into focus the real gifts of Karen Carpenter the drummer. [. . .]

According to friends and family, Karen took the drums very seriously from the start, spending endless hours practicing. Her brother Richard recalls, "She seemed to take to them in nothing flat." In time, Karen came under the influence of the Dave Brubeck Quartet, with drummer Joe Morello. So keen were her ears that she soon taught herself the intricate, odd-time rhythms of Brubeck's "Take Five" and "It's a Raggy Waltz." Karen had been playing little more than a year by this time.

The first incarnation of the Carpenters as a working group came in the form of the Richard Carpenter Trio. Consisting of piano, bass, and drums and performing strictly as an instrumental combo, they won first prize in the Hollywood Bowl Battle of the Bands in 1966. The trio can be heard twice on *From the Top*, a four-disc boxed set that offers a complete overview of the group's recording years. [*From the Top has since been revised and re-released as* The Essential Collection (1965–1997).]

The first example is a rendition of Duke Ellington's "Caravan," where we hear a very young Karen playing with assurance and technique. After a respectable display of swinging and comping, she launches into a solo that can best be described as an explosion of energy and chops. The next tune, "Iced Tea," is a jazz waltz with some intricate, classical-style snare drum work, and a short solo that adds up to a real tour-de-force for a drummer just past her sixteenth birthday.

In 1969, the Carpenters recorded their first album for A&M. The album, originally released as *Offering*, was later reissued as *Ticket to Ride*. On this disc, nineteen-year-old Karen plays drums on all the tracks, and also sings lead on the lion's share of the tunes. The drum track on "Your Wonderful Parade" has Karen overdubbing snare and bass drum parts to create a huge drum-corps effect. "All I Can Do" is an up-tempo jazz tune in 5/4 that swings from the word go. Here we witness a drummer in full command of her technique, assured and full of fire, playing imaginative fills and great hand/foot combinations. Her drumming is alive with the joy of self-discovery.

In 1970 all the pieces came together for the Carpenters on their recording of "Close to You." "When the producers finally decided to go with professional musicians," recalls studio legend Hal Blaine, "they talked to Karen about my playing drums. It was fine with her because she and Richard really wanted a hit.

"I always said that Karen was a good drummer," Hal insists. "I knew she could play right away when she'd sit down at my drums on sessions. She played on a lot of the album cuts, and she played when they performed live, as well. But after their third or fourth hit, I remember saying to her, 'When are you going to get off the drums? You sing too good, and you should be fronting the band.'" In time, it was decided that Karen would remain behind the drums on the up-tempo numbers, and come down front to sing the ballads.

"Karen was a very good player and very knowledgeable about the drums," recalls former Carpenters drummer Cubby O'Brien. "Some of the things we did together weren't easy. Richard wanted things played exactly like the record. We worked out all the drum breaks from the records, and I played exactly what she did. The whole idea of bringing me in was to get her off the drums so she could *sing* more. But Richard had grown up with her playing, so it was hard for someone else to take over the drum chair."

One of the things that Karen and Cubby did together can be heard on the Carpenters' *Live at the Palladium*. A percussion feature was arranged where Karen would move around the stage and play various configurations of drums and percussion. The medley of Gershwin tunes kicks off with a stop-time rendition of "Strike Up the Band," where Karen fills in the spaces like a great tap dancer, dividing this rudimental workout between the head and rim of the snare drum. Moving to full drum set, she sails into some fast swing on the hi-hat, while maintaining a samba ostinato with her feet. Jumping out from behind the kit, she moves to timbales and cowbells for a brief Latin turn, trades solos with Cubby O'Brien, and ends it all on her multi-tom set for the big finish.

In 1973, work began on a new album, *Now & Then*. After using session players for their three previous recordings, this one was cut almost entirely with road musicians—with one exception. Karen returned to her roots and supplied the drum tracks for every song [with the exception of "Jambalaya (On the Bayou)," which was tracked by Hal Blaine]. On "This Masquerade," Karen lays down a Latin rhythm that can only be described as elegantly hip. With a stick and a brush, she weaves an almost ethereal groove. Hi-hat accents and an uncluttered clave offer a textbook example of musical and creative drumming. Towards the end, she plays some fills that break up the time and are phrased in a very personal manner.

Karen Carpenter was a more accomplished player than most people realized. No less a figure than Buddy Rich considered her to be a superior player. "I remember one time when Karen and I went to see Buddy's band," says Cubby O'Brien. "I knew Buddy fairly well, so before the show I took her backstage to meet him. I said, 'Buddy, this is Karen Carpenter.' He said, 'Karen Carpenter, do you know that you're one of my favorite drummers?' As tough as Buddy could be on drummers sometimes, he always respected someone who played the instrument well." [. . .]

Once, when asked how she hoped time would view the Carpenters, Karen said, "We want to be remembered for our contribution to music. That's the main thing in our lives: to present what comes from within us through our music. We want to be remembered as good musicians and nice people."

And this is precisely how we'll remember Karen Carpenter, who, to the end, always considered herself a drummer who sang.

THE CHORAL SOUND
OF THE CARPENTERS

Frank Pooler

The Choral Journal, 1973

It is well known that on their recordings, Karen and Richard Carpenter sing all of the vocal parts using the over-dubbing process, which was pioneered by Les Paul and Mary Ford in the late 1940s.

In a recording studio, it is possible for two people to "stack up" as many vocal parts as desired (Carpenters lay down a 13-part, 39-voice chord in "I'll Never Fall in Love Again"), but at the present time Richard and Karen prefer to record in four-part harmony because that is what must be used on stage by the "in person" Carpenter group.

The comment, "You sound different or better on records," has never been heard from any of the millions of people who have seen and heard the group in concert. The usual audience and press commentary is that the "live" and the recorded Carpenters are identical in vocal sound. This parallelism is not an accident. Richard and Karen are determined that the "in person" vocal sound be of the same quality as that of their recordings. Previous to their first concert engagement in February 1969, Karen, Richard, Doug Strawn, Dan Woodhams and Gary Sims (the singing Carpenters) rehearsed seven days a week, twelve hours a day for six months.

Throughout this article reference is usually made to recordings because while the "in person" Carpenters are not readily available, their recordings *are* and the vocal sound is the same.

The original Carpenters are highly skilled choral singers and were selected by Richard Carpenter for that reason. Their vocal ensemble sound is based on absolute vowel uniformity and a frontally focused brilliant "ē" vowel. The razor-sharp "ē" at the end of "Road Ode" ("roads of sorrow coming to an end for mē") and the "wē are" background to Karen's solo in "Hurting Each Other" are typical examples of the Carpenter tonal foundation. All of the other vowels and voiced consonants seek to maintain that knife-edged "ē," which is often produced while wearing what the group calls a Disneyland smile. (Richard and Doug Strawn formerly performed at [Disneyland].)

The "ah" sound used as a vocal background to instrumental solos in the fade-out choruses of "Goodbye to Love," "Help!," and "Close to You" and the melismatic "oo's" in "A Song for You" and "Piano Picker" and the "wo's" in "Do You Know the Way to San Jose?" possess the greatest possible similarity in vocal timbre to that "ē" which is produced when prefaced by an explosive "f" or "p" consonant.

Those singers have both ear and breath control. Their rendition of "Love Is Surrender" gives but one example of the vocal control that can move an absolutely unified sound through all registers of the voice and from a soft to loud dynamic level with unyielding equality of color. The tonal unity commencing with the words "day after day as I wait for the man" from Richard's arrangement of Burt Bacharach's "Knowing When to Leave" is high voltage ensemble singing.

Carpenters also make frequent use of dramatic tonal change-up with an extremely breathy quality which Richard calls "airy." It is produced by releasing a large amount of breath previous to the attack of tone. An audible exploding "h" in front of the word "I" renders a windy overcoating to the phrase "I may go wrong and lose my way" in "Do You Know the Way to San Jose?," "Close to You," "Bless the Beasts and Children," and "Superstar" are a few examples of songs which utilize the soft "airy" sound as vocal background in the slower moving ballads.

Carpenters move easily within this bright to breathy color spectrum. In "Baby It's You," the solo and ensemble quality changes from a pleading husky "many, many nights go by" to a harsh, biting "it doesn't matter what they say." These tonal contrasts are nearly always related to a change of textural mood and are dramatically convincing. They display that distinctive interpretive vocal coloring characteristic of the Carpenters' style.

Richard speaks of two kinds of popular songs: those which can be delivered in a "conversational manner" where the vocal tone quality changes as contrasting moods are suggested in the lyric ("Baby It's You," "Superstar," "Bless the Beasts and Children"), and those songs with "neutral" texts and melodies ("Close to You," "For All We Know") which do not demand dramatic emotional changes.

The December 23–30, 1972, issue of *Opera News* contained an article entitled "A Question of Magic" by Denis Vaughan. Mr. Vaughan dealt with several techniques used by Sir Thomas Beecham in conducting Mozart operas. One of these techniques was to "add occasional accents, always organic and justified by the melody, but nearly always irregular and in asymmetrical patterns." Vaughan could have been writing about a particular stylistic tendency of the Carpenters. When they choose to use "irregular accents" they achieve them by exploiting the percussive power of certain consonants. The explosive power of the sharply accented "p's" in "pumpin'" and the savage hiss of the "s" in "gas" give to the phrase "and all the stars that never were are parkin' cars and pumpin' gas" (from "Do You Know the Way to San Jose?") a sardonic, driving, pounding finish which contrasts sharply with the legato delivery of the lines which envelop it. Similar treatment is accorded the consonants "d," "ch" and "b" in "I'll Never Fall in Love Again" in the words "don't tell me what it's all about" and "out of those chains that bind you."

Unexpected accents frequently occur in the vanishing vowel of diphthongs, "walk on by" (bah-ee), and the second syllable of two-syllable words is often socked for dramatic purposes as in "never think-ing of my-self" from "Reason to Believe."

The Carpenter style often adds to this practice of irregular accentuation by inserting "w's" or "h's" before vowels within certain words and within melismas for purposes of accent (a device which had been used earlier by the Beatles and the Bee Gees). A few examples of this practice occur in "make it easy on yourself" (yourse-welf) and "don't tell me what it's all about" (abou-wout) from the "Bacharach-David Medley" and "think I'm going to be sad" (sa-had) from "Ticket to Ride."

The group also exploits the fact that some words "feel and sound good in the mouth" and they attempt to communicate that feeling and sound for its own sake as well as for making a word or phrase intelligible to their audiences.

Richard has discovered that in certain contexts some words are extremely difficult to coordinate. Recently after working all night on the word "won't" he finally had to call it quits without recording a track he would use. The difficulty lay in the fact that "won't" is naturally difficult to sing and in the song being recorded it occurred as the first word of the phrase "won't come back from . . ." The attack was high, loud, and preceded only by a drum break. The word "we're" causes similar difficulty for the same reason in "Our Day Will Come" when they sing "we're too young to know."

An interesting use of the "r" is discernible in Carpenters' performances. The harsh final "r" is, according to normal choral practice, omitted in "Mr. Guder" and the internal "r's" in "earth" and "birth" from "Crescent Noon" are de-emphasized to the point of omission. However in "Top of the World," the "r" in "world" is given a purposeful country rasp and has caused several critics to wonder where Karen acquired a new accent.

Carpenters are concerned about impeccable intonation, blend, and balance. Their methods of achieving these choral basics are not unusual. Each member of the group possesses an unusually excellent sense of pitch and chordal balance. They strive for high thirds, exact octaves and perfect unisons. Thirds tend to be more prominent than fifths and very little vibrato is tolerated in the ensemble work.

All concerts are amplified. Unlike many pop groups who merely tap the microphone to see if it is "alive" and leave the balance to the sound engineer, Carpenters spend from a half to a full hour before each concert balancing first the voices and then the instruments and finally the combination. One member of the group is always out in the house and bears the responsibility for the "sound balance." Richard attempts through his sound system to give each show, no matter what the acoustical condition of the hall, a large cathedral-like resonance.

[Richard] Carpenter shares with other choral musicians the unending search for the right material. The easiest method for him, as for other choral directors, would be to wait and see what is a "hit" or what is working well for comparable groups. But he prides himself that his repertoire is distinctly his. Recently, when another group recorded a song Carpenters were using in their show and the recording became a big hit, Richard withdrew the piece from his concert program rather than risk speculation that he was "cashing in" on someone else's success.

The Carpenter book has been culled from literally hundreds of songs and "demo" records sent to Richard from all over the world. When a song is finally selected for a Carpenter arrangement, the first criterion must be that it gives him a strong emotional reaction; it has to raise "goose-pimples." The words of the song must also be appealing, not only to him but to what he conceives of as the average record buyer. The lyrics can't be "far out" or suggestive because Richard feels strongly that the average buyer really doesn't care to purchase records with texts of this kind. The melody should be capable of sustaining varied harmonic support, and good possibility for choral arrangement must exist.

The Carpenters know what they like and [why] they like it. Their personal musical style has elicited a great deal of criticism from several pop-rock critics who refer to their music as being "slick" and "superficial." But at concert after concert, the finest studio musicians in the business, who come prepared for boredom, lead the roaring standing ovations and leave praising the technical virtuosity and personal musical integrity of a group which has concertized throughout the world, has performed with the Minnesota Symphony, and has sold over twenty million recordings in a little over two and one-half years.

Richard and Karen are becoming interested in recording with larger vocal forces. A sixteen-voice children's choir was used on "Sing" and a sixty-voice choir will not only "back up" Karen's solos but will be featured in contemporary compositions for choir alone in a forthcoming Christmas album.

Their influence is rapidly expanding. Music educators throughout the United States have been instrumental in securing Carpenter concerts for their localities and conventions of both the American Choral Directors Association and the Music Educators National Conference have extended invitations to the group to share with them the choral sound of the Carpenters.

Part II

TOP OF THE WORLD

IT HAPPENS IN THE
MIDDLE OF THE ROAD

CONFESSIONS OF A CARPENTERS FAN

John Tobler

1974

N ot so long ago (a matter of months probably), there was a very distinct dividing line between music which appealed to rock fans and
the more generally acceptable, bigger selling records bought by what is
termed the "middle of the road" market. To a large extent, this barrier
has now been broken down, in my view mostly because of two groups
of performers, the now defunct Bread and the very much active Carpenters. In fact, the trend continues, a good example being the latest album
by Andy Williams, where he is backed by the sort of musicians you
might expect to find backing John Lennon.

Such a move is not the reason for the Carpenters' widening appeal,
for even on their first album, *Ticket to Ride*, they had the help of Joe
Osborn on bass, who has played on record for many of the West Coast
progressive groups over the years. It's my opinion that the duo's ability
to appeal to most record buyers lies in the fact that they are able to select
tuneful and catchy songs, but can arrange and present them in a way that
is not offensive to any but the most diehard avant garde fan.

The start of my own appreciation of the Carpenters was hearing "Goodbye to Love," which was released as a single from their fourth album *A Song for You*. The tune must be familiar to practically everyone, and it's certainly one of Richard Carpenter's best compositions, but what made it so astonishing for me was the guitar solo towards the end of the record, which could easily have been played by some progressive hero of the ilk of Jimmy Page or Jeff Beck.

Many of my acquaintances were similarly impressed, and a number of people, myself included, could be seen stealing surreptitiously into our favorite record shops and whispering our requirements to an astonished assistant who probably thought we'd lost our minds. Shades of prohibition!

It was with great relief, then, that the news was received that the Carpenters' next album would contain a long medley of pop hits of the sixties. To some this seemed to make Karen and Richard more acceptable, and while it may have alienated some of their older fans, who seemed to feel that such music was rather too noisy, it surely attracted a great many other people caught up in the curious phenomena of nostalgia, which seems to have gripped Britain during the last year.

If 1973 was the year in which you became anywhere between twenty-four to thirty years of age, there was a very good chance that you had the original singles which the Carpenters were re-creating, or at the very least had heard them often enough for a chord to be struck in your memory.

It may be a sad comment on each of our lives, but the less complicated years of the early to mid-sixties certainly seem to strike a sympathetic chord in our minds, and memories of the Beach Boys in their original candy stripe shirts (black and white), and all those chanting girl groups like the Crystals and the Chiffons seem to bring a smile to the most hard-nosed among us.

Now if the Carpenters had tried clever updating tricks with those songs of my heritage, I might not be writing this. But they didn't, and that medley on the second side of the *Now & Then* album is so affectionately performed that I'm really looking forward to seeing them perform live in England this February, when it's certain that they'll bring back a lot of happy memories to people like me.

Of course, not all that the Carpenters play comes into that revived category. Since acquiring the two albums I've mentioned, I've also become sufficiently interested to investigate their previous work, which for the most part is contained in three albums, chronologically *Ticket to Ride*, *Close to You* and *Carpenters*, and found that in each of them, there is very definitely something which is quite specifically to my taste.

Perhaps it's to cater [to] latecoming Carpenters fans that a new album [*The Singles 1969–1973*] is being released to coincide with their British tour.

As might be expected, this contains twelve of their biggest hits, which together make a very attractive proposition for the record buyer. I'm unable to detect a weak spot in the choice of material, although it should be noted that the aforementioned "oldies" medley doesn't feature, as it is undoubtedly too long for inclusion, apart from the fact that it in no way fits the concept of the album.

However, the old adage about the only certain things in this world being birth, death and income tax can now be definitely rewritten—a fourth certainty has appeared, and that is the Carpenters' new album, and their European tour will be among the great successes of 1974. Actually, it's equally certain that I'll be there to watch.

CONCERT REVIEW

SAHARA, TAHOE, AUGUST 24, 1973

Variety, 1973

It's no secret that the Carpenters, with their tender songs of broken hearts and young love, have revolutionized the music scene and shattered trends to the far reaches of rock. They are wildly popular at the Sahara Tahoe and breathless approval is audible among under-30 customers.

Lyrics to some songs are pitched to adolescents and lush orchestrations occasionally pile up like whipping cream, but the sound is distinctive and sometimes touching, arrangements are sensitive and Karen Carpenter handles her sure, melodious voice impressively.

Particularly in an era of flaming creatures and wildly mannered femme singers, Karen Carpenter, who sticks to the music, stands out. Her phrasing is controlled and stylized, harking back to band vocalists of the past. She holds her notes and sings the music as it's written, and the voice, while not of great range, is becoming a rich, well-seasoned instrument, pure and melodious within its limits.

Chief fault in her stage delivery is a distracting tendency to overact her songs. Voice is sufficiently expressive to allow her to stand motionless behind a mic, and it's unfortunate that nightclub pressures force her into unsuitable liveliness.

The Sahara Tahoe show, titled "Now & Then" after their latest album, is a satisfying blend of their best music and some pleasing forays into the tunes of the '50s and '60s.

"Rainy Days and Mondays," "For All We Know" and "Goodbye to Love" comprise bows to the past and loud applause greets their present hit "Yesterday Once More." There's also "Top of the World" (recently made popular by Lynn Anderson), a country-style song, orchestrated in the group's style, and given Karen Carpenter's impeccable delivery.

Distinct separation of the show into old favorites and period medleys may seem anticlimactic to Carpenters fans whose biggest thrill is to see their big hits performed live. Oldies are solidly successful, with Pete Henderson participating amusingly as backup and with skill and assurance for solo and duet work with Karen Carpenter.

Tony Peluso, their lead guitarist, supplies amusingly overbearing D.J. intros, and Richard Carpenter, seldom heard as a soloist, acquits himself well with "Book of Love." Otherwise, it's Karen Carpenter all the way, with fine versions of "Johnny Angel," "Leader of the Pack," and "Runaway." Her "Jambalaya" is certainly different than more raunchy versions of the song, but the careful, stylized treatment is a pleasant alternative.

They have the good fortune to be supported by Skiles & Henderson, who add a lively note to this heavily musical show. Their comedy, with classic sound effects and unlikely props, plays well with their participation in the Carpenters' show, culminating with a wild, strobe-lit sword fight with drumsticks.

THE CARPENTERS

SOFT ROCK AND 14 GOLD RECORDS

Frank H. Lieberman

Saturday Evening Post, 1974

A typical hot Southern California afternoon. Smog. Bright sun. A bumper-to-bumper drive back from suburbia to the press agent's Beverly Hills office. ("You'll have no trouble writing about them. The few hours you just spent with them plus all that other time. . . .")

Continual talk about how fantastic Richard and Karen Carpenter are added to the haze in the air. Every time a song finished on the radio, he pushed a button to find something else. "The commercials are awful." I was thinking more about food. My interview with the Carpenters, one of many the past few months, was at 11:30 a.m. It was now 3 p.m. They didn't feed me. I was starved.

Great. Honest. Real. Just normal kids. The adjectives continued to flow like a press release. So did the acid in my empty stomach. It was easier to nod in agreement. "If you need anything else, just call my secretary and she'll set up a phone call with them . . . I don't think you will, though; they did answer all your questions very completely and openly."

Finally. The Beverly Hills office. Downey—the Carpenters' retreat, about a thirty-minute drive from downtown Los Angeles—seemed a day's ride away. An ice cream store across the street. And no ticket on my car. It was worth it after all . . . I guess.

Listening to the tapes, I wondered what it would be like living in that fancy house with its luxurious Japanese garden and high, insurmountable wall around it. The wall wasn't really there . . . or was it?

"We've been called sticky sweet, Goody Two Shoes and squeaky clean," said Richard in an interview at the time of their first White House appearance. "But it's all relative, isn't it? We came along in '69 right in the middle of acid rock, when all the performers had this negative sort of 'take me as I am' attitude, never concerned about their stage appearance. And then we walk out, just normally clean. I mean, most people shower, right?"

Of course, that afternoon Richard and Karen had looked immaculate. They have every time I've been around them. Were they dull the first time I saw them at the Hollywood Bowl. It had to be one of the most boring concerts of all time. But that audience loved them. They cheered. And cheered. Two encores, if I remember correctly. My review wasn't very complimentary.

I looked up the telephone interview I had with them prior to that concert. Boy, did some of the answers illuminate today's session. Egads. Honest, real. All the press agent's (the same one all the four years) terms. I used them, too. Maybe, just maybe, he was right. Nah, nobody's perfect. Are they?

The career of Richard and Karen Carpenter is a story of blind faith, of being musical mavericks during the heyday of glitter rock, and of waiting and believing in themselves and their sound. (They sure do. I listened to other interviews with people ranging from an underground Los Angeles paper to a totally naive older woman's free-lance assignment. The answers were all the same, just like the way their music has been described.)

The Carpenters' music has been called by many labels—soft rock, easy listening, pabulum or homogenized rock. Critics shout it's commercial; others say it's reliable. But no matter. It's successful, and despite contrary claims, success is what it's all about.

Is that the key to the music industry? Dollars and cents? Do great sales dictate creativity? In many cases, yes. In the Carpenters' situation, I don't think so.

The Carpenters' popularity increased as reaction to harsh electronic hard rock began. In contrast to rock's loudness, the Carpenters' musical effect is to soothe, to pep up or to amuse. It is quieter, using the same electric guitars, drums and horns as rock, but not as loudly. In contrast to the angry anti-establishment lyrics of so many rock songs, the Carpenters lean toward songs that talk about love in the rain or sitting atop the world. [. . .]

At age twenty-seven and twenty-three respectively, the brother-and-sister combination claims fourteen gold records ($1 million in sales each), three Grammy Awards, and the loyalty of a huge contingency of fans.

Karen twirls her hair. Stares at the ceiling. Glances at the many gold records hanging on the wall. She was tired of the interviews the press agent had arranged. Sure, he was doing his job. But she was home. No airplanes. No Holiday Inns. She makes a face at the woman doing the interview, later saying, "I hope she didn't see me. But those questions! Who cares?"

Richard returns from escorting the woman to the door. Her time was up. I had another crack at them. But then, I was different (though the answers seemed the same). After all, I was writing a tribute (the Carpenters were paying for it) about Richard and Karen for [*Billboard*,] a national record trade publication.

I kept picturing all the interviews and all the time I had spent with the Carpenters. It was late evening and I couldn't wait to finish transcribing the tapes.

Richard was explaining their success. "We've built a large following because it seems that the people understood us, and most critics didn't. (Me neither, at least at first.) I love rock. I enjoy [Frank] Zappa, the Beatles, and dozens more. (The shelves loaded with various types of albums proved his point.) I know we're not rock. We're pop. But we're not that kind of bland, unimaginative pop music that is so often associated with the term 'easy listening.' We don't just cover other people's recordings. I think we are a little more creative than that. We do our own arranging, our own orchestration. We try to bring our own interpretation to a song."

The perfect sound. Nah, nobody's perfect. Are they?

My wife reminds me of the late hour. "Just a few more minutes." Simple answer. Effective. Like the Carpenters' lyrics, I thought, but they are only words. Isn't there more to a performer, whether it be a solo art-ist or a group? Yes. Then couple the Carpenters' musical intention with their public relations image . . . and instant establishment success.

Soft rock stars, like the Carpenters, are proud to belong to the estab-lishment. Right? Their lifestyle as well as their music reflects traditional middle-class American values. It's not personality that sells their records. I know for sure it's not their gimmicky theatrical antics on stage. They simply don't have any.

Maybe it's because Karen would rather eat a candy bar for quick energy instead of an amphetamine. Or maybe it's because they're made of sugar 'n' spice and everything nice.

Richard describes their image as "garbage" with an accent on the "bage." He admits they've had to put up with a great deal of social image "with our music coming in second. It has nothing to do with the music, how we record or play it. It's mostly garbage that came from the early literature. I never cared for it, and still don't . . . pushing this ridiculously clean image that hardly anybody fits."

Both claim they're "starting to overcome it." Judging by the editing of the record publication story they did, the process may be a slow one. Richard says that he and Karen "have reached the point where we can't hide our feelings just because somebody is not going to like it. We are expressing our minds, and I don't think our thoughts vary much."

Life for Richard and Karen Carpenter is their music. It has given them everything they've wanted. They realize as entertainers they owe the public "something" for accepting their talents, but insist, "this doesn't give the public the right to decide what we do with our lives or how we should think."

Richard and Karen are both concerned with their appearance, espe-cially when it comes to publicity pictures. Watching them pick prints from a photo session is like a Looney Tunes cartoon. They can't be touching each other. "Someone might get the wrong idea. Like we were married instead of being brother and sister."

Richard is good-looking, according to a survey I conducted with some of my female friends. The males I checked with felt Karen was "a cute cookie who needed a new hairstyle and some different clothes."

Karen's stage wardrobe is limited because of her first playing the drums and then coming to the front to sing.

But despite the limitations, the Carpenters' stage presentation draws capacity crowds throughout the world and usually excellent reviews. They magnificently re-create their record sound on stage. And again, Richard is the mastermind.

Richard started music lessons at age twelve and studied classical piano at Yale while the family was living in New Haven, Connecticut, where both were born.

While Karen's interest was in everything but music, Richard loved it all and had access to his father's extensive music collection, which included classics, big bands, jazz, Les Paul and Mary Ford, Red Nichols, and Spike Jones.

"The first group I was in was horrible," smiles Richard, who also maintains a love for fast cars. "My hair was plastered back [he now, of course, subscribes to the dry look] and I wore glasses [now it's contacts only]," he explained. "With two guys in their twenties, we formed a group and got a job at a New Haven pizza dive . . . and were we horrible."

The family's move to Southern California ended Richard's fling, but it didn't take him very long to launch his West Coast activities.

It was 1963. Richard was a senior at Downey High school and continued his piano studies at the University of Southern California. He had hitched on to another group—similar to his previous one—and played at all the typical nightspots in the area.

"I'm still not athletically inclined," grins Richard with a nod of agreement from Karen, who also avoided gym class the same way.

Karen, the idol of thousands of girls for her cuteness, her career, and for having an older brother, started drumming when she was sixteen. Through subsequent group transformations, first as the Carpenters Trio (with a friend), then as Spectrum, a larger band, she developed into the lead singer.

"But we were all so young, we couldn't get any work," recalls Richard, "so we entered the Hollywood Bowl Battle of the Bands—Los Angeles's super-competitive, nonpro musical derby—as a jazz instrumental group."

"It gave us encouragement," adds Karen, "but nothing really developed from it as far as a career was concerned." All despite winning several trophies, including the sweepstakes.

Spectrum had become the Carpenters by 1968. Karen and Richard were doing all the singing, and they were still without a contract. Then in 1969, a friend of a friend of a friend, as Richard describes it, brought one of their tapes to Herb Alpert at A&M Records. He liked their work and signed them.

The Carpenters' first album was *Offering*, from which the single "Ticket to Ride" was released. The second LP was *Close to You*, which has sold four million copies.

Again it was Alpert who was the messenger from heaven, presenting them with the opportunity to record "Close to You."

Burt Bacharach had brought Alpert the song which he wanted the singer-trumpeter to record on his own. (The song had been written six years earlier and lay buried in Dionne Warwick's first album.) But Alpert decided against it because he didn't want to sing the line, "sprinkled moon dust," and gave the lead sheet to the young Carpenters, who were rehearsing on an A&M soundstage.

Richard tells the story of how it sat on his piano for weeks before they recorded it. And some more incidents about their highly successful career. Included was their 1970 appearance on *This Is Your Life*.

"I didn't even know who Ralph Edwards was," laughed Karen when recalling the television show. "And I didn't know it was back on the air," chimed in Richard. "We both thought it was a bit strange to be on that show," he added. "After all, we had only been in the limelight for six months at that time."

The Carpenters' success has sprung from Richard's devotion and belief in the unusual sound he created. He is the mastermind behind it all. Yet he isn't the star. In fact, on the early albums, despite doing all the work, he didn't receive any credit.

Does it bother him? He answered, "That's not right. Let me start again." Another try. Hesitation. "My end of the thing is not a whole ego-building thing as far as what the public realizes. Karen is the star. She's the one who gets the letters and requests for autographs. I don't get much attention, everyone's mostly interested in Karen . . . she's the lead singer and the featured part of the act.

"My end is selecting material, arranging, orchestrating, production, names of the albums, selecting personnel for the group, the order of the show and how to improve the show. They, the audience, don't realize what I do. They don't know I've written several hit songs; it's always Karen. Which is fine. It's the same way with Donny and the Osmonds. But to me, I know what I've done. Even though a lot of people and critics don't like it, the fact is it's very commercial. It's well produced and it feels nice to me that I selected an unknown song and made it a hit. That makes me feel good, and sure, it feeds my ego."

The Carpenters' newest album is also Richard's product. It's entitled *The Singles 1969–1973* because he doesn't like the term "greatest hits."

"I feel it's really an overused thing," he says. "Individuals and groups with two or three hits all of a sudden put them on one album, use filler for the rest, and title it 'great.' This album contains eleven true hits, yes, but it wasn't just slapped together. We've remixed a few, recut one and joined a couple of others. It's simply something I feel we owe to our audience and ourselves."

Following the "Close to You" success came "We've Only Just Begun" and then "For All We Know" from the motion picture *Lovers and Other Strangers*. Along with being their third consecutive gold single, the tune won an Oscar for best song of the year (1970) from a motion picture.

In quick succession came "Rainy Days and Mondays," "Superstar," Hurting Each Other," "It's Going to Take Some Time," "Goodbye to Love," "Sing," "Yesterday Once More" and "Top of the World." They won their third Grammy award in 1971 for Best Vocal Duo.

"Music will always remain a part of our lives," says Richard. "How much of an impact we'll have is hard to say. Acts have gone up and set records, and then all of a sudden the public has had enough of their sound. They never totally leave, but they don't enjoy being at the top. It's not the happiest thing to think about, but it's fact.

"That's why I keep the public in mind and try to stay on top of all the successful products. I pay close attention to what our public seems to like and really respect their wishes. What so many critics and artists forget is that the public puts you on top and in the limelight. Going along with them isn't copping out, especially when you enjoy your music and what you're doing like we do."

Another thing Richard and Karen cited is that many people forget that they're normal people.

"The rock thing has made so many people's thinking so freaky," says Richard. "We come along as average people and because we're not painting our face, and because we dress up for a performance, we're not 'hip.' I know the music business is always searching for a new leader. Everyone 'who knows' claims there has to be something new and different. There has to be a new Beatles; or an attempt to make glitter rock the new trendsetter.

"Maybe there doesn't have to be something or someone new for a while. Sure, the '40s had Sinatra. In the '50s it was Elvis. The '60s belonged to the Beatles. So naturally something is expected for the '70s. And in trying to find that special thing, the oldies, the roots of rock, have been pushed into the limelight.

"I feel as long as everyone is searching, it just isn't going to happen. You can't manipulate success and tell the public, 'Look, here's your new leader.' When glitter rock hit, the 'who knows' were claiming it was the force of the '70s. While it's very successful, it obviously isn't to the '70s what the Beatles were to the '60s. Obviously, they were wrong.

"What these people don't realize is that Sinatra, Elvis and the Beatles still have the same magnitude today. They haven't faded . . . their makeup hasn't worn off."

THE CARPENTERS

THE SINGLES 1969–1973

Marcello Carlin

Then Play Long, 2011

"Think I'm gonna be sad . . . Loneliness is such a sad affair . . . Come back to me again and play your sad guitar . . . Makes today seem rather sad . . . Sing of happy, not sad . . ."

You don't have to know the ins and outs of Karen Carpenter's life to realize the mood which prevails throughout this collection; the word keeps recurring throughout the record, its feeling all-pervading. And while I am not necessarily an observer who bases his judgment of art on the life lived by the artist, it is impossible from these dozen selections to avoid the conclusion that Karen was not a happy person. Even when she essays happy, as on "Top of the World," she never quite convinces the listener; her brightest thought is "I won't be surprised if it's a dream" and her shaky transition throughout the phrase "be the same for you and me" finds her on the verge of suppressed collapse. As with Perry Como, she cannot quite make "Sing" sing true; she is constantly trying to convince herself that happiness is a good idea.

But flawless sadness was what 1974 Britain seemed to want, indeed, luxuriated in; this was its year's biggest-selling album, only beginning to step outside the top ten in November (and it did not leave the top five until September). Part of the duo's core appeal was that they sounded like no one else in their time, be it pop or rock or even easy listening, and it is true in the context of 1974 number-one albums that they still did not. Everything on the record sounds [as though it's been] beamed down from above, even if its words are frequently more in keeping with hell than heaven; it is quite convenient to assume that the Carpenters might have been among the most radical of pop groups, even if their radicalism had only extended to not sounding like Slade or Foghat.

The Singles 1969–1973 is not quite the straightforward greatest hits album it might initially appear; the majority of its tracks featured remixes, re-recorded lead (and harmony) vocals and, throughout side one at least, a spotless segue complete with new orchestral introductions and interludes. That this would herald a lifetime of endless tinkering with the same material suggested that the Brian Wilson influence was more encompassing, or possibly engulfing, than was sometimes apparent. The album begins with the piano/vibes introduction to "Close to You," recalling George Crumb as much as Burt Bacharach; Karen sings the first two lines before a bass slide and decisive snare drum usher in soaring strings, followed by a harp, and then an oboe/strings theme—traveling in less than a minute from *Makrokosmos III* to Vaughan Williams' *A Pastoral Symphony*. All very grandiose [. . .], it goes straight into "We've Only Just Begun," the bank commercial that Richard Carpenter decided to turn into a hymn.

Actually, the Beach Boys connection is deeper; Tony Asher, the *Pet Sounds* lyricist, had originally been approached to compose the lyrics to the Crocker Bank ad but fell ill and recommended that Paul Williams take over and articulate the music of Roger Nichols. Both of the latter were writers and performers with a history of enterprising *avant*-MoR work at A&M—hear, if you can find it, 1968's extraordinary *Roger Nichols and the Small Circle of Friends* (the CEO of Crocker Bank certainly did, and approached Nichols to write the jingle)—[in the Carpenters' recording,] all is smooth and hopeful; Nichols and Williams might have written it, but only, I suspect, the Carpenters could have derived hymnal salvation from a bank ad—and, as the "Walrus"/police siren piano chords prove, not to mention Karen's anguished multiphonic "live" in the second verse (a regular trope which Karen would practice when she dropped her emotional guard; see also, out of many examples, the "wind" in "wind up" in "Rainy Days and Mondays"), the future is not quite as bright or uncomplicated as she would like. Similarly, "Top of the World" plays like a simulacrum of a jaunty country song (that high pedal steel sustain which occurs like a wraith after all but one of the choruses), but the main interest here is Richard's arranging and producing—as with "Penny Lane," he subtly alters the mix throughout the song, emphasizing different instruments at different points; the pedal steel, the harp, the Fender Rhodes.

A solo piano passage welcomes a swooning orchestral re-entry, followed by more solo piano, then strings and a strangely harsh-sounding cymbal, and finally cascading tubular bells, strings and harp, all of which alight upon the most desolate Beatles cover I can think of; again, Karen does her best to inject more life, less neutered deadness, into her vocal than the 1969 original. For example, in the rise to the final chorus, she now sings "Ohhh . . ." as compared with what sounds like "Hell . . ." in the original—but I wonder whether the original blankness didn't make for a more affecting performance. It's as if the sixties have drained away, and they know it; before [the Beatles] have announced their official split, [the Carpenters] are already mourning for [them] (and indeed the 45 of "Ticket to Ride" sold better immediately following the Beatles' split than it had done in the two months previously)—Karen's ["don't care"] is a terrifying admission of nothingness and the Beatles' own "My baby don't care" sequence is jettisoned altogether from both readings; it is replaced by a distant wall of harmonized sadness. Welcome to the seventies; *still* goodbye to the sixties, even almost halfway into the next decade.

The blankness drifts easily into "Superstar," that lament for lost rock ("But you're not really here / It's just the radio"). Karen's vibrato is again teary but there are hidden dramatics; the thunderous low piano which rumbles into the picture following Karen's aghast "wait." Note also the especial subtlety; much was made of the rewrite of the line "I can hardly wait to *sleep* with you again" into "I can hardly wait to *be* with you again"—and yet they kept the line "What to say to make you come again?" Strings and trumpet move into a reluctant climax before a harp flourish presses everything down again. The segue into "Rainy

Days and Mondays" is hardly noticed, and yet this song—another Nichols/Williams composition—gets surprisingly close to the knuckles of the Carpenters' sadness; "Talking to myself and feeling old," murmurs Karen at the beginning, before progressing through the song. The key word is "down" at the end of each chorus; the first Karen weeps in that multiphonic despair again, but with every recurrence she puts more and more force and confidence into the word. It's what "they used to call the blues," but she is not alone. "Run and find the one who loves me" is, however, a strange expression of relief, and Karen's performance now becomes more attacking, aggressive. "No need to talk it out / We know what it's all about" and the meaning of the song suddenly becomes clear, the hidden radicalism revealed—how many hit songs have there been about that time of the month? As Karen continues her gradual emotional opening up, she climaxes on a nearly triumphant "get" before taking the "me down" down to restless quietude.

An oboe bridges "Mondays" to "Goodbye to Love," [with] Karen's new vocal echoing against piano as though in a dungeon. Sung in a deceptively reassuring G major, the self-constructed despair of the lyric chases itself around its own labyrinth (the long sequence in each verse where Karen sings a complex two-octave line over fourteen bars without pausing for breath), trying its worst to convince itself that giving up on life is the best option, but the pain can scarcely be concealed, which is why Tony Peluso's fuzz guitar solos make such an impact (and provoked hate mail from MoR fundamentalists and even Adult Contemporary radio boycotts) since it expresses everything that Karen cannot dare to articulate; it also reminds us, not before time, that apart from Brian Wilson, the Beatles and Bacharach, another of Richard Carpenter's main early influences was Frank Zappa. Were the Carpenters an extended Ruben and the Jets–type study of "easy listening"?

The segue/suite idea does not extend to side two, whether through loss of interest or other reasons, but this side does spotlight the duo's attempts to pick themselves up again. "Yesterday Once More," their biggest British hit single, was allegedly inspired by the revival of interest in pre-Beatle pop at the time (and if so it anticipated *American Graffiti* and *Happy Days*, even though it didn't dare get its hands dirty) but there seems to be a much greater process of mourning at work in the song. It contradicts itself—Karen sings of happy times but then says that these old songs can make her cry "just like before"; and who are those "they" to whom she first sang them? A word here for Joe Osborn's bass, which effectively provides a third "voice" throughout the Carpenters' work; on "Yesterday Once More" he is particularly inspired, virtually weeping behind Karen in the first verse before blossoming out (and note also the importance of the Farfisa organ, just before the climax to "Goodbye to Love" and throughout "Yesterday Once More"). It sounds to me as though they are looking to recapture or retrieve something greater and deeper than golden oldies, and for the complete picture I would really have to refer you to side two of *Now & Then*, wherein the song bookends a long medley of oldies (complete with Peluso's camp DJ routine and phone-in quiz). [. . .] The Beach Boys' "Fun, Fun, Fun" notwithstanding (and even that was recorded on New Year's Day 1964), there is nothing in the oldies medley beyond the autumn of 1963 and that, redone in the 1973 style, the old songs sound sterile to the point of being scary.

They do a fair job on Carole King's "It's Going to Take Some Time" with Karen's new love resolutions ("I can't make demands . . . I'll learn how to bend") marred only by a clumsy modulation after Bob Messenger's flute solo. Then the forlorn "Sing," despite the efforts of the Jimmy Joyce Children's Choir (read what you will into *that* name)—the first time that the voices of actual members of Generation X (the generation/movement, not the Bromley punk band) are heard in this tale—and then "For All We Know" with Osborn's high-pitched, questioning bass. Unlike the fairly unambiguous path of "We've Only Just Begun," this song is sung in the foreknowledge that everything might not be perfect (as emphasized by Karen's strange English pronunciation of the word "know"; see additionally her "down" on "Ticket to Ride" and her "over" on "Top of the World") and so happiness seems as elusive as ever.

"Hurting Each Other" dates from 1965—originally recorded by Jimmy Clanton, subsequently covered by *inter alia* Chad Allan and the Expressions (who eventually mutated into the Guess Who) and the Walker Brothers—and is the nearest the record gets to open emotional candor; it's the only point where the kettle threatens to boil. [. . .] Karen puts extra measures of pain and bewilderment into the song, finally

climaxing in something not far away from a shout: "CAN'T WE STOP?
GOTTA STOP!"

And so the record stops, save but to welcome back the opening theme
and the song ["(They Long to Be) Close to You"] where it all, effectively,
began for the Carpenters—and, again, it was a song with a history dating
back to 1963—and it still sounds immaculate and felt, so much so that
you don't realize that, far from being a happy ending, she doesn't have
him; "Just like me, they long to be . . . close to you." Her contralto is
as lost as ever, but the musical cushion is impeccable; Richard's harpsi-
chord, barely perceptible underneath the piano, Chuck Findley's cheeky
Herb Alpert tribute in the break, above all, the oceanic "Waaaaaaaah!"
which feels like the singer's head emerging above water for the first time,
having scuttled underwater, searching for she knows not what, and feeling the warmth of the sun (you see the Beach Boys subtext sneaking in
there again?)—the song is about breathing in fresh air for the first time,
the Girl in the Bubble breaking out and connecting with the world. Or
so she hopes. Happiness is as uncatchable a horizon as ever [. . .] but you
know that she is intently thinking about these songs, even as she sings
them—and what are the two of them really thinking? I sense the Carpenters' key work as a kind of numbed, shell-shocked reaction to something that has been lost—and in the world of Watergate in particular, we
feel, underneath the layers of smoothness, a rumble; perhaps even a buried rage on the part of a people who felt that those who were supposed to
govern them and watch over them had just packed up and left with their
money. [The Beach Boys'] *SMiLE*—which the Carpenters can't *not* have
heard—may yet prove the other end of this telescope.

THE CARPENTERS

FORBIDDEN FRUIT

Tom Smucker

Village Voice, 1975

The Carpenters were one of those groups I thought I shouldn't like but kept thinking they sounded *good* when I heard them on the radio. Being the person I am, I both set up and felt compelled to break strictures against enjoying them, driven to taste the forbidden fruits of middle-class culture.

The posters for their *Now & Then* album on the subway walls enticed me, with the Matisse-like super-real album cover. Karen and Richard are frozen in a moment in time, driving an air-conditioned sports car down a Southern California suburban street. Nothing is happening but the moment is so perfect, so normal, that it's luminous. Like those opening scenes in a monster movie that are so average you know something weird is about to happen.

And so I rehearsed how and where I would attempt my Carpenters' record purchase. Trying to overcome my worst case of consumer stage fright since I first bought rubbers years ago. What would the man behind the counter say when I walked up with my Carpenters record? Would he yell out something embarrassing to his buddy at the other end of the store?

But A&M Records saved me. They put me on their freebies list just long enough to send me *Now & Then* in the mail. In a plain brown envelope. I didn't know what it was when I opened it, honest. For all I knew, it could have been something good, like Phil Ochs. Or Herb Alpert. And once it was opened I had to take it home and play it, right?

What a record!

Karen Carpenter has a voice in the great tradition of Judy Collins, Joan Baez, and other white middle-class women. Somehow expressive and full of allusion in its basic mournful/depressed impressiveness. Both presenting the surface of middle-class life and suggesting its deepest hidden feelings. Like the cover of *Now & Then*.

Karen's [voice] is the ultimate for me. Both more bland (or smooth) and more resonant than any other. And, woven into Richard's fabulous Beach Boys/Beatles/Bacharach–inspired arrangements and productions, musically intelligent and a joy to listen to.

When I went to see them at the Westchester Premier Theatre last Monday I was both excited and apprehensive. I half expected a blinding suburban epiphany. But I also thought, because of their prowess in the studio, that they might be exceptionally lame as a live group.

I shouldn't have worried. For all the Carpenters' overdubbing and studio intelligence, Karen's voice is still a natural marvel. As fantastic as her recordings from the moment she opened her mouth.

And although their live sound could never match the intricacies of their studio work, it was still polished and flawless. Karen, Richard, and the band flubbed less than five notes all night. The essence of "tight."

But their live stage presence was nothing like what I expected. I guess I thought visually and physically they would be as tight and polished as their sound. Or at least some kind of ultimate suburban symbol. Like a singing Tricia Nixon maybe. But both Carpenters are angular and almost artless on stage. Looking normal the way you and I look normal. Just regular folks who are really into their music.

Unfortunately, tight live music runs the risk of not involving the audience, and for this reason I most enjoyed the "sloppier" oldies medley that closed the show. My friend Ray, who likes jazz more than me, was more impressed by Karen's flawless run through a long Bacharach medley. And I'll have to admit she looked most at home singing this stuff.

Their new album is supposed to be out in a month. In the meantime, I highly recommend their greatest hits package—*The Singles 1969–1973*. Unlike most other compilations of this type it really flows and holds together on its own—aided by some slick additional studio work from Richard. Buying it in person once I already owned *Now & Then* was almost effortless, too, as it turned out.

UP FROM DOWNEY

Tom Nolan

Rolling Stone, 1974

Karen Carpenter, the solo singing half of a brother and sister musical duo that has sold over 25 million records worldwide, has classic "good looks" but with something extra. It is the something extra that makes her interesting to look at, some unrealized firmness in her features, a womanliness she does not always allow herself to express. It comes out when she sings—in the emotion that makes her voice intriguing and beguiling.

Karen insists on the right to be normal, even though she is a celebrity known all over the world, but it is impossible for her or for her brother Richard to regain the placid existence of their youth.

At a back table in Beverly Hills' La Scala restaurant, Karen described some conditions that would tend to make an "ordinary" life impossible for her. While everyone else at dinner (including her brother) was enjoying sumptuous pasta, she had before her a simple green salad and iced tea. She was, as usual, on a diet.

"A lot of kids write and ask me for advice," Karen began.

"Some of the things they ask are normal. How do you get into the business? How do you learn to sing?

"A lot write and say they were hung up on drugs, but since they've heard our music they've gotten off of them.

"But a lot of kids who write have mental hang-ups. They're lonely, they want to know why their parents don't love them, why do their brothers and sisters hassle 'em. They haven't had a good life at all, and they just live for our music.

"They ask for advice that I'm not capable of giving. Because I'm not a doctor. It's hard to tell someone how to live their life even if you know 'em, let alone if you've never seen them. It's hard. It really is.

"One girl, her boyfriend had gone to Vietnam and gotten himself killed. She wanted to kill herself, and [asked] what should she do? I said, God, don't kill yourself! I mean . . . what do you tell 'em?

"Another girl, in Phoenix . . . Remember, Richard?"

"Oh yes," Richard Carpenter said, looking up from his meal. "The first time we played Gammage Auditorium. That big hall Frank Lloyd Wright designed."

"This girl. It was her mother's third marriage. The stepfather hated her. Truly sad. What else, Richard?"

"Something to do with her *brother*," Richard said slowly. "I can't remember."

"The ones that are really . . . freaky, if you answer once and they write back, then I give them to our manager, Sherwin Bash. You can't really get involved. It gets too heavy. You have to handle each one in a different manner. When you're playing with personal feelings, with someone who's that hung up on you. . . ."

One of the first times the Carpenters worked with their current opening act was in a huge coliseum in Houston. During Skiles and Henderson's comedy turn, a young man walked up the ramp to the stage and sat down at Karen's drums. Skiles and Henderson thought maybe the Carpenters were putting them to some kind of test, and the group supposed the guy at the drums was part of the comics' act.

He punched a policeman who approached him and was forcibly carried off, shouting, "Don't touch me! I'm engaged to Karen Carpenter!"

At the jail it was found he had on his person a wedding ring and airplane tickets for the honeymoon.

Another man who inserted himself memorably into Karen's life began his courtship with a letter which she received while they were playing Tahoe. Torturously scrawled like a five-year-old's mash note, it read, "Guess what. I've been waiting all this time to marry Melanie but it looks like it's not gonna come off, so you know who I picked to be my next old lady? That's right, Karen—you!" She and Richard laughed and kept the letter just for kicks, as they keep all the "strangies."

Three months later a GTO with JESUS SAVES stickers on the back bumper pulled up in front of the home in Downey, California, where Richard and Karen lived with their parents. Their father was in the garage working on a car. The fellow in the GTO got out and asked him if Karen was home.

"Yes," said her father, who cannot learn to lie.

"I'd like to speak to her."

"I really think she's busy right now."

"Oh," the fellow said, "she'll want to speak to me."

"Why is that?"

"Well," he explained, "you know all those songs she's been singing for the last four years? She's been singing them to me."

He showed up the next day, and the day after that. They came to recognize his car as it approached, the GTO of this guy who was not playing with a full deck, the guy who had written the letter they laughed at in Tahoe.

The night Richard and Karen went to the [Muhammad] Ali–[Ken] Norton fight at the Inglewood Forum with Herb Alpert, they returned to find the GTO parked and empty in front of their house.

While their parents were away GTO had pried open a door, setting off the burglar alarm. The police had come instantly. GTO had been very calm. He was not there to rob anything. He was engaged to Karen Carpenter and he had just come in to say hello.

They locked him up for 72 hours, after which he returned for his car.

He sat in the car for another day.

A neighbor called the police. As he was leaving, the black-and-whites pulled up, fencing him in. That was the day Karen had had enough. The police said they couldn't arrest him; all they could do was escort him to the city line, to Norwalk, mere minutes away.

"Look," Karen said, "let's be serious about this. The guy has broken into my home. I don't know anything about the law. But don't tell me I'm supposed to be calm about this guy sitting and staring at my house, looking for me. If you just take him to Norwalk he'll turn around and come right back here."

Sitting there, day after day, staring at the house.

The police said that he had spent some time in a home. He had been in a mental home.

The police wanted her to go outside and say hello to him. Since he wanted so badly to speak to her, maybe that would satisfy him. She told them they were crazy.

The final day of his vigil he got out of his car and walked to the far end of the house. Perhaps that's where he thought her room was. He stood there ten minutes and at the top of his lungs screamed her name, over and over. . . .

"Some people center their whole lives around us," Karen continued. "They only live to see us, to hear us. That's getting awfully heavy.

"People get so *involved*. It's sad to see kids *cry* if they can't get backstage to see us. They go to sleep with our album covers. Sometimes their mothers send them to be autographed. Especially *Close to You*. You should see them . . . all crumpled up . . .

"Only the really important letters are handled personally. There was a 12-year-old girl in Utica, New York, who was dying and who wanted a drum set. We got her the drum set. She was supposed to die a couple months before we played Utica, but she wanted to see that show so bad that she stayed alive for it. A few weeks after that . . . that was it. That also happened with a little girl in Notre Dame.

"It's weird to think you could have a meaning like that for someone, to make someone go on living. That's a hell of a responsibility. Someone loving something that much, to keep them alive. . . . It's a very strange feeling, to think you could have that much . . . power . . ."

Karen concentrated on articulating thoughts she did not seem often to entertain. "That you could mean that much to someone. It's an eerie feeling. I *don't dig* being *responsible* that way.

"I mean . . . we only wanted to . . . make a little music. . . ." [. . .]

Richard Carpenter is technically handsome but really much more interesting looking than that easy term implies. His face reflects his sarcasm, talent, arrogance and pride; his mere good looks are a product of careful grooming. He is a creature of his own design. As assiduously as he has done everything else, Richard transformed himself from a gangly, short-haired, horn-rimmed music student into a chubby fellow with Prince Valiant bangs, then into a thin young millionaire with a certain poise and Sebring cut.

Richard never stops working. It is he who is the driving force behind the Carpenters. It is he who selects the material, arranges it, makes most important decisions and in general keeps the ball in the air. If he is not actively making music, he is thinking about it. His preoccupation extends from the most obvious attention to his own group's performance, through a general and encyclopedic awareness of current pop product, down to the tiniest particular factors bearing on actual sound: that the turntable at L.A. radio station KIIS is a mite slow, for instance, and that KLOS's is a bit fast. Recent cuts he likes include "Puzzle People" ("a *perfect* track!"), Paul Simon's ballads ("great strings, great everything") and "Jet." Among the pop musicians he has most admired are Frank Zappa, Brian Wilson and Jim Morrison.

Music is almost his sole interest in life. He does not read books. He is not concerned with politics and feels no affinity for either major party, although he was outraged at the 18-minute gap in the White House tapes and the lenient sentence given Spiro Agnew, two developments which managed to come to his attention.

"I'm not into much besides my music," he says frankly. "And cars. And investing my money. I like to have money, because I like what it gives me. I like to buy nice clothes. I like to eat well at good restaurants. If I hear about some new amplifier or something I want, I like being able to say without thinking twice, 'Yeah, get it.' "

He did not always have that option, and some of his single-mindedness may come from remembering the financial difficulties experienced earlier in his life when their parents worked wonders with a lower middle-class income in order to give their children what they wanted.

"When we were trying to make a go of our music," Richard said, "our parents bought everything they could afford for us. We had a drum set, a piano. Basically the whole thing. But we couldn't really afford to buy amplifiers, or an electric piano, or even mic stands.

"When we wanted to buy a tape recorder, to make demos of this first group we had . . . Dad, he wanted to get it for me, but we just couldn't swing it. It took us months to save enough even to make a down *pay*ment on a little Sony."

The Carpenters' early history is not as smooth as some might assume. Children of a lithographic printer, they grew up in New Haven, Connecticut, where 16-year-old Richard studied piano at Yale. The family moved to California in 1963, to Downey, a low-lying, bland suburb near L.A. International Airport. Richard continued his music studies at Cal State Long Beach, where he became interested in vocal arranging and was accompanist for the school choir. A few months after high-schooler Karen had begun playing drums, the Carpenter Trio was formed—a jazz instrumental group consisting of Karen, Richard and a bass-playing friend. In 1966, the trio won a city-wide "Battle of the Bands" televised from the Hollywood Bowl, with Richard taking the Best Instrumentalist award as well.

The trio was signed to an abortive contract with RCA, and some instrumental tracks were cut which pleased no one. Karen had started to sing by this time, but RCA was not interested in listening to her. While Richard and Karen Carpenter were recording light jazz instrumentals for RCA, the company was also cutting vocal tracks with a young unknown singer named Herb Alpert who was unsuccessfully trying to stir up RCA interest in an idea he had for a trumpet record.

When the trio disbanded, Richard and Karen became the nucleus of a vocal group called Spectrum which stressed the harmonies Richard had loved in choral work. Spectrum included four other members—all of them Cal State students—two of whom would eventually find a home in the Carpenters' organization: Danny Woodhams, who sings and plays in the Carpenters' touring band, and John Bettis, a tail end folkie who became Richard's lyricist.

Spectrum, all dressed alike and singing original compositions, not pop hits, had difficulty getting gigs. For the year they were together (1968) they mostly played Hoot Night at L.A.'s Troubadour Club, waiting their turn to appear for 15 minutes on the same stage as other unknown hopefuls like Jackson Browne and Brewer and Shipley. After some unsatisfactory contract talks with White Whale Records, Spectrum disbanded.

Richard and John Bettis worked at Disneyland for a time, singing on Main Street dressed in 1900s ice cream suits, writing songs on Pepsi napkins during spare moments.

Soon Richard created a vocal sound similar to Spectrum's with a new group made up of just him and his sister Karen; they achieved harmonic blend through overdubs. Demo tapes were cut in the garage of well-known session bassist Joe Osborn, and Richard made the rounds of the record labels as he had done for Spectrum. He was turned away at the A&M gate, but in 1969 a friend of a friend got the Carpenters' tape a hearing from that company's now famous cofounder Herb Alpert. Alpert gave the Carpenters freedom in the studio, said nothing when their first album stiffed, and brought them "Close to You," a little-known Burt Bacharach–Hal David tune which became their first Number One single.

The rest is well-known. Twenty-five million singles and albums sold. (Even their atypical debut LP, *Offering*, is headed for the million-dollar mark.) Three Grammy awards, phenomenal concert attendance in all countries, with concerts bringing them up to $30,000 a night. The Carpenters refrained from issuing figures telling their monetary worth, but they do state they are both millionaires. Their investments include two shopping centers in Downey and two apartment complexes, one named "Only Just Begun" and the other "Close to You." According to the success ethic, they should be completely untroubled. Life, alas (or fortunately), is not that simple.

The Carpenters have real pressures and problems, hard feelings and confusions which few would associate with the image of the group. Richard and Karen themselves are far from fully acknowledging these feelings. They suffer under strains which even they only dimly comprehend.

The Carpenters seem to be going through what they would like to be a transition period. They have an idea of what they are unhappy with but apparently no clear picture of what would make them more content. They would like to change the image people have of them. They would like to change their way of life. It is just that they are not at all certain what they would like to become. They are reluctant to give up the sheltered existence they have known, and change is such a foreign concept to them they can only approach it with great caution.

Well into their 20s, they still live with their parents in the suburb where they grew up. They are about to move from Downey at last—not into two separate homes, however, but into one home for the two of them.

There is evidence the Carpenters' special circumstances have made it especially difficult for them to break old habits. Their parents have remained parents. When told that Richard and Karen would be driving back to Los Angeles immediately after the final evening performance of a recent Las Vegas engagement, their mother warned, "*I wish* they wouldn't do that. They are just too *tired* after a show."

The Carpenters are protected from outside stresses not just by their parents but by a retinue of publicity and management people who carefully screen anyone wishing to make the acquaintance of Richard and Karen. One of the things Richard and Karen are particularly sensitive about at the moment is their home in Downey. It was decorated in their parents' taste, which embraces a Japanese garden, artificial waterfalls, and AstroTurf and was probably always meant to be a present to the elder Carpenters.

Although unsure of where they are going and how to get there, they are on firmer ground discussing grievances incurred in getting where they are.

During dinner at Au Petit Café, a Hollywood restaurant the Carpenters frequent, Richard and Karen made forays into personal territory. Or rather, Richard expounded while Karen demurred to his lead. Richard had many things he very much wanted to discuss. It seemed he had had few opportunities to explain himself on these points, and what he wanted most was to be understood.

He was openly angry about the Carpenters' image, about the wholesome halo made to hover over the two of them from the very first. The problem, he thought, began and was perpetuated by the publicity pictures and album covers prepared by their record company.

"The pictures, the album covers, the eight-by-ten glossies." He sighed in disgust. "There had been no brother-sister act since Fred and Adele Astaire. They just hadn't known what to do in a photography session. You can't be embracing. And yet . . . they wanted that.

"We didn't say anything when we were getting started except 'yes sir.' So they said: 'OK, sit on the floor back-to-back and smile. Put your arm on his shoulder and smile. Richard, put your arm around her waist and smile.' Every stock Steve and Eydie pose you could imagine.

"In Europe, just last month, it was the same thing. Press conferences with 80 photographers, all saying, Smile! Cheer up! Come on, smile, smile, smile! I'm *sick* of smiling. But they're all upset if you don't. So we oblige them, and we get it back in the press. 'The sticky-sweet Carpenters—*still smiling those Pepsodent smiles!'*

"This . . . *thing* they've built up, where it's implicitly understood the Carpenters don't smoke, the Carpenters don't drink. Never would swear. Never would listen to rock music. They can't figure out how the fast car could have gotten in there. It's like we're Pat Boone, only a little *cleaner*. As if all we do all day is drink milk, eat apple pie and take showers. I don't even *like* milk.

"Not that we're totally opposite from that; we're not. But there's an in-between, you know what I mean? I don't drink a whole hell of a lot. I do have wine with dinner. I voted to make marijuana legal. I believe in premarital sex. But then, I *don't* smoke."

"The image we have," Karen said, "it would be impossible for Mickey Mouse to maintain. We're just . . . normal people."

Richard returned to the subject of press photos and album covers. "Some I can stomach, as far as sending 'em out with the press kits. But I'm still waiting for something that really knocks me out. And some, especially that *Close to You* cover . . . zero imagination.

"They took me to Mister Guy's for that, outfitted me in all this stuff that didn't fit worth a damn. I can't buy stuff off the rack. I have big shoulders and I sort of taper in. I said, It doesn't *fit*. They said, You let us worry about it. The coat had to be pinned. The coat is held . . . in . . . with all these pins, all the way down, just for the picture. Cashmere coat, must have cost 250 bucks. Super expensive pants. Shoes. The whole outfit.

"They give her some expensive dress and then they take us and sit us—for an album cover that's sold four million copies or something— took us to Palos Verdes, have us scramble down a 200-foot embankment. Waves splashing over the $400 outfits. Freezing, sopping wet. We're supposed to record that night. And they sit us on a rock. And here's this amateur right next to us, some amateur just out on the weekend, takin' pictures of his girlfriend—the *same* identical pose! And I'm thinking . . .

something isn't *right* here. . . . 'OK, sit,' they say, and 'OK, smile!' And there's the album cover.

"When they brought it in I said, 'I don't like it.' They said, 'Learn to love it.'

"I have never learned to love it. I hate it.

"That's all the early stuff was, the *same old thing*, whether we did it at A&M or whether we went to this guy or that guy. And it still is!

"The *Song for You* cover. Whew . . . it's hard to explain. They came up with this heart, against a big red background. I said, 'It's gonna look like a Valentine's Day card.' 'Oh no, you're wrong,' they said, 'this is hip, it's, it's camp. People will look at this and they'll say, oh yeah it's the Carpenters all right, but they're putting us on.' I said, 'They're gonna think it's a Valentine's Day card.' I mean, that's what it looks like: a bunch of syrupy love songs, all packaged up with a heart on the front.

"On top of that, they put these stickers with a picture of the two of us, cheek to cheek, smiling . . . *in the heart*! It looked so . . . *sweet*! So . . . lovey dovey!

"Then they decided they wanted to redo it, *after* it was released. Probably the first album that ever sold a million copies that they took back and redid the cover. They thought it would be 'improved.' It was worse. I mean . . . they're experimenting on *our album cover.*

"The cover for *Now & Then*. That was supposed to be—very original—a picture of us standing in front of the house, smiling. I said, 'No. No no.' Then it was, 'Well, what else can we do now that we're here, how about if you get in your car and drive down the street.'

"Immediately someone sees the picture of us in the car and says, 'You're not smiling. You look mad.' 'No,' I said, 'I just don't smile when I drive. If I were smiling it would look like a 1952 DeSoto ad!' "

The photos and the album covers contribute to an image which is then reacted to by the media, a process which really exasperates Richard.

"This guy from Louisville, who went on and on about 'the vitamin-swallowing, milk-fed Carpenters.' You could just read between the lines, he was so up*tight* that we wouldn't give him an interview. 'I'll show them!' The most inane things . . . Remember, Karen? About . . .

their songs are about . . . Karen falls in love with someone who's test-piloting an airplane, and the plane crashes, and . . . it was so ridiculous we kept it.

"We've narrowed the interviews we give now down to . . . practically none.

"This DJ from Toronto called me up on the air. It was different, I'll grant you that. He opens up by saying, 'What's the difference between you and Paul and Paula?' 'There were two of them. There's two of us,' I said. 'That's where it ends.' 'OK,' he says, 'what about Sonny and Cher?' "

Karen: "She's thinner."

" 'All right,' he says finally. 'I know where it's at. We might as well bring it out. I've listened to the lyrics of your songs. I know that Karen's singin' 'em to you. I know they're about incest. You want to talk about this?' I couldn't believe it. I was stunned. I tried to explain, absolutely not. Imagine—*I tried to explain!* 'I don't even write all of those songs. They just happen to be love songs. Karen sings them. I sing and arrange. We happen to be brother and sister.' "

"I remember how you threw the phone down when that was over."

"Yeah. That was the last *phone* interview we ever did."

"In Toronto, when we did the oldies medley, some writer thought we were a group from the fifties and that those were *our hits!* How do you deal with people who have the intelligence of an ant?"

"We get good reviews, but they're surface good. 'They were here. Boy, it's nice to see an all-American group. The audience was dressed neatly. The music wasn't too loud.' They never get into *why* the music's good. *Or* bad. It's just image.

"I wouldn't *mind* a bad review of things that *are* bad."

RICHARD CARRIES A great many things in his head. Every pop hit since 1962, for instance: theme songs from all the fifties TV comedies and every detail of the Carpenters' struggle to be accepted. To an outsider their rise may seem meteoric, but for Richard it is an ongoing story, with past details as fresh and clear as yesterday's rehearsal. Bitterness is one of the qualities he subliminally projects, although he hastens to cover its traces when he becomes aware of them.

One of the Carpenters' first gigs was a charity show where they met Burt Bacharach, who complimented them lavishly and asked them to prepare and perform a medley of his tunes for another upcoming benefit. Initially he gave them carte blanche, but when he heard the medley Richard had arranged he dictated all kinds of changes the day before the show, necessitating frantic all-night work from the group, who had to learn a radically different medley from the one they had been rehearsing for weeks.

When Richard first told this story, the confusion and hurt he felt at the time lay heavy in his words, but as Karen embroidered the incident, essentially repeating what he had said, his attitude reversed completely and he finished by denying any thoughtlessness or folly on Bacharach's part, as if it were necessary that he officially remember his relationship with the man who wrote "Close to You" as nothing short of perfect. There are touchy areas, places he is not willing to probe. He fills his conversation with verbal shorthand and clichés: ". . . *type of thing.*" "*I was stunned.*" (Karen, too, on the brink of a revelation about someone, will stop short and say instead, "Well . . . she's quite a character.") [Richard] has no time to probe those areas. He is busy working, maintaining the style of life and work he and his sister have become accustomed to in the last five years.

"It all changed very gradually," Karen said.

"For a long time it was the same," Richard picked up. "First of all, you don't get a royalty check for six months. In six months, we had three gold records: 'Close to You,' 'We've Only Just Begun' and the *Close to You* album. But we were still living at our old house, still living in the same neighborhood, with the Number One record in the United States and it was *odd.*"

"Then we decided to move, to the other side of the tracks," [Karen said.] "There's a street in Downey that's both north and south of the tracks. We were south of the tracks."

"Right. There're actually tracks in Downey to be on the wrong side of. We bought a place right around fall of '70 when 'Begun' was out, and we moved in December, when 'For All We Know' was released."

"Even so, we were scared."

"Well, you know *some* royalties are going to come in, you just *know* it. You've sold those records. But you still haven't seen it. We were wondering if we should buy a place that cost so much."

"Then the first royalty check came. Herbie [Alpert] signed it himself and he'd written 'hello' all over it, made all kinds of little drawings . . ."

"Yeah. And it was for 50." Fifty what? "Fifty thousand."

"I'd never seen anything like that in my whole life," Karen recalled. "We sat and stared at it all through dinner. I'd never seen that many zeros . . ."

"That's when you start noticing a change. That's an awful lot of money, you know? You still feel the same inside. You're still the same person, but to come from the financial situation we grew up with right into staring at something like *that* . . ."

"It takes a long time for it to sink in. There are all these habits you've been brought up with all your life. You don't just go plowing through a store, buying everything you like. I'm getting better at it, but . . . compared to a lot of other people, what I buy is nothing. Like my accountant told me last week to go spend some money."

"He was kidding, Karen," Richard smiled. "That was humor from the accountant." But Richard grew reflective.

"I never thought it would get as big as it has," he said. "I never thought it would have as many pressures as it does. How could you imagine it? Before, when the two of us were going to college, it was just screwing around. We rehearsed and said, 'Someday we'll make it,' and . . . no worries. What worries? Our biggest worry was not being able to afford some microphone we wanted."

"The first thing you know you need to do is get a contract," Karen said. "If you're lucky enough to do that, you say, 'I've got to have a hit.' When you get your hit . . . "

"Everyone tells you, 'That's not enough. You need another one right away. You don't want people thinking you're a one-hit group, do you? There are lots and lots of those around.'

"Waiting for our second hit, we were in New York to do the [Ed] Sullivan Show. 'We've Only Just Begun' had taken off, but WABC hadn't put it on their playlist yet. I was worried about it, because WABC was the biggest, the most important station in the world. And they weren't playin' it, and I was worried. Then ABC went with it, and it was the last station, and I knew the record was a smash, I knew we had our second Number One.

"Then the promotion man in New York says, 'I gotta tell ya, kids, the whole ball of wax . . . is three. Three, it really puts you in the money.'

"I suppose the guy was serious. I guess he really believed that and the whole thing, but . . .

"Ever since then it's been, 'OK, get an album out, OK you gotta go here to perform, OK you have to do this, OK now that.' Sometimes I feel like a big . . . like a robot.

"And yet . . . I can't *complain*. This is what we worked for. It's all stuff I want to do. I *want* to play the *Warsaw Concerto* with the Boston Pops. I *want* to record a new album. I *love* to go out and perform.

"It's just so exhausting. We haven't had three days off in all these years, not three days where we were totally free of interviews, rehearsing, composing. It's become a business, whether we like to think of it that way or not. Even though it started as music, and it still is music, you've got like 30 people working for you, and a corporation, the whole thing." The Carpenters' corporation is dubbed "Ars Nova." Richard is its president and chief decision maker. "You get problems, things you never thought you would have to deal with, things you never knew *existed*. What it's like to have people working for you, keeping them all happy."

"And while all these people are working at the things that have to be done, nothing can be done without an OK from us. So we have to think about all those things still.

"It's not like being a doctor, where you work hard for so many years and then at last you've got your practice, your office, your regular routine. Your El Dorado. In the record business you can have money piled up to the ceiling. You can say, 'Well, I could retire tomorrow.' But you don't *wanna* retire. So you always have to worry about that next hit.

"It got to me. I had like an anxiety thing happen to me. It was November of '72. We were out for too long. We were out for six weeks of one-nighters. We didn't have a single in release. It was in between 'Goodbye to Love' and 'Sing.' And there's always, like for the person picking the single and doing the creative thing, there's always that nagging thought: 'Will we *find* another single?' On top of going from city to city to city, six weeks of dingy weather, each day more rotten than the last. Business was good, crowds were good, the group was fine, but . . . Holiday Inn after Holiday Inn . . .

"It just got to me. One night—man, I just didn't know what—it just hit me.

"What happened is, a lot of little things started goin' wrong. Which doesn't mean anything. Every now and then you have a concert where a lot of little things go wrong. I got up there, I didn't like the feel of the place. Which doesn't mean anything either. We've played a lot of places just like it. It was a big domey . . . ice rink. It was freezing, and . . . and there was this rumble. The acoustics were so awful, and I hear this rumble, and . . . then there's a mistake in the music . . . then a chord fell out . . .

"I felt like I was losing control. I mean, I never felt that bad. I mean you can't describe it. You just get scared and you-don't-know-why type of thing. 'I-don't-wanna-be-here. I-don't-wanna-do-this-show.'

"But you're onstage. What are you going to do? *What* are you going to *do*? I was so afraid, because I didn't know what was going to happen. I felt I was really going to lose it.

"There was just something, some part of my mind was telling me not to. 'Don't stop. You can't just walk off. You have to finish the show.' I mean, all those people there . . .

"So then by that time we were getting into the second part, into the oldies medley, things I could do without thinking much, and . . . I got control of myself. We didn't stop or anything."

Having said this much, Richard seemed to want to retreat from the episode.

"Evidently I just wasn't in the greatest frame of mind. I mean, who's to say? I can't tell all the things that led to it. Ordinarily, and ever since then, if the flute player's mic falls off or something, we roll anyway. But I just . . . I felt it was really gonna . . . get me."

Karen clutched at herself, gripped by a comic phantom. "Aah—it's got me!"

"Not funny," Richard said levelly.

"Oh. Not funny."

"I did *not* enjoy it."

Chastened, she said, "Well, I knew *something* was going on. I looked over at him and he had the weirdest expression on his face."

Richard said, "Well it wasn't a nervous breakdown. I've never had anything like *that*.

"Just about then, that article about the Beach Boys was printed in ROLLING STONE. Someone showed it to me, and I read about Brian Wilson freaking out on that airplane. And I said, gee, maybe that's what's . . . happening to me. Brian, of course, being the genius that he is, could handle that.

"No, I just felt it was time to . . . pull back a little.

"But who would have thought it could get even that heavy? I mean, who knows about anxiety when you're 20, and you're doin' the things you love. Lugging big amps onto the Troubadour stage for Hoot Night. Having a wonderful time.

"Then you get all the things you've worked for so hard for all along, and it *changes*. And there's lots and lots of *pressure*. But still . . . it's something you want to do!"

What would happen if the group took things at a slower pace?

"I don't know," he said, as if he had never given it thought. "It wouldn't affect record sales or anything. The part we'd have to cut down—which we are, bein' we cut the summer tour—is the concerts. We can't cut down on recording. We only come out with one album a year anyway, so . . . That's what it would have to be.

"The way I see it, I mean, we have to cut down a little. It was getting to be too much. Now we've had the Europe thing, now we have the Japanese thing, and the summer tour, before that the April tour, and . . . yeah, May. It was too much.

"But it's what we worked for, you know. And we really. . . . It's exhausting, and it's a lotta problems, but I still. . . . It's something we like to do. The whole thing is.

"But we have to cut down."

"I want to start cutting down."

WHEN THE CARPENTERS tour certain parts of America, it would not be much of an exaggeration to say that Richard and Karen are like visiting deities. A paucity of entertainment in these areas combined with the Carpenters' huge appeal ensures almost entire towns will turn out for their concerts. Thus it was in Beckley and Wheeling, West Virginia. In Richmond, Virginia, and in Hershey, Pennsylvania. They bring glamour to scenes of devastation, to small cities scarred by open mines and strewn with tornado debris. Their limousine glides through narrow streets suited to Dublin slums, past felled trees, railroad yards, mounds of coal, wrecked house trailers. . . .

Glimpsed from the driver's seat the three figures in the rear look like a Fellini parody of *Don't Look Back*. Karen, in dark glasses and fox-fur collar, chews gum as she gazes at the dreary town gliding by. Randy Bash, Sherwin's daughter and Richard's girlfriend, her gamine face animated or bored, hangs on Richard's arm and on his every word. Richard, projecting nervous hauteur, holds in his lap the Sony CF550 cassette player–radio which he personally carries everywhere. Richard tunes the radio to the local pop station—he imitates the morning man's nasal boss-jock tones. "Yes, they've *got* that *sound* here in St. Clairsville, Ohio!"

The clackety-click of tapping on metal in time to the music: Karen's long carmine nails.

In every town they play, mention of their names brings smiles to faces young and old. "They're really special. Lotta groups been through here, but . . . they are the only ones *really worth seein'*." Their records are on all jukeboxes, squeezed between the country records that predominate. Muzak plays their hits, and Karen and Richard prick up their ears, comment on the arrangements. This is Carpenter country. (But then, so is Las Vegas. So is Europe, and Japan.)

They are quite gracious when asked for autographs, considering how often they are approached in restaurants, after concerts, while riding in limousines. "I'm going to act like a fan now," a driver will announce. "My other daughter would never forgive me if I got one for her sister and not for her," a woman at the Sheraton Inn will say ingratiatingly as she begs for a second signature. Approached during breakfast in Richmond, Virginia, by a rotund and particularly nervy fellow bearing five napkins to be individually inscribed, Karen blurted in disbelief, "Oh, f—!"

◆

KAREN IS IN some ways like a child, which is not surprising. A star since 19, a committed musician even longer than that, she probably missed out on one or two normal stages of adaptation to "the real world." Richard is similarly detached, but he is older; Karen at 24 most noticeably shows the effects of an early success. She has been sheltered and pampered and behaves accordingly. Finished at lunchtime with the gum she often chews, she drops it unwrapped into a clean ashtray, where it glistens wetly like a kitten's tongue throughout the meal. She is capable of doing childlike things with the unself-consciousness of a ten-year-old: Giving directions to some destination, she uses her body like a walking car, *driving* down an imaginary boulevard, pivoting herself to the left for a turn. . . . Onstage she sometimes projects the air of a spoiled, slightly heartless prom queen toying with the emotions of the audience, a willing collective beau. "There she is," one of the Carpenters' band muttered sourly one morning as Karen and her hairdresser/wardrobe girl, laden with traveling bags and beauty kits, descended downstairs to a Sheraton Inn lobby. "The princess."

But petulance or overobvious use of privilege are mere compensations for being in a position she is not truly able to enjoy. She is the star of the show, but her lot seems more like a band singer's of an earlier decade, the amiable thrush along for the ride; except Karen rides private jets instead of band buses, and there's not much hearty fraternization going on. The partially forced naïveté, the occasional bitchiness on the road, the comic Imogene Coca mask which fits her so imperfectly are all forms of a will which cannot find its proper outlet. So long has she deferred to her brother, it seems, she cannot express a distinct personality of her own. The two of them are like a couple married too long, in whom passion has been replaced by accommodation. When agreed-upon patterns are deviated from, the transgressor (usually Karen) is quickly slapped down. Then again, Richard can be stronger only because Karen lets him.

The closest she is to her brother is when they are making or talking about music: During a rehearsal, discussing a four-bar break, the two of them will suddenly burst into song as if they possessed ESP. On tour, huddled over a coffee-shop table, discussing the chart positions of their latest releases, she consoles him when their single hasn't debuted as high on the Top Hundred as might have been hoped. At other times, when she needs reassurance from him, at least in public he isn't there. So Karen retreats into giggles and facial takes, becomes a gum-chewing comedienne or a spoiled princess who doesn't allow herself to think out loud with strangers. Or close friends? Or even alone?

When she really comes alive is when she sings; she changes completely. Joking or talking one moment, she becomes a different person the very next, as soon as she opens her mouth. Out comes that unique and wonderful voice, exactly as on record, expressing fascinating contrasts: chilling perfection with much warmth; youth with wisdom. Then she seems to be someone who knows something of life. She must be aware of the transformation she brings about, yet when asked to describe what happens at such a moment, all she will guardedly say is, "I don't know what you mean. I'm not thinking of anything in particular. I'm just . . . trying to get it right."

AT BREAKFAST IN the coffee shop of the Beckley Ramada Inn, Karen said she had a sore throat.

Richard had a complaint of his own. The group had ordered an expensive piece of sound equipment from the firm that supplies the hardware for their concerts, and the equipment was months overdue. Richard seemed in some way to blame Karen, because her sometime boyfriend worked for the firm when the order was placed. He began nagging her in a scolding manner.

"We were supposed to have that thing by January. *Then* we were going to get it for Europe. *Then* they said it would come in time for *this* silly little tour. And now—they're telling us, wait till Japan. Karen, I want that $15,000 back."

Karen floundered, out of her depths and for once in more human waters. Piteously, unconsciously touching her throat, she said, "Look, Richard. I don't know anything about that equipment. All I know is, I don't feel very well."

Elliot Abbott, Sherwin Bash's dry-humored representative, began uncharacteristically to hum "Tea for Two" in a strained and significant voice, as if to remind them of a writer's presence at the table. They didn't notice. Richard stared at his sister as if she were pulling feminine rank on him by having a sore throat, but for the moment he let the matter drop.

The waitress—this one had decided to treat the Carpenters as just plain folk—brought the news that there was no orange juice this morning.

"No *orange* juice?" Richard slumped against Randy in astonishment and mock despair.

"Gee, I guess this is gonna be the first time in 17 years that Richard hasn't started his day with a big double glass of orange juice," Karen offered. Richard nodded like an endearing little boy. His disappointment was partly comical and dispelled the previous moment's mood, but it also betrayed a real letdown. Not a $15,000 letdown, but certainly something worth remembering.

"Boy, there've been a lot of firsts on this tour," he said. "No grapefruit yesterday, no ice cream the day before . . ."

"*No vanilla ice cream*," Karen said with wonderment. "I almost died when I heard that one. Could *not* believe it."

"And now this."

ALLOWING FOR UNFORESEEN mechanical annoyances, the show itself is as seamless as could be. It never varies. It features all of the Carpenters' many hits: "Rainy Days and Mondays," "Top of the World," "Close to You," "We've Only Just Begun," all the others. There is a fun oldies medley, narrated in terrific boss-jock fashion by superb guitarist Tony Peluso, the man responsible for the incredible solo on "Goodbye to Love."

The Carpenters' conservatively mod wardrobe consists of expensive and attractive "semi-hip" ensembles, generally embroidered or sequined denim suits. Karen and Richard's patter has been created for them by a professional writer, and they speak it word-for-word during every performance.

"How many of you remember the Mickey Mouse Club? You do? I want you to think back to the end of the show, when the camera would focus in on two of the littlest Mouseketeers: Karen and Cubby. Well, I'm not the same Karen. But the newest member of our band *is* the same

Cubby! Ladies and gentlemen, let's have a big round of applause for our drummer, Cubby O'Brien!"

When they speak nonmusically to their audiences, for some reason—insecurity? a misguided sense of propriety?—they become something very close to the image of wholesomeness they are so weary of. They are here to present a series of tunes as professionally as possible, and there will be no nonsense please!

The music is wonderful. Karen sings like a dream, a wish fulfilled, a sorrow resolved in the telling. Richard conducts from his electric keyboard with the precision and brilliance that has won him respect as an arranger and producer from such peers as Henry Mancini and Burt Bacharach. When Karen plays the drums she flails away with unthinking enthusiasm; she is a very good drummer. It all makes an excellent show.

In Wheeling, West Virginia, the Carpenters play two shows back to back in the Capitol Music Hall, home of the WWVA Jamboree, a well-known counterpart of the Grand Ole Opry. The hall holds approximately 3,000. Both concerts are sold out, and an official guesses that if a third performance had been scheduled it too would have attracted a capacity crowd.

The Wheeling audiences are respectful without being dull, enthralled but enthusiastically appreciative on cue: the kind of audiences Richard likes. The setting helps—a marvelous, ratty old theater with proscenium stage, velvet curtains, balconies—"A dump," as Karen says. The night before, in Beckley, the Carpenters had played semi-in-the-round in a domed athletic stadium, and the informal atmosphere had encouraged a lively cheering and whooping which Richard had found rude. Here in Wheeling the loudest sound except applause to be heard from the other side of the footlights is a shushed and sibilant hiss, a whispered chorus of many young women singing softly along with Karen on "Close to You."

One of thousands attending the first show of the evening is an eight-year-old girl named Karin, who is dying of cancer. She weighs 40 pounds. Her fondest wish was to see the Carpenters perform in person. This was arranged for her by the men who are serving as the Carpenters' drivers in Wheeling. There is no limousine service in Wheeling or St. Clairsville, the town in Ohio across the river where the group is staying; these part-time chauffeurs were recruited from their usual jobs as drivers for the town's private ambulance service and funeral home. Through their work they had heard of Karin, and they made possible the special treatment which allows her attendance tonight.

Karin is lying on the wide shelf of a balcony, looking down on the stage from the left. Sitting behind her in aluminum folding chairs are her mother and a hospital nurse. Karin rests on a litter, dressed in pajamas, covered by blankets, supported by pillows. She clutches a teddy bear to her side, and in one attenuated hand is a tattered Kleenex like a paper lily. When introduced to someone saying he is with the Carpenters, Karin beams suddenly with an intensity that is hard to bear. The skin on her face, on all her body, is sparse and taut, barely covering the bones. Her head is skeletal and looks enlarged, too big for the wasted frame that carries it. Karin reminds one of embryos photographed in the womb, but her gaze is informed with a century's wisdom not native to the unborn, nor to eight-year-old humans. Her being has taken on through pain a beauty it seems blasphemous to contemplate. With great effort she summons the energy to speak. "I really like their songs," she says. "I really like to listen to them."

In each of their concerts the Carpenters perform their hit "Sing" with the help of a local children's choir recruited from whatever town they are playing. The Wheeling Elementary School Choir is in tune and particularly well-kempt, fresh-faced and exuberant as they cheerily endorse the virtue of facing life while delivering your personal melody. "Aren't they somethin'?" Karen Carpenter asks, and the audience applauds its endorsement of these adults of the future, and Karin applauds them too.

The Carpenters' unofficial observer leaves the balcony before the concert's finale, before the end of the show that someone has stayed alive to see.

As the Carpenters finished, there was much applause from their second capacity audience of the night, but the cheering faded and stopped before the hem of the curtain had quite touched the boards of the stage of the Wheeling Jamboree. As her brother led her off gently by the arm, Karen asked in subdued alarm, "What was—what happened? What went wrong?" Richard, walking her briskly toward the stairs to the basement dressing rooms, amused by her faith in the infallibility of their magic, said with a chuckle, "Well honey, sometimes it just doesn't . . . work. . . . ."

THE 12-PASSENGER HANSA jet was less than full. Murky weather enveloped the small airfield and promised a bumpy 40-minute trip ahead. Police cars had stood guard around the Carpenters' two chartered planes. Autographs had been extracted in return for a swift departure: Sign these albums, and you're free to leave.

Now, inside the small craft, a stewardess prepared to quietly distribute orange juice, coffee, beer, vodka; copies of *Time, National Lampoon*, ROLLING STONE. She made no announcements. The Carpenters had made it clear at the start of this tour they wished no extraneous disturbances.

It was a short field. The pilot took all of the runway to lift the Hansa up into the bleak gray morning.

Karen confessed to her hairdresser she had chosen the wrong color socks the night before—orange instead of tan to match today's slacks—then settled back, no one beside her, resigned to the flight.

Richard, eyes closed, his head on Randy's shoulder, seemed to be listening for the sounds of the landing gear retracting. He counted the thuds with the fingers of his right hand: one . . . two . . . three. . . . He nodded, satisfied. He gave himself up to sleep.

Below, through drizzle and hazy clouds, a grim panorama of American landscape inched by beneath the plane carrying Richard and Karen away from and toward what they had created for themselves.

THE CARPENTERS

AN INTERVIEW

A&M Compendium, 1975

Nearing the end of the sessions for the new Horizon, *Richard and Karen Carpenter took a few hours to discuss the album and their music in general, as well as matters of image, taste, style, and the like, with several* Compendium *[A&M Records newsletter] staff members. What follows are excerpts from the conversation, which took place at Hollywood's Au Petit Café on a late-March evening.*

[*Compendium*]: I think a good place to start is with this album, which has been a long time in the making, and possibly where it is in relation to your earlier work.

Richard: We're spending a lot more time, not just in selecting material, but in every last thing that has to do with the album. We're getting into a lot more stereo effects than the other albums had, not gimmicky type things—things that have been happening lately in recordings, like stereo drums. We used to record the drums on two tracks; one track for the kick drum and another track for the rest of the set. We use four tracks now for drums, one for the kick, one for the snare, another one for the left tom-toms, and another one for the right tom-toms. In a lot of our recordings, there has been a much thicker snare sound. We've really wanted to get into that and it takes time to EQ each different thing and experiment. Now we spend hours with the drums. We try them in a certain place, use a certain mic, listen to it, EQ it, get another mic, bring it in, try that out. Same with the piano. We played it in Studio D with the top almost down and a cover over it, then we rolled it into a booth that was meant for strings, to keep leakage down to a minimum, and opened up the top to see if the sound would be better, which it was. But all of this takes time.

C: Do you generally have a conception or is this a process of open-ended experimentation?

R: Yes, it's that more than anything. I listen to a lot of records and I try to keep up with what's changing. I like to keep up with it—you don't *have* to, don't get me wrong. You can turn out an album that doesn't sound as good as *Band on the Run* or *Fulfillingness' First Finale*, and it's not going to make any difference whether it will sell or not, but it makes a difference to me.

Karen: We've just spent a lot more time on everything.

R: For example, I used a Harrison-style guitar part on "Yesterday Once More." Now if we use that effect, we'll record it once then go back and tune the guitar slightly flat, and then double the part—to give you a real nice spread, a fatter sound, and a sound that comes out of both right and left channels, but again, this takes time.

K: We're into using different mics for backgrounds, different mics for leads. There's so much to get into, all the things that we never had time, or stopped to take the time to get into.

C: It must piss you off sometimes, in terms of patience, having to wait for the right combination of elements before you can do the thing that you're really there for.

R: That's one of the things I'm really there for, so *that* to me is as important as the actual performance. It doesn't frustrate me to do that. Also, we're recording at 30 inches per second which cuts down on your tape hiss, and we're going with Dolby right from the ground up, where we used to wait until we would go to the two track to use it—it makes for a very quiet recording. We're using 24-track too. Anytime you use Dolbys all the time, anytime you use 24-track all the time, being very sophisticated equipment, you have more breakdowns than you used to have. One breakdown at least per night, with one thing or another. The board, or the tape machine, the Dolbys, a mic, or whatever.

C: And you just patiently go with it.

R: The only thing that's frustrating is that you start worrying about the money you're spending after a while, and the time spent. If we had done this album like we did the other ones, it would have been finished, but we're going through a lot of changes and we're learning a lot of things, and I really find it to be a nice experience.

C: How close are you to finishing it?

R: Oh, we're on a sustained forge, this last week we've picked up, so I would say we're about 85 percent done. We'll have it done by May 8th. We tried computer mix, we thought that would be a good idea, and it turned out not to be a good idea. But we blew two weeks on one song, "Solitaire," it just wouldn't go together, and we couldn't figure out why. I've never had that happen before. I've had times where I thought the arrangement was finished, and we'd go into mix, and then I would hear something else, and we'd run into a studio and put it on. But we're past that point. Everything was on it, and it still didn't sound right, and it turned out we just couldn't get the natural flow of the thing with the computer mix. You can just sit there and do one thing at a time. You may be getting two bars of piano that need to be brought up at the end of the song, and you have to wait and let it go through the whole song, sit there and then raise it up and then start over.

K: It was very boring. We never got the right feel.

R: It took us two weeks to really find that out.

C: It's reassuring to know that human ears are still preferable.

R: There's something spontaneous about doing it all at once. With 24 tracks, you need three people to mix it.

C: And there's still something tactile about sitting there and moving all those things, right? It's part of the process.

K: Panic.

R: The computer mix hasn't worked for anybody that I know of yet, but for somebody it may be great.

C: If you're really concerned with a quiet recording, I think what you really have to do is to supervise the mastering.

R: Well, we have the top guy in town today—Bernie [Grundman]. I would never worry about it. I'll be there for the mastering, but he's great. The trouble is, after all the trouble and expense of going 30 Dolby and all this, the quality of the disc itself isn't so hot anymore. You get surface noise, even though you've gone through the trouble of making a totally quiet recording.

C: It's really maddening, because that's usually what you hear on a contemporary album. You don't hear the studio hiss in the tape.

R: No, you hear surface noise. I bought an American *Band on the Run* with "Helen Wheels" and when I went to England, I got ahold of a British one and the difference in the quality is frightening. The English one is so much better. The American pressings are just terrible.

K: They've gotten worse.

R: Australia makes the best in the world, because they have such a little output, that they're hand-checked. I went into the factory, and they have a woman that has a light and takes each album and checks it for flaws. Japan pressings are impeccable, and so are the English. I knew that for years. I had a friend who was going to England years ago, and asked me if there was anything that he could pick up for me, and I said please get me an English *Sgt. Pepper* on Parlophone. I wanted to hear it next to the Capitol one, and even back then, before we got into the vinyl shortage and the quality trouble that there is now, the British pressings were much better.

C: It varies here from company to company.

R: Yeah, A&M is better than normal, Elektra is very good, I'll tell you, MCA . . . I don't know if you've listened to any newer Elton John things, but the end of "Harmony" on the *Goodbye Yellow Brick Road* album, for example. I mean, the level of surface noise . . . I can't believe it.

C: So this will certainly be the most sophisticated Carpenters album.

R: Yes, technically and performance-wise. Material-wise, I can't really say, unless I'm too close to it, that it will be all that much different. There's a lot of ballads, a lot of love songs, definitely, so that people that don't particularly care for our music, who consider it real sentimental or gooey, or whatever, are still going to feel that way, I think.

C: You're taking more time finding the tunes, right?

R: Oh, yeah. Far more time.

C: What prompted you to do that?

R: I just got into this thing where I wanted every song to be strong enough to be a single. We've already got two on *Horizon*. "Solitaire" is a single, "Desperado" is a single, "[(I'm Caught Between)] Goodbye and I Love You" is a single, and I think "Happy," which we didn't think was until it was finished, is strong enough to be a single. What I'm getting at is that there [are] six or seven songs that could be singles. They aren't going to be, but that makes for a damn good album.

C: Is that your prime criterion in selecting the tunes?

R: I like things that don't sound like fillers, throwaway cuts or whatever. I like to find songs that I can do a decent arrangement on, that I can feel inspired by when I hear the tune, and tunes that the people who buy your records are going to like. The Bacharach-Davids aren't together, the Williams-Nichols aren't together; people we used to get material from, they're not writing together anymore, so it makes selecting harder.

K: There was a period when we were looking and there just wasn't anything we wanted to cut.

R: Then all of a sudden, two or three things came along.

K: So that's why it took so long.

R: I've selected a lot of songs that really go down into Karen's lower register, because I think she really sounds good that way.

C: The first note on "Only Yesterday" is low.

R: And "Solitaire" has a rather big range. That's a Neil Sedaka tune.

C: I was really impressed with the single, because it is so free of any sort of gimmick, it's just a real straightforward song.

R: I was trying to write a song that had the feel of the Sixties. The castanets, the chimes. And yet part of it has a sound of the Seventies—the spread of the guitars, the saxophone through tape delay.

C: Who's the sax player?

R: Bob Messenger. He's played on all our records. He's in our backup group. The guitar is Tony Peluso.

C: He's terrific. The solo on "[Please] Mr. Postman" is nice. . . . Richard, I recall that you had a really interesting definition of soul, in reference to some criticisms about your music, and other people's music, for that matter.

R: To me, soul is a word that can be applied to all forms of music. Soul is feeling. And soul doesn't have to necessarily mean black feeling. So a critic may not like our music and say it has no soul. It sure as hell does have soul in its own way. It doesn't have maybe inflected black soul, like Gladys Knight or whatever, that type of thing that soul has come to mean.

What I'm getting at is Joan Sutherland has soul when she sings opera. Tchaikovsky had soul, he most definitely did when he composed. So did Rachmaninoff or Fats Waller, or it can go into a hell of a lot of different directions. And our music, in its own way, has as much soul as Gladys Knight or Stevie Wonder, it's just not the same type. What you're referring to is that article that said Olivia Newton-John is so lacking in vocal definition that she actually made us sound like we had soul. It's a ludicrous statement. Soul isn't just something black. To me, Cole Porter, Irving Berlin, Burt Bacharach, [and] Paul Simon have plenty of soul.

C: The word has just been overused and misused, which is something the critics have missed in your music, extending the meaning of soul.

R: I think so. A lot of our music is judged by rock standards. It shouldn't be compared to rock. It's pop. It's not pop like Muzak pop. See now that's another thing. If you're going to put us down, that's okay. People are entitled to their opinions. One of the English pieces said, and it's a tired cliché by now anyway, that we sounded like Muzak. That's really tired stuff, to call somebody you don't like who's easy-listening Muzak. I think somebody mentioned about David Gates' first album that it's the same old Muzak stuff. That's not true. Muzak, if they're going to get into saying that, doesn't even have any vocals. It's all instrumental. We have some fairly strong backbeats and a lot of things that would definitely not get played over that at all. Maybe next to Grand Funk, or Led Zeppelin, or whomever, it seems very quiet, but next to Muzak, it sure as hell isn't quiet.

K: It's the same as us being termed easy-listening.

R: It may be true, but it's progressive in its own pop way. In other words, we introduce songs. Easy-listening artists will cover whatever's been done. You'll get three or four easy-listening albums a year that are nothing but covers of what's been in the Top Ten the past two or three months. They're thrown together, some arranger does them. A producer picks the stuff, they get an arranger, the vocalist comes in and puts the whole album together in two or three days, and they throw it out and call it *Tie a Yellow Ribbon* or *Rainy Days and Mondays* and *Sing*. Songs that John and I wrote—like "Yesterday [Once More]," "Goodbye [to Love]," "Top of the World"—got a lot of covers. It's not your average easy-listening act by any means.

C: I don't think your music has been characterized that way because of a lack of artistry but because of its accessibility. The kind of music you are alluding to is accessible to people because of a familiarity with the tunes. And your music, even though it's fresh material, has an immediate engaging quality. You're working with conventional forms.

R: Oh sure. It's standard type stuff. I never said it was all that different.

C: There's something to be said for working within the limitations of convention or a particular form.

R: It has a sound. You know it's us as soon as you hear it.

C: I think the fact that your records are so successful established them as an institution better and faster than any other artist in the world. When you put a record out, within three months, it's an established part of our culture.

R: Most become standards. Granted, "Postman" isn't going to be, and maybe this new one won't be either. Take a look at "Close to You," "We've Only Just Begun," "For All We Know," "Rainy Days and Mondays," "Hurting Each Other," "Sing," "Yesterday Once More," "Top of the World," "Won't Last a Day," they've become standards. The least successful went to [number] 12. "Ticket to Ride" didn't do well, but since "Close to You," there hasn't been one that's gone below 12. And ten of them so far have been million sellers. And ten of them have gone top three. "Superstar" didn't get too many covers, because of the lyric content, I guess. I know Vicki Carr did it. But there weren't that many vocalists that did "Superstar."

C: Did you ever really get annoyed or fed up with the whole critical thing, the misconception of you, and said well, if that's what they want, I'll do a rock and roll album.

R: Hell, no. I don't take critics seriously. We couldn't do a rock and roll album that would sound right. That's not our thing. I love rock. It's not like you can turn around and say, okay, let's do a rock and roll album, because there's no way we could do it justice. It wouldn't sound right.

C: Your music has undergone a dramatic reevaluation by the rock press. When the *Singles* album came out people were calling us [A&M] up and asking for a copy of the album. They were embarrassed at first because they liked rock and roll, they liked things that they could talk about in print without going out on a limb. And then the reviews of that album, when they came in, were much more positive. I think what happened was all those songs were a part of everyone's lives because they were on the radio in the cars. Together they made a very deep impression on people. And they said, "Oh, yeah, some of that stuff is really good." The *Singles* album revealed a technical efficiency of arranging and writing, and with a series of singles. But when it was all there on a record, that brought together a lot of different elements, the reviewers began to understand.

You made a comment, Richard, about putting all the singles on one album, which hadn't really been done up until that time.

R: Yeah. First of all, if you're lucky enough to be able to split it up and actually have an album with everything on it a hit, which very few people have, it would be divided into two volumes. Bread, two volumes. Creedence Clearwater [Revival], where they could have had an album beautifully done with all hits, had two albums. We were the first to put them all on one.

C: Did you remix any of the songs?

R: Oh yeah. We recut "Ticket to Ride" from the ground up. Remixed "Hurting Each Other," most of them.

C: Do you think the critics understand the complexities of what it takes to put out a Carpenters song?

R: No. Because they always say our music is not complex. I still don't know what they're getting at. They should be there when we're putting it together. It's anything but simple. There is a hell of a lot going on in something like "Only Yesterday." Arrangement-wise, different colorings, it would get technical and boring to explain how many different things are on that record. And how much time is put into it. Not only the engineering, but in the arranging as well.

After the mistake of doing the *Calendar* piece, we made another mistake in doing the Bowl. And that Channel Seven Barney Morris thing. I turned it on, and it said "Coming up, the king and queen of the bubblegum music world, the Carpenters." This guy had no idea. This music isn't bubblegum music, whether you like it or dislike it, it sure as hell isn't the 1910 Fruitgum Company.

C: Have you ever wanted to produce someone else?

R: No, I don't have the time, so I don't give too much thought to it.

C: What are your own musical tastes in records, either sonically or in terms of the aesthetic in pop music and rock and roll?

R: My favorite group is the Beatles. American group—Beach Boys. Mothers of Invention. I've always liked Steely Dan and a lot of others.

I know I'll leave out someone. Doors. David Gates. I think some of his things are incredible. His voice is incredible. Not really heavy music, but damn nice pop music. Elton John, although I like his earlier stuff better. Neil Diamond. Always a [Harry] Nilsson fan. Randy Newman.

C: Do you like the Byrds?

R: Oh, I think they were terrific. Cat Stevens. Again the earlier things better than the newer stuff.

C: What singers do you like, Karen?

K: As [a] vocalist, I think [Barbra] Streisand is unbelievable. Dusty Springfield. Ella Fitzgerald.

R: You see, I'm leaving people out like Oscar Peterson, Spike Jones. Red Nichols.

K: Bing Crosby, Perry Como. Dionne Warwick.

C: So you have a well-stocked record cabinet.

K: Very wide selection. Well, Rich, from the very beginning, would sit and listen to music. I didn't get into music until I was 16. Almost forgot earlier Presley.

C: Those records are a good example of intensity over technological precision, because they're *really* primitive.

R: But they have *it*. I really got off on ["Surfin' Bird"] by the Trashmen. "Dancin' in the Streets."

K: My taste naturally evolved from what Richard liked, I was totally into whatever he listened to. But my dad was into classics and pop, not rock. He was more into vocalists, like Crosby, Como, crooner types.

C: When did you first start writing?

R: I started when I was in the eighth grade. Started writing with John [Bettis] in 1967. A lot of things that were on the first couple of albums were written by us back into the Sixties.

C: Do you feel like you're into a highly creative period of time now as a writer?

R: Absolutely not. It's nice that everything we've written from "Goodbye to Love" on has become a single, and a hit. But there haven't been that many new songs. But back in the late sixties, we didn't have albums to record or roads to go on. We had this gig at Disneyland, and we used to spend time there writing songs.

We got fired from our gig at Disneyland. We weren't very company oriented. The songs are now more commercial than they used to be, but they aren't being turned out in numbers like they used to. Between production, touring, and all the business, I find it really hard to write.

C: What are your reviews like of your concerts?

R: Fifty-fifty. They very rarely even get into the music at all. The reviews concern themselves with audience dress, the fact that there aren't that many blacks there, et cetera. They complain about the way the stage looks, which is ridiculous. One person showed up at the sound check in the afternoon, and did a review of the sound system.

C: Do you like performing?

R: Oh, yeah.

K: We know what's right and what's wrong with our performance. There are some nights that no matter how hard you try, it just doesn't go right. Ninety percent of the critics you run into, they walk in and they have already judged you before they've even seen you. They might as well print the article before coming. They print what they think we will say, it doesn't matter how we feel, what we do or say.

R: Oh, yeah. Squeaky clean ivory babies. Things that were said that weren't true, things about being asked to do "The Way We Were" on the Academy Awards and turning it down. We were never asked to do anything on the show.

C: Has it changed any in the last few years?

R: No. Only the *Rolling Stone* piece. Finally, someone presented a nice— not all pro, but not snide—objective article. I couldn't believe it when I read it. I really felt that it was good.

C: How do you feel about being one of the top five guaranteed acts in the country?

R: I'm proud of it. We work hard at our career. I think it's something to last five years. The new album and single are doing really well. All the concert business is doing fine. Things in Japan are even better than when we went over there. It's bigger in England than before.

C: You probably rank higher getting a record on the Top 40 than anyone.

R: I think it's Elton John and us. I'm really proud of that.

K: It's an unbelievable feeling to have things like that happen. We never look at it as a surefire thing. We never take it for granted that anything will make it.

R: I read an article on Elton John where he's really on his singles and what is happening with them. I sure as hell do worry about that too. He calls radio stations and checks chart listings. And that's the way we stay on top of it. I love the business end of it. I really like singles. I think the single is really an important thing, even though it doesn't make you the kind of money an album does.

C: The magical thing about singles is that they are so concise. You have two or three minutes to say something different—to have an impact on people. It's one of the most concise mediums of expression.

R: There are not that many artists that have had one hit single after another. When the price of singles went up, the sales went down. Singles are made out of such crappy material that it's unbelievable. Distortion, everything. It's trash compared to albums.

If you want to make money off a record, you should make it off an album. Not a single, save them for promotional things. Never think about royalties and money coming from a single. Even though we sell quite a few. To me, it's to help the album. The *Song for You* album did two million and *Close to You* did more like four. If "Top of the World" had come out instead of "It's [Going to] Take Some Time," the *Song for You* album would have done another million units. It was a stronger single than "Goodbye to Love" was. *Close to You* had two monster hits on it to promote it. And the Tan album was one of two that had three gold singles off of one album. Blood, Sweat and Tears' second album, with "Spinning Wheel," "You Made Me So Very Happy," and "And When I Die" was the other one. *A Song for You* had "Hurting Each Other," but [it] came out four months before the *Song for You* album came out, so it was already an oldie. "It's [Going to] Take Some Time" went to 12, which is nice, but not compared to what our other records did. "Goodbye to Love" went to seven, which again was nice, but wasn't a million seller. It took up to "Top of the World" to get a smash [single] off of that album. And it upsets me because that's my favorite album of ours. I wish it had done better. If "Top" had just come out at the release time of *A Song for You*, it really would have sent that album higher than it went.

C: Don't you think it's all a point of timing, in getting the single out at the right time?

R: Absolutely. The single got Elton John back. The *Elton John* album and *Tumbleweed Connection* did very well but *Madman Across the Water* didn't do as well. Same with Neil Diamond and the *Stones* album. They didn't go top ten. Elton and Neil fell a little less with each release. Neil Diamond went and put out *Stones*, which went to 14 or something. The *Stones* album had "I Am, I Said" in it, but again, like "Hurting Each Other," "I Am, I Said" was released months before the album, so it was an oldie by the time *Stones* was released. Neil Diamond was like us. He would sell a certain amount of albums but if he had a hit single he would sell more albums. Then he came out with "Song Sung Blue" and that did it. That came out and then the album. *Moods* went number one. The Elton John live album didn't do well. The *Friends* album didn't do well. And he had several singles, like "Levon" and "Friends" and "Tiny Dancer" and "Border Song" and ones that weren't doing well at all. I mean they were long and they weren't getting too much airplay and they didn't go top 30. I liked *Madman Across the Water*. I really thought it was terrific. But it didn't do all that well, compared to some of his other things. Because he hadn't had a top-ten record or a top-20 record since "Your Song." He went a hell of a long time without a hit single and then "Rocket Man" came along. "Rocket Man" went to seven, which is only as high as "Your Song" went. Compared to his new records, that's really nothing. Like "Lucy" or "Don't Let the Sun" or "Philadelphia Freedom."

K: Was "Daniel" right after that?

R: No, that was during his streak, which hasn't stopped. But no, up until "Rocket Man" he hadn't had a top-20 record since "Your Song." And boom. *Honky Chateau*, "Rocket Man" was from that. "Honky Cat" next and then came "Crocodile Rock" and et cetera, et cetera.

C: "Crocodile Rock" was the one that got him the crossover play.

R: But album-wise, *Honky Chateau* went sailing right up to [number] one because of "Rocket Man." Look at Roberta Flack. "Killing Me Softly." She had this huge big hit with it, but she waited months before she got the album out, and it went to [number] three. I'm not saying that's bad, but I'm saying if it came out as "Killing Me Softly," the single, was peaking, it would've done better. Now she's putting out a *Feel Like Making Love* album, when the single, "Feel Like Making Love," was a hit six months ago.

C: You might say that you guys do the same thing.

R: Sometimes. I wish we had had the *Song for You* album when "Hurting Each Other" was [number] one, but we didn't. "Postman" was number one in three trades at the same time. The ideal thing would have been to put out the *Horizon* album the week that "Postman" went to [number] one.

C: So your greatest success has been in developing the single both as an art form and as a commercial entity.

R: Yeah. How many people can you name—and I'm not on an ego trip, this is a fact—that have had hit singles, one right after another after another? It's a type of thing where it takes a certain talent to be able to pick something that becomes a hit single. You used to hear, "Well, you've gotten to that point that no matter what you put out . . ." Bullshit. Harry Chapin followed up a number-one smash with a number 43 without-a-bullet record. Neil Diamond would do it consistently, top ten and he'd put out ["Soulai Món"] and it would go to 30. Then he'd put out something [that] would go top three, then he would put out "He Ain't Heavy, He's My Brother," which would go to 20. Then he would put out something that would go top five, then he would put out something that would go to 14. Each record has to stand on its own. The Beatles did it. Creedence did it until they split. The Jackson [5] did it for a while. But we've been going now for five years, with 14 consecutive top-12 records, and I really am proud of that.

K: Everybody used to say, "You can't keep releasing ballads."

R: You think of each record for what it is.

C: Your first album, *Ticket to Ride*, is interesting. It sounds like a lot of Sixties groups. Not exactly psychedelic, but sort of ambitious.

R: That album, I had in my mind finished years before we got the contract. That wasn't where I was at the time when we signed [with A&M], and some of it could have been a lot better, but you can hear that the ideas were there. Time-signature changes, extended solos, and things that we don't do now. I should've just forgotten it and gotten down to where I was at at the moment. But it was like I had to do that album, I didn't care if we had gotten signed in 1980, that was what the first album was going to sound like. And that's what we did. And that's why there is such a big difference between the *Close to You* album and the *Ticket to Ride* album. I just happened to hear something from it the other night on KNX and got out the album and listened to it, and it's really different than the other stuff we've done since.

C: People still say around the country that if you redid "Ticket to Ride" it would be a number-one record.

R: Yeah. We redid it for the *Singles* album and it's right where it should be, but I don't know about releasing anything more that's old, after "Won't Last a Day."

K: "Ticket" is great.

C: Are you going to put out "Desperado"?

R: I don't know yet. It doesn't matter, but I don't think the rock people are going to dig it at all. Our stuff is polished, because I believe in production and all. They'll probably call it slick.

C: That track has an emotion and intensity that is new to your style.

R: I think so, too. I hope you're right.

K: The same thing happened with "Desperado" that happened with "Superstar." That song had been around and been done by a few people.

C: And lyrically, as far as that goes, people don't remember that "Superstar" is about what it's about.

R: Well, we had to change that one line, or it wouldn't have been a hit. "Hardly wait to sleep with you again," which I think she put in just for shock value. I changed it to "be" with you. It never would have gotten to the top 40 otherwise. Now you can get away with "made love in my Chevy van," and [Paul] Simon can get away with "making love with Cecilia [up] in my bedroom," but he couldn't get away with "crap [I learned] in high school." They made Lou Christie recut "Rhapsody in the Rain" because he said "making love in the rain." And "in this car love went much too far" had to be changed to "love came like a falling star." It still got the point across.

C: Remember, he used to have a fortune teller tell him what singles to release? And he wrote some single about her.

R: "The Gypsy Cried." That was right before "Two Faces Have I."

C: They have testing services now.

K: What is that?

R: For "goose-bump reaction?"

C: Have they ever tested a Carpenters record?

R: I don't know. See, now they have "goose-bump effect." That's the thing that [Robert] Hilburn is missing. He's into lyrics. He's not into music. I doubt he could ever get a chill from music. Look what he has to talk about. I really like lyrics. Newman's lyrics and Joni Mitchell's and many more. But hell, it's a chill factor that comes with good music. You can get off on a song for its feel or its raunchiness—like I really got off on [Led Zeppelin's] "Black Dog" and "Whole Lotta Love." You don't get a chill from that, but you get something else, it's really hard to describe. Like "Bridge Over Troubled Water"—you get a chill. At least I do. But

I think that judging from the rock critics' point of view, they never get that, the sheer beauty of the music.

C: It's not just the words, "Sail on silver girl," but it's everything that's happening in the song at that moment.

R: I'm glad you brought that line up. It chills—beautiful.

K: The bridge in "Old Friends."

R: Chills in "Something So Right." Maybe you wouldn't get from "Kodachrome" but you still dig it for different reasons. You brought up two lines that got to you, both lyrically and musically. "Desperado" is a chill song, both the music and the lyrics. It's there. It's there in a lot of these rock acts, even though they concentrate on other things. The Eagles even though they're not a hard-rock act wrote a song like "Desperado." It's like a spiritual. Something that was written 200 years ago. Or [like] Led Zeppelin would write "Stairway to Heaven." You see it— the chill factor. Or Lennon could turn around and write "Imagine" after "Helter Skelter." Or Mick Jagger, "As Tears Go By." I just think there are people that are just not touched musically and that's what I'm getting at with soul. There's soul in the music we've brought up. Not black soul, but it's soul. It's right there.

THE CARPENTERS

AN APPRAISAL

Tom Nolan

A&M Compendium, 1975

The seeming inevitability that is one hallmark of art. A "seamless" per-
fection, the result of so much painstaking effort, so well conceived it seems
effortless—and hence is criticized as "simple." "Please Mr. Postman":
Caucasian angst. What we critics call "quotidian sorrow and joy." I love
the Carpenters.

THOSE UNFAMILIAR WITH the Carpenters' origins might be star-
tled to hear their atypical debut LP, released as *Offering* and later retitled
Ticket to Ride. Some of the later elements of the Carpenters' style are
present, to be sure—a relatively polished production, Karen's distinctive lead on many tracks, and even a foreshadowing of their subsequent
breakthrough single in the lyric of the Richard Carpenter/John Bettis
song, "Someday," in which Karen sings the very precognitive phrase
"close to you"—but the record is unmistakably a product of the pop-
rock mainstream of its time.

The a cappella "Invocation," beginning side one echoes the choral
religiosity of the Beach Boys' "Our Prayer." "Your Wonderful Parade"

is prefaced by Richard declaiming a circus barker's sleazy-surrealistic monologue à la Herman Hesse via Joseph Byrd, leader of the art-rocking United States of America; while the song itself could have been written by Van Dyke Parks for Harper's Bizarre. Other influences discernible throughout include the Mamas and the Papas, We Five, and early Nilsson. There is restrained use of the then-*chic* toy, phasing. There are tempo changes; soft but extended jazz-like solos; shimmering Buffalo Springfield-type guitar—and a Buffalo tune, "[Nowadays] Clancy [Can't Even Sing]"; as well as the folk-rock staple ["Get Together."] *Offering* tends toward being the sort of album many rock critics were encouraging at the time: a post-folk, soft-psychedelic Southern Californian mini-oratorio.

By the second album there has been an enormous change. With *Close to You*, Richard and Karen have become what the world knows as "the Carpenters," and although they have not yet acquired all the refinements of their style and sound, they are firmly based in them. With two huge singles—the title song, and the even more definitively-Carpenters "We've Only Just Begun"—they have hit their stride, and strongly. With this disc they simultaneously attract the concentrated affection of their newfound fans and the hostility of another segment that has distrusted them from first hearing. They are both loved and hated from the very moment they are noticed at all. Why?

American popular music has always reflected the aspirations and intended identities of its listeners. The mothers and fathers of rock criticism in the Sixties "discovered" that fans were buying more than music; they were purchasing lifestyles. But it was ever thus: Okies paid for Hank Williams' beatific moonstruck grin as well as for his 78s. Swing nuts must have made some connection between [Gene] Krupa's goofy gum chewing and those crazy drum choruses; his *attitude* was as attractive as his art. So here are these neatly dressed kids, a polite-seeming brother-and-sister team, materializing like a weird hallucination in the midst of acid-rock and offering their alternative to "In-A-Gadda-Da-Vida," singing of all things a *bank commercial*. The grumbling began, and grew louder in proportion with their success. You'd think they were an arm of the government, the way some people reacted! What was it they thought the Carpenters represented? Domesticity, perhaps? The nuclear family? Saturdays spent shopping for sofas at Sears? Capitalism itself? There were those so turned off by what they thought they detected beneath the music that they spoke of the Carpenters as the enemy.

The enemy. Imagine. Poor Karen and Richard! Just trying to make their music . . . All this rancor. . . .

The music, though, continued to improve. It reached a new level with the album, *A Song for You.* This was perhaps the first Carpenters LP to receive a *very* great deal of loving care, and it remains their finest overall effort, as well as being Richard's favorite. The material is excellent, the arrangements and production are faultless, and Karen sings with increased maturity and sophistication.

Throughout they had remained true to their vision, their identity, their roots. Eventually they paid tribute to the latter with great style, in the extended oldies medley that comprises the entire second side of [*Now & Then*]. Hearing Richard and Karen interpret the Beach Boys at one generational remove is similar to witnessing the Wilson family cop psychic riffs from Chuck Berry; there is an homage here to truths learned from things of the past, and there is also distance enough for a personal expression to have developed. Through the format of guitarist Tony Peluso's flawless evocation of the spirit of deejay-dominated Sixties pop radio (as effective in its brief duration as the entire *Cruisin'* series), the Carpenters distill the heady, sometimes comic, but ultimately poignant essence of our adolescent fantasies. Those who criticized this medley for not having the identical production values [of] a Ronettes single were very far from an appreciation of its special value. It would be a pointless exercise to recreate these numbers note-for-note; Karen and Richard instead summon up those aspirations and illusions of adventure and happiness that made our sophomore years bearable even as they catalogued our frustrations. (We'll have fun-fun-fun—and our day will come.) The fact that Richard himself is now a skillful producer of pop dreams satisfyingly completes some kind of circle.

Now the Carpenters have finished recording what is in many ways their most ambitious album to date: *Horizon.* The technology alone has consumed a great deal of energy, with scores of separate mikings making the production definitively "state-of-the-art." But above, before, and beyond the sound—which Carpenters' aficionados will expect to be impeccable anyway—is the music. Some of it is already familiar to us:

the hit singles "Please Mr. Postman" and "Only Yesterday." (Notice how easily and quickly the Carpenters made the transition from the unblinking optimism of "We've Only Just Begun" to the sweet wistfulness of "Yesterday Once More" and "Only Yesterday"; apparently the existential distance was never that great.) Other tracks include a 1949 Andrews Sisters tune, "I Can Dream, Can't I?" which features the Billy May Orchestra; a song Richard's collaborator, John Bettis, considers their best-ever composition, "([I'm] Caught Between) Goodbye and I Love You"; a four-and-a-half-minute version of Neil Sedaka's "Solitaire"; and—most exciting of all—the Don Henley-Glenn Frey ballad, "Desperado." Richard is expecting the biggest critical sneers yet when the latter track is released, because of its "underground" popularity (though a highly respected song, it has not yet been a hit single). He may be happily surprised. A critical reevaluation of sorts seems to have begun with the release in late '73 of *The Singles*, the Carpenters' greatest hits collection.

Whether or not "Desperado" gains the nod from *Rolling Stone*, it certainly will please those attuned enough to Karen and Richard's work to be appreciative of exciting developments in it. Karen's singing on this track is especially moving; she utilizes a hitherto-unheard lower register, with startling effectiveness.

Horizon is about to be released as I write this. I have a hunch it's going to make my summer.

CONCERT REVIEW

RIVIERA, LAS VEGAS, AUGUST 24, 1975

Variety, 1975

K aren and Richard Carpenter, with backup quintet, have firmed up their previous mushrock displays into more solid overall presentation. Current fortnight with Neil Sedaka is the best combination for them so far and in musical selection the Carpenters' roster is put together very well. Audience reaction is overwhelming at times.

Karen Carpenter, fortunately, is out front from her onetime scrunched position behind drums, moving around, communicating well in song projections and friendly girl-next-door talk. But, she is terribly thin, almost a wraith, and should be gowned more becomingly. Brother Richard is a confident leader from his keyboards, directing Cubby O'Brien, drums; Dan Woodhams, bass; Tony Peluso, guitar and organ; Doug Strawn, amped clarinet; and Bob Messenger, reeds. Dick Palombi takes his cues to direct the strings and other sections of his orch. Put together, the sound is full when needed, lean as required, with the total orchestral finale a most effective affirmation at curtain.

Sedaka generates enough excitement in his opening 40 minutes to indicate future headline status. His in-person ambience is so very much different from the almost effete manner with which he purrs on disc-clicks. The live Sedaka's warbling quality is potent, filled with nuances and contrasts with vinyl rounds as he becomes a definite personality. He moves well, can shout and boogie along with the best of them and in the Carpenters' seg, when he reappears with Karen to belt out "Superstar Medley" of the '50s and '60s, the session really fires up. During his opening period, seated at the keyboard, he puts out Sedaka hit after hit and gets his crowd up and yelling on "Music Takes Me," prompting a standing ovation opening show.

LIKE TV DINNER
FOR THE EARS

Dave McQuay

Columbia Flier, 1975

A spaceship landed in Symphony Woods at Merriweather Post Pavilion last Sunday. The Martian didn't have time to park it over in the Mall in a legitimate parking space because he was late for the Carpenters concert. He had heard about the Carpenters for years and thought a few of their hits weren't bad. The songs weren't funky, but they were slick and catchy, and the Carpenters had developed a strong following in the Milky Way. Even low-class Venusians knew how to hum "Close to You."

So since Marty was circling the earth at the time of the concert (it was an old habit of his—he was a planet voyeur), he zipped down a few million miles to take a look at the intergalactic superstars.

He levitated himself over the pavilion fence and took a seat.

He had missed Skiles and Henderson, a comedy group that opened the show, but he had never heard of them anyway. Neil Sedaka was playing. Every spaceman knew who Neil Sedaka was.

He was one of the smartest writers in the music business who poured out hits such as "Breaking Up Is Hard to Do" and "Calendar Girl" in the late '50s and early '60s, faded out of sight, but kept writing for other groups and came up with a dozen more hits, including "Working on a

Groovy Thing" for the Fifth Dimension. Sedaka was a writer's writer and knew every trick of writing Top 40 music. Now he was recording again for Elton John's Rocket Records—a noble name for a record company, the Martian thought.

Sedaka was sounding better than ever, even though he was short and fat and balding and 36 years old. But he was always smiling. He looked like a happy bowling ball. The Martian thought Sedaka looked and sounded [like] what Elton might be in 15 years. He was a good showman with good, slick songs and the crowd loved him and called him out for encores.

So what if he sang like the star soprano in the boys' choir who just discovered his voice was changing. "Laughter in the Rain" is a fine bit of sentimental schmaltz and the slow piano solo of "Breaking Up is Hard to Do" drove the Martian to happy tears. He remembered the first girl he went steady with in junior high.

The Carpenters came out, and the Martian was confused. Richard had a higher voice than Karen, and he was just as pretty. He had thought Richard had been lead singer on all their hits—another male chauvinist letdown.

They began with "We've Only Just Begun," a clever opening, and the Martian surveyed the crowd. There were a lot of high school rings and hand-holding.

The hits flew by, every one neat and tidy and three minutes long. There were no surprises. Who wanted surprises for $7 a ticket? They wanted to hear "For All We Know," and they wanted to hear it sound like the record. So why didn't they stay home, save their money and play the records? Marty was puzzled.

Because the Carpenters are not musicians. They are personalities. They are stars, and they give their audience exactly what they want. The Martian knew earthlings didn't read their best writers. Who wants to put up with Tolstoy? They wanted Harold Robbins and Jonathan Livingston Seagull and Rod McKuen. They knew what to expect from these people. The Carpenters are like a TV dinner for the ears. Richard is the hash browns and Karen is the applesauce. And everybody's happy. Who needs surprise?

The highlight of their set was a rock and roll medley. "Little Honda" and "Leader of the Pack" still bubbled with charm, but middle-aged parents were clapping to them. They were the same songs parents so bloodily scorned a dozen years ago. Does this mean Mom and Dad will be dancing to "Bennie and the Jets" in 10 years? Why didn't parents like the songs when they were released? The Martian theorized that they were threatened by the music's immediacy. He remembered how his parents broke his radio after "Satisfaction" was played every half-hour. Parents accept even the nastiest rock songs after a decade because then the songs are no longer immediate. They become cute relics, old novelties.

Still, for all their whiteness and milksop stage presence and Karen's phony Annette Funicello aren't-we-having-fun smiles, the Carpenters have a slick, tight band, and it was worth half the price of admission to see Cubby O'Brien, the old Mouseketeer, on the drums. And then, another blast from the past took the stage—Neil Sedaka!

It was perversely funny to hear Richard, Karen and Neil sing together. They were all altos. It was [as] if David Seville had turned Alvin and the Chipmunks loose.

[Sedaka] rocked the show up with a few oldies, and they broke into an uptempo "Breaking Up Is Hard to Do." After all these years, what a fine song! Even the Martian sang along. Then Sedaka rolled off the stage and Marty took one last look at Karen before he left.

He had seen old pictures of Karen and she had looked as foxy as a sponge. Now in her pink and orange gown with her bare midriff, she looked like the most expensive candy in the dime store. Almost sexy, young, tanned and thin, but a little too sweet. If it weren't for her teeth. . . . She could give Carly Simon a run for Teeth of the Year. He wondered what she would be like if she let down her hair and enjoyed some late-night pleasure.

Assuming Karen Carpenter lets down her hair is like picturing Doris Day playing strip poker. Karen Carpenter would never let down her hair. It would spoil her makeup.

The Martian heard the audience clap. Even the applause was immaculate—rhythmical, polite, no one out of step. It was like hearing an army of Pat Boones marching. Then he realized that the Carpenters would become the Sonny and Cher of the 1980s—TV stars who would sing their old hits and tell old Johnny Carson jokes. He smiled sadly and whistled "Eight Miles High" on the way back to his spaceship.

Venus and Mars are all right tonight, he thought, but earth ain't so funky after all.

THE CARPENTERS
"NAIL" NEIL SEDAKA

Rona Barrett's Hollywood, 1975

Whoever said, "When you're hot—you're hot!" could probably win a belly laugh from singer/composer Neil Sedaka. In his case, Neil would more than likely change that saying to "When you're hot—you're fired!" because that's what he's alleging just happened to him.

Neil, a popular figure in the music industry, has, according to critics, made a highly successful comeback to his career. Not only has he recently had a solid half-dozen of his compositions among the Top Ten, but he had been on a three-month tour with the brother-sister singing team, Karen and Richard Carpenter.

A week after opening at the Riviera in Las Vegas, Neil was no longer in the throes of ecstasy over his successful return. He had been informed by the Carpenters managers that he would not continue with the group to a planned Japan tour. "I'm in the state of shock," Neil commented upon learning that he'd been fired. "It was Richard who first suggested I tour with them. It was a wonderful trip—every performance was filled with ovations." And before Neil reportedly had time to draw his next breath, the comedy team of Skiles and Henderson replaced him as the Carpenters' co-headliner at the Riviera. "They felt I was too strong," Neil says and admits that he was told at the dinner show on a Wednesday evening that it was his final night—and that the six remaining days were paid off. Apparently, the Carpenters' contract with the Riviera calls for them to select and pay the co-headliner for their act—and the move had been swift and final.

Not surprisingly, many entertainers appearing in Las Vegas at the time were not only as shocked as Neil was—they were outraged at the way the whole situation had been handled. Neil completed his final two shows and also informed the audiences of what had happened. To his credit, Neil stressed that he did not harbor any bitterness or resentment towards either Richard or Karen, expressing only a deep sorrow about the dismissal.

However, some of Neil's friends were less hesitant in making their opinions clear. Elton John, who has been mainly responsible for Sedaka's comeback, called him immediately upon learning of the action to express his own sadness and to say that he would have gone on stage for Neil's finale had he not been on the stage of the Troubadour the same night. Steve Lawrence and Eydie Gorme, one of the industry's most respected and talented husband-wife teams, invited Neil to join them on their Caesar's Palace stage to tell what "happened." But, again, to Neil's credit, he refused the offer saying: "I don't want to bad-mouth the Carpenters."

The ovations which had literally been showered on the act allegedly played a big role in Neil being fired. In his column reporting the incident, Army Archerd wrote: "It was these ovations—*for Sedaka*—that keyed the eventual firing, insiders say, but Sedaka would not admit it." As for Mr. Sedaka, Neil's only comment—again—was: "That's not for me to say." All Neil would provide was: "They felt I was too strong. I guess I was going over better than they had expected."

In talking to reporters later, Neil informed the press that Richard had not even spoken to him about the firing, but that "Karen was in tears in the wings and she said, 'I'm sick over this.'"

While Neil was kept busy explaining his sudden absence from the billing, it was noted that neither Richard nor Karen made themselves available for comment—to anyone.

Some sources say that one of the "difficulties" which Neil mentioned in his statement could easily have been when he introduced superstar Tom Jones and Dick Clark from the audience. This is a gesture almost expected of any headliner—to introduce other celebrities who might be sitting in the audience. "They are both close friends of mine," explained Neil. "And I've written songs for Tom. It's the first time I've ever been asked to leave because of good performances.

"I feel badly such talented people should have such insecurity," Neil said. "And, ironically, they have a current hit record, 'Solitaire,' which is my composition."

Whether or not the Carpenters will answer the charges—implied or openly voiced—that Neil was dismissed simply because he was receiving more attention than expected is anyone's guess. As we go to press, no one associated with the Carpenters—including the manager [who] told Neil he was no longer working—had offered to explain their side of the unfortunate situation.

A further note of irony was added when, as a result of Neil's "freedom" being learned by the rest of Las Vegas, offers from *every* hotel in that entertainment capital (including the Riviera) began pouring in for him. And, it seems, each one made the offer to Sedaka as a long-termer. In fact, the Riviera began almost immediate negotiations with Neil—directly—about his appearing again on their stage. "I have been assured we will be doing business together in the future," Sedaka admitted.

In the meantime, support for Neil has been shown from every corner of the industry. Even if he had not received all the ovations—even if his talent was not evident in the fact that he has *six* songs among the top-rated in the nation—even if other top performers had not invited him to air his views on their time—it's still very obvious that Neil Sedaka does not have to worry about his comeback at all.

He has *arrived*—and, from all indications, will stay.

CARPENTERS— GOOD, CLEAN, ALL-AMERICAN AGGRO!

Ray Coleman

Melody Maker, 1975

Richard and Karen Carpenter have decided to fight their whiter-than-white image, and declare themselves as "ordinary folk who take a shower and yet get bad-tempered like anyone else." In a six-year build-up to their current status, the Carpenters have achieved plenty but said little. Their music is straight pop, with little rock connections. "Do we have to apologize for that?" demands Richard. The Carpenters talked in two sessions in Los Angeles.

◆

Karen Carpenter is a student of needlepoint and makes cushions. She finds it relaxing, especially on the road during those interminable journeys.

Richard Carpenter is an enthusiast of fine wines, and knows a good year. He's been known to choose a restaurant only because of its wine list. He even smells the corks.

Neither of these two characteristics will help the Carpenters' reputa-tion in the area they seek to conquer: the gentle persuasion of the self-appointed hip.

But then, it's hardly what they do or even look like that's caused Richard and Karen to sell nearly 30 million records, including ten gold singles and five gold albums. It must be something to do with their music. And breathes there a man with soul so dead that he cannot accept their recorded beauty?

WHEN THE BOOK of popular music in the 1970s comes to be written, the Carpenters should figure mightily in the chapter on quality music. . . . It's been said that the blandness and safeness of their sounds is in line with the uncertain times in which we live; and with the post-Nixon determination of President Ford for everything to be super-wholesome, non-controversial. Middle America personified. That's perhaps partly true, but the shame here is that Carpenters' music seeks no categoriza-tion, and waves no flag for anything except excellence.

Their music transcends barriers. And yet, while rock itself has been allowed to settle into music-making with little outward message—the voices of revolution have long subsided, or at best have a hollow ring—the straight contemporary pop of the Carpenters is not allowed by many rockers to exist without a great deal of sneering.

Fine music alone isn't enough, apparently; Richard Carpenter's short hair and his sister Karen's girl-next-door appearance don't equal rebel-lion or, indeed, take any stance at all except that of creative, melodic pop musicians.

Thus, we have the increasingly wide gulf between public taste and the hard-line radicals who want change, an end to conservatism. And still the Carpenters claim audiences right across the age spectrum: their recently canceled British tour was to emphasize that their audiences stretch from age nine to 90, and that classy music in any form will never go out of style.

Excellence in all forms of music demands recognition, and it seems to me that the Carpenters—quite aside from their re-statements of fundamental values in popular music—represent standards which should never become blemished by irrelevant commentaries on their appearances. Many artists of sheer genius, after all, have hardly looked hip.

MEETING THE CARPENTERS, one becomes acutely aware that they are hurt by the knocks which have unnecessarily overshadowed their successes. Yet nobody produces all those gold records without intense dedication, and undoubtedly the nervous energy expended by Karen was responsible for her collapse and cancellation of the British tour. For six years, she had been playing the role of "just another member of the band, the one who sang." Feminists may choke and chauvinists will laugh, but the reality proved otherwise, according to her boyfriend Terry Ellis (he's also their manager now, and regular *Melody Maker* readers will remember that he's the manager who steered Jethro Tull).

"Girls just can't take that life without something going wrong," Ellis observed.

From "Close to You" and "We've Only Just Begun" through to "Please Mr. Postman" and "Desperado," the Carpenters have given us peerless popular music.

And remember: even though they work in the pop area, most of their work is self-composed, and arranged by Richard with spectacular precision and inventiveness.

It's worth remembering, in this latter half of the Seventies, that for the opportunist who fancies a hit and is blessed with a good ear plus some vocal/instrumental talent, there's a gigantic catalogue of many thousands of good songs that can be converted into hits. No need to go to much trouble writing and arranging. Flip through the archives and recycle an oldie! The Carpenters have not relied on this safe method, but have produced quality popular music.

In the [following interviews], the Carpenters stake their claim to posterity.

KAREN: I WAS ALWAYS A LONER

On Playing Drums

What's more important to you, singing or playing drums?

They're both special to me. I love to play, I really do. And when I started there were very few female drummers, but I didn't start playing just to be a gimmick.

It was different and I realized it was something new, but at the same time I took a lot of pride in knowing how to play my instrument.

People will ask me: "Is it hard to play and sing at the same time?" No, because it was something that just came naturally, and for the first year and a half to two years we were on the road, I played the whole show and I never thought twice about it.

I didn't need anyone to do my playing, just like I didn't need anybody to do my singing. But as we got bigger and Richard started to realize that there had to be somebody fronting the group, I happened to be the only girl in the group who was doing the lead singing, everybody was looking at me.

And I said to Richard: "Oh, no you don't," because it hurt me that I had to get up and be up front. I didn't want to give up my playing. So singing was an accident. Singing seriously came long after the drums.

When we started we had an instrumental jazz trio. That was Richard, myself and a gentleman by the name of Wes Jacobs who is now with the Detroit Symphony.

And he played phenomenal stand-up bass. I think I was 16 and Richard was 19 and Wes was 22. That was 1966.

So it kinda happened like in the summer time when we were all off from school and the trio had been together for a while and we just spent six months playing, and we entered the Hollywood Bowl [Battle of the Bands] in '66. And we won it, in our category; Richard won outstanding instrumentalist.

We did "Girl from Ipanema" and Richard's arrangement involved about six different time signatures, and then we did another tune he wrote himself called "Iced Tea" that he put the tuba in, to display Wes's talents, because he was phenomenal.

About that time I think I was singing if we just played a gig or something, you know. If we played a wedding and somebody wanted me to do "Yesterday" I would sing it.

But basically I was the drummer in the band. I remember when we walked into the Bowl there were 20 acts on the show and I was still new to the drums; it took me a while to set them up. We'd only been together for like six months, and what was even funnier, I couldn't lift them. I couldn't move them, so I had to have everybody carrying my drums.

And then I'd put them together.

I mean, all the guy drummers were hysterical and then we won. They were so funny. But I definitely take drums seriously. I have five sets of drums.

When we finally made the decision to get another drummer we were very picky about who we got, because I like a certain style of playing, and I wanted somebody who played like me, because that's what we were used to. And we've always been lucky with drummers.

On Her Voice

At what point did you actually sing your first note? And why? How long was the drumming without singing going on before you sang?

When I was about 13, Richard used to write songs, and he went to college at the time and he had two friends who used to have him sing, he used to accompany them at school.

I can't really remember why I started to sing, I really don't. It just kinda happened. But I never really discovered the voice that you know now, the low one, until later, when I was 16.

I used to sing in this upper voice and I didn't like it, I was uncomfortable, so I think I would tend to shy away from it, because I didn't think I was that good and I wasn't, but I hear tapes now of my lower voice and you can tell it's me but I sound country!

It's kinda corny to listen back. We had an original recording of Richard's songs that I sung, and the range was too big. I'd be going from the low voice to the high voice and even though it was all in tune, the top part was feeble and it was different—you wouldn't know it was me.

Then suddenly, one day, out popped this voice and it was natural. When I was in college, the chorus conductor was a very big influence on Richard's ideas of putting a vocal group together; he heard this voice and he wouldn't touch it, he said I should not train it, it doesn't need training, it's arty and natural. And the only thing I did work with him on was developing my upper register so I would have [a] full, three-octave range. So it really helps.

You'll only hear me "up" on records as a background. Like in "I'll Never Fall in Love Again," there was a 13-part chord that covered three octaves and it took Richard's lowest note and my top note to get it.

Richard also has a great falsetto, so between the two of us we can practically cover anything. Something else you don't think about is being able to sing in tune—thank God I was born with it!

It's something I never thought about. When I sing, I don't think about putting a pitch in a certain place, I just sing it.

What singers are you particularly in awe of?

I always liked Ella Fitzgerald, Nilsson and David Gates has one of the best male voices ever. Perry Como is absolutely fantastic. I like Dusty Springfield, Dionne Warwick. A lot of different types of singers, and for different reasons.

Do you want to be remembered as a classic singer? A lot of people regard your voice as one of the best in popular music. Do you really regard yourself as someone to be remembered in the history of popular music?

I sure hope so. I'd be a fool to say no. That is the ultimate compliment, to have respect not only from your fans but also your peers and other singers.

To have that kind of a reputation and to have it to stay, it would be fantastic and it's really nice to know that other people think that something you yourself have is that special. It's a great feeling.

Do you practice drums? Do you study other drummers?

I haven't practiced since the day we went on the road, no time. When I first got my set I was 16. I played for a year before I ever studied. I just picked it up.

The full set, not just one drum, it was the whole set. It was something that just absolutely came [naturally], it just felt so comfortable.

When we were little we played instruments too. I played accordion for two weeks, I played piano for two weeks, I tried the flute; like every kid, you try every instrument in the book and it wasn't until I went to high school that I tried drums—to get out of gym, which I didn't like because it was at eight o'clock in the morning and they expected you to do silly things, like running around a track at [eight] o'clock and I just couldn't. I wasn't into it, you know. So I got out of gym.

Richard was good friends with the band conductor and he got me into a marching band. When that happened, all of a sudden, because I hadn't played anything, they gave me bells to play, and the bells marched in the drum section and one of my best friends was the top drummer of the school and I used to watch him every day.

One day I picked up a pair of sticks and it just felt natural and when I told the band conductor I wanted to play drums, he looked at me like I was out of my tree, you know. He said that girls don't play drums. I said that if I can carry the thing, I can play it, and it was heavy but I loved it, and from then on that was it.

After I played for a year I went to Drum City in Hollywood and studied for about a year and a half and then we signed with A&M and that was it. When I was studying I was very into Joe Morello and Buddy Rich.

But I shall not play drums quite so much on stage in [the] future. When we were on this past summer tour, Richard decided he wanted me up front the whole time, just to get a different look.

I do want to play, but we're going to treat my playing as something special, rather than just having me ending up as the drummer that's backing up the group.

There's a way to do it properly and that's what we're going to do. Because I do want to play, absolutely.

(At this point, Carpenters manager and Karen's boyfriend, Terry Ellis interjected: "Over my dead body.")

On Brotherly Love

What are the handicaps, if any, about working with your brother? Does it pose any problems? Do you ever feel too close to each other for working well?

No. We've always been very, very close and this brought us even closer.

The thing that works with the two of us is that we've both got separate things that we do that complement each other and it really helps.

And my knowing the way he thinks as well as I do, and the same for him, makes it a lot easier to work, because there's a lot of people that couldn't work the way we do, which is, I guess, kinda strange.

We could walk into a studio and Richard won't even know what he wants, and yet five minutes later we can be cutting something and I can just tell what he wants.

On Competition

Well to really be in there solid you've gotta have friends, you know, and so you hope for hit after hit after hit. A lot of people would say now you've had a couple of hits you can try anything, the radio stations will play it, the people will buy it. BALONEY!

You have to watch everything you put out and with each hit you get, you have to work five million times harder. You know, each time you turn out a hit record, you go: "Oh man, I've gotta do it again," and, you know, your odds come down, and anybody who believes that line about "I have my hit record, now I'll just put out the same track with a different lyric over it," they go up and down so fast you can't even remember their names.

It's their own dumb fault because anybody who treats the business that way, doesn't deserve to be in it. Because this isn't a game, you know, it's a highly respected, smart business.

NOBODY knows until a record goes out, it's played and they buy it. Very few are just automatic, out-and-out smashes and if you get one in your entire career you're damned lucky.

Once you've got the one you pray for the next one. And every time a record comes out we watch every radio station that picks up on it, day by day, reports, charting, numbers, sales, because that's our business.

There's not a day that goes by that we're not buried in the charts of the music papers.

You know, if you're gonna be in it, you've gotta know what you're gonna be in because the competition in unbelievable. Also we keep watching what we're up against.

There's not that many that have come through and are just hanging in there every time they come out with a record. The Beatles, the sheer pleasure of the Beach Boys coming back, they're excellent, utter heaven.

I mean just knowing there's a Brian Wilson around is enough to make you go to sleep at night. I mean it. Genius is walking around.

One who's very upsetting is David Gates. He's so overlooked, so incredibly talented. He not only writes his tail off, but that voice, my God, it's gotta be one of the all time greatest male voices ever.

After he left Bread, it was really upsetting, to see all that talent being overlooked.

On Femininity

When you're on the road, as the only lady in the band, do you feel equal to any one of the men in the band and one of the gang, or do you stand up for your feminine rights, say, to have things carried for you?

For as long as I can remember I was always part of the gang, but at the same time they would open a car door for me and carry my luggage.

But the whole group is very, very close and I had a good time. For a long time we packed all our own equipment, I packed my own drums, and then I helped pack the truck. We set up all our own sound systems.

Then I'd go in the dressing room and set my hair, then I'd iron all the clothes for the guys. But the whole group worked and did everything.

As time went on, I became more the girl of the group but I never felt out of place because I was so close to everybody.

It was quite a while before I even carried a hairdresser, another girl. I didn't carry a hairdresser for about three years, but before that there was just me and the guys. We had a ball, a real good time.

It's nice having another girl, but you know, it's a very closely knit group, we always have been, so it works both ways. Now I go either way between being the lady of the group or part of the gang.

Depends on what kind of mood I'm in or what the situation is but they're very respectful to the needs of a girl.

Going on the road is a very hard thing you know, especially of it's seven to one, but I never found it uncomfortable. They're all very protective and they always have been.

Is that what you wanted?

I never had a boyfriend on the road, I didn't agree with it. Not only didn't I agree with it, but I never met anybody I wanted to have on the road—it's the same thing [as] guys carrying wives, or women, on the road.

We tend to think when you go out you go to work. I was always more of a loner because it's different for a girl on the road, you just don't walk up to a guy and say: "Hi there." Also I'm pretty shy, I'd never do it, never.

On Illness

All my strength is not back yet and that alone gets me upset. I'm not used to being slower than I normally am. Being idle is annoying because I never have been, from working on the road to coming into town and going right into the studio.

We haven't had a vacation the whole time we've been in the business. Until in the middle of the *Horizon* album. I went away for four days and I didn't know what to do with myself.

Richard and I have never had a vacation. And it's stupid for the two of us to let it get carried to that amount of work and it turned out to be harmful to me. It's going to be a whole learning process to me to do things in a different way [and] to really seriously calm down and do things at a slower pace, because I'm very regimented. I cannot stand to be late.

I go to bed at night with a pad by the bed and the minute I lie down it's the only quiet time of the day. My mind starts going: "This has gotta be done, that's gotta be done, you've gotta call this."

Then I find myself with a flashlight in bed writing down about 50 things that have to be done by 10 o'clock next morning. It's not the best way to be. It's better to hang loose, but I'm just not that type of person.

"Stop worrying," they say. That's a riot. You never calm down, recording an album. You would get to four or five in the morning, then drive home and get a couple of hours sleep and be back in the studio by noon. It's going, going, go.

Richard's creativity was definitely cut back because of our ridiculous schedule. We got to a point where he was not interested in going to the studio, and he hadn't written for a while. He was totally exhausted.

When I saw that, that upset me. And I said, well we gotta take some time off so we cancel a tour and end up in a studio. He said no he doesn't wanna do that, so the next thing we know there'd be a TV show booked or something, so we were never alone.

To get any proper kind of rest, you know he didn't want it. And we were in the middle of a song for the new album I got, I had been singing straight for three or four years without a break and I finally got so wiped out. I got sores on my vocal cords right in the middle of a song for the new album and my doctor said, "I don't want you to sing for a month."

I said, "What do you mean not sing for a month? I'm in the middle of an album." I was home for two days [and] then I was back in the studio.

Do you take any particular care with your voice? Gargle?

No. Absolutely nothing. I've had other singers ask me how I warm up, what do I do to prepare for a show. I say: I walk out on the stage and open my mouth!

On Their Image

How conscious are you of the Carpenters' public image? Does it matter to you at all?

Oh, we've given it an enormous amount of thought. It started on the wrong foot because it's a brother/sister team. He's totally shocked the industry.

A lot of people, because they did not know how to handle it, ended up trying to throw us into a Steve and Eydie or a Sonny and Cher.

They would take our publicity pictures with us cheek to cheek, you know, they were just all wrong.

Being brother and sister, which was again different in this business, it ended up being a kind of goody-two-shoes image, and because we came out right in the middle of the hard rock thing, because we didn't dress funny and the fact that we smiled, we ended [up] with titles like vitamin-swallowing, Colgate-smiling, bland, Middle America.

The fact that we took a shower every day was swooped on as symbolic. I mean, it's all nonsense. I know a lot of people who take a shower every day, I know a lot of people who smile.

In an interview once, somebody asked Richard if he believed in premarital sex and he said yes, and the woman wouldn't print it! We were labeled as don't-do-anything!

Just smile, scrub your teeth, take a shower, go to sleep. Mom's apple pie. We're normal! I get up in the morning, eat breakfast in front of the TV, watch games, shows.

I don't smoke—if I wanted to smoke I would smoke, I just don't like smoking, not because of my image. I wouldn't kid myself about it.

I mean, we're not lushes or anything, we're very into wine!

I remember one concert; it was in the middle of the summer someplace, and we were having a rehearsal and some people got in to watch the rehearsal, and the guys in the band had beer on stage, because it was 95 degrees.

Well, we got letters, you know; absurd. "The nerve of you, drinking beer." It just got carried to a point where it was nonsense.

And reviewers didn't like the fact that anybody clean was successful. And the more successful we got the more they attacked our image.

They never touched our music. We would get critics reviewing our concerts, they'd review the audience, they'd say how ridiculous that somebody came to see the Carpenters in a tie.

What the hell's that got to do with our music? And our capabilities as music makers! It's ridiculous.

We've had shows that we knew were not right, something might have been out of tune.

But nine out of ten reviews would either review our clothing or the way the stage looked, by making fun of the fact that we carry a lot of equipment.

We're very dedicated to our business. Our life is our music, creating it. We try to do everything with as much perfection as we can. We have certain beliefs, certain loyalties to ways of doing things. You know, it's just nice to be treated the way you are, just like two human beings.

In Defense of Richard

You know, there's so much in Richard, just so much that hasn't even been touched. He's so talented [it] just makes me weep that everybody just walks right by him. They never give him any credit but he does everything. He's the brains behind it.

Everything else is him. And yet I get cracks like, well, what does the brother do? Or you know, I get the impression that it's really nice that I've brought my brother on the road.

Look what he's produced. There are 16 gold records, he's produced one of the most successful acts in the world. And nobody gives him any credit, he never gets referred to as a producer, or as an arranger, and they walk right by him as a writer. Richard and John Bettis are terribly overlooked as writers.

I really get upset for him because he's so good and he never opens his mouth; you know he just sits back and because I'm the lead singer I get all the credit.

They think I did it and all I do is sing. He's the one that does all the work. There isn't anything I wouldn't do for him to give him the perfection that we both want.

How long do you like to live with a song before you actually put it on record? Do you need to get inside a lyric or can you go cold into a studio?

One of the things you learn, working with Richard, is to be able to do anything, any time, and because he knows me so well, he knows I can do it. I recorded "I Can Dream, Can't I?" and I didn't know how the damn thing went, and I kept saying, "Rich, you gotta let me know how this tune goes."

He wanted to record it live with a 40-piece orchestra. We're both working on the whole thing, and he wanted to do it live and I didn't even know how the song goes and he said, "Oh, I'll give you a tape. I'll give you a tape," and a month went by and I never got a tape and finally I got it and it was so funny, I gotta play this tape that he did.

He did it one morning on a piano and he was reading off a lead sheet and he gets halfway through really good, you know, and the song is kinda strange and parts of it are a little light. He got to this part and he must have gone through it about 20 times to get it right and then finally when he got through to the end of it, it was such a joke, I had no idea how it went but I was so hysterical.

I was listening to it on a Thursday driving in on the freeway and he wanted to record it Friday morning! He never knows what he wants until it's time to do it and he'll hand me over a lyric sheet and I'll be [all] right. But we had trouble on the last album.

We were both so tired, so we came home from a five-week tour on a Monday at 12 o'clock and went in that night to record and worked all night. Many days like that.

And on my parents' 40th wedding anniversary we worked all day, ran to the anniversary dinner and then went back to the studio at one in the morning to cut the two things at the beginning and the end of the album, "Aurora" and "Eventide."

Richard made *Horizon* in the worst state I've ever seen him in. I mean we had got to a point where we didn't want to go to a studio. It was work, because we were so exhausted and we've never had that.

We've always been, "Hey, I can't wait to get into the studio," but that last album just drained everything, every drop of blood out of us.

When it was done, we weren't glad it was done, we were upset with the way it turned out. Richard can work unbelievable hours, but this last time it was getting to us.

But now it's gotta change. The two of us can't go on like that. The way that things have happened in the last six months, we're just fed up with being treated like two things that the blood spurts out of.

On Audiences

What sort of audiences do you think you attract?

All ages, and a lot of different types. We attract a lot of families. At our concerts we see a bunch of kids and their moms and dads. A lot of long-haired people love our music and a lot of long-haired people can't stand our music.

We appeal to housewives, we appeal to a lot of kids, but not in the numbers like the Osmonds, or David Cassidy.

Except we did one concert, a special event for youth, or teenagers, it was something like 15,000 kids, all under 10 and we almost died.

But we went on, and I was flabbergasted because I stood there and sang "Rainy Days and Mondays" and I saw a baby sitting there singing every word with me.

It was a riot, just a riot, and they were quite responsive. In our fan club, we get letters from an 80-year-old grandfather and also an album sent by a mother of a three-year-old that was crumpled to bits because the kid took it to bed with him every night.

We had to sign and send [it] back, because the kid won't go to sleep without the album.

Did your criticism in the Melody Maker *of Mott the Hoople represent a hatred of rock or what it stands for? [Editor's note: In an interview conducted a year earlier, Karen jokingly referred to the group as "Moot the Hopple," calling them "the most amateurish group I've ever seen." Richard added: "They're a joke . . . let's get back to the music."]*

No. I love hard rock—or some of it. There's a lot of it I don't like, but then there's a lot of soft rock I don't like.

I really don't know what made me say that about Mott the Hoople and after I'd said it I could have died.

It got to be a standard joke in the business because we're so different, Mott the Hoople and the Carpenters. It was one of those things you regret saying. To take in all of hard rock—absolutely not.

It's like somebody saying to us, if you like it why don't you do it? That makes about as much sense as Grand Funk [Railroad] doing "Close to You." We're all good at what we do, and I think it would be an insult to hard rock if we did it, because we're not hard rock people.

I may not like everything, but if it's good, I've gotta say, "Hey, that's good, but it just doesn't appeal to me." Not just because I don't like it, it stinks. That's not very bright. I apologize to Mott.

RICHARD: WE'RE NO ANGELS

On Their Image

Do you think your success is partly due to the renunciation of heavy rock or even acid rock? Do you think, had you come along in 1967, you would have flopped?

No, because it's just a whole different audience—one's rock [and] the other's pop.

In 1968 Herb Alpert comes out with a Bacharach/David composition "This Guy's In Love with You," which could easily have been "Close to You."

[It] went to number one, sold a million and a half copies. It was pop as opposed to rock. "Close to You" could have been a hit in 1954!

And you know, Marty Balin wrote a love song on the [Jefferson Airplane] *Surrealistic Pillow* album called "Today"—"Today, I feel like giving you more than before." Gorgeous! That's nothing but a love song.

Right smack in the middle of the acid rock movement, the premier acid rock song was a love song!

And with us, our type of music, especially "Close to You," could have been a hit in 1940, 1950, 1960—it could have happened any time for us.

But it happened in the Seventies, beginning of a new decade, decline of acid rock. People are disgusted with this whole thing of drugs and long hair and although we, the Carpenters, are not claiming anything, a whole lot of people used it for *their* stand!

They take "Close to You" and say: "Aha—you see that number one? THAT's for the people who believe in apple pie! THAT's for the people who believe in the American flag! THAT's for the average middle-class American person and his station wagon. The Carpenters stand for that and I'm taking them to my bosom." And BOOM—we get tagged with that label.

Well, I just don't believe in that. You try to tell those people that I have every Zappa record, every Mothers [of Invention] record, every Beatles record, that I disagreed with Art Linkletter (TV commentator) when he blamed the Beatles for the death of his daughter.

I got so upset when this whole "squeaky-clean" thing was tagged onto us. I never thought about *standing* for anything! I mean I realize

Presley came along and you can argue whether he filled a void when James Dean was killed, but he stood for something. Rebellious teenagers and all that.

Were you interested at all in the youth culture?

No, I mean, I was Middle America; I mean middle class, housing development, the whole thing. And when I first heard Elvis's music, I didn't know what he looked like.

We had some types on our street who leaned towards the black leather jacket, and got in trouble, but they didn't take to me.

In fact, they used to get roughed up for it and where they may have looked up to Elvis because of what he stood for, all I've ever been into is music.

I heard "Heartbreak Hotel," "I Want You, I Need You, I Love You," "Don't Be Cruel" backed up with "Hound Dog" and liked it immediately because of the music, not because of what Elvis stood for.

Same with the Beatles. I had to order a Beatles record and I heard it and played it for about a week on radio station KRLA, which at the time was the number one station in California.

In August of '63 they played "From Me to You," which got absolutely no response at all, and I loved it. It excited me, everything about it was new.

I went to the record store and I said I want a copy of "From Me to You" by the Beatles, and they laughed at me. "The Beatles, there's no group called the Beatles."

I said, "No, I heard it on KRLA. It's called 'From Me to You' by the Beatles."

They look it up. "You're right, well we don't have it in stock, we'll order it for you." They released it later as the flip of "Please, Please Me," and it got well known.

The copy I've got is a collector's item. It was on VJ Records and very, very few of them were made, because it was backed with "Thank You, Girl."

I've always made a practice of looking [at] who wrote what. So I looked at the Beatle thing, saw "Lennon/McCartney," looked at the flip, saw "Lennon/McCartney" [and] figured they were a duo.

Later I saw a picture in a magazine which said the Hot Beatles, and I thought, "Wow, different looking." And there were four of them. FOUR of them?

What? You didn't put together a group with a drummer and rhythm guitarist, you didn't think about it!

But anyway, I kept checking to see if any [Beatles] albums were put out, I couldn't find anything on the Beatles until six months later, all of a sudden [. . .] "I Wanna Hold Your Hand" and boom, the Beatles.

But to me it was always their music. Only their music. I never felt them representing anything. I was never into the youth rebellion.

That's why it hurt me to be put down and classified into the reverse category. People who immediately took to us were the enemy. They were against us.

There're certain groups I don't care for, but that doesn't mean just because somebody's on hard rock, that I don't like them.

Art Linkletter was a fool, to come out with that when his daughter died. I think it was right during the time that *Sgt. Pepper* was popular and he came out and said "My daughter's death was the fault of the Beatles," and since that time he's taken back his statement.

You know it was his daughter that overdosed, man, it wasn't the Beatles. The Beatles didn't come to his daughter and say, "Hey, overdose."

But, ah, you know people could blame anything on the Beatles. Now they can use the Carpenters to describe a lifestyle if they wish, because there's nothing fresh, like in the Sixties.

Young kids are more sophisticated. You've got the Four Seasons, one of my favorite groups, and Neil Sedaka, and how many other people from the Sixties all getting hit records in the Seventies because the people remember how things were before the energy crisis and before things got so tough.

People are going back to the Sixties and Fifties because [those] were times when they were happier, so they're buying music by artists who were famous that day. Standing ovations for Simon and Garfunkel [are] coming back again.

So many people wish the Beatles were back together, because there's nothing now to make them forget Simon and Garfunkel, or the Beatles, or so many of these acts from that time.

I'd love to see the Beatles and Simon and Garfunkel get back together. There's something that happens with these sort of groups, even if one person in the group is the guiding light. But when the stars of the group go on their own it's never the same.

David Gates when he left Bread, John Sebastian when he left Lovin' Spoonful, John Phillips when he left the Mamas and the Papas, and so many others.

When they were together you say, "Hey man it's really mostly Gates, mostly Sebastian, mostly Phillips." And this gets in their mind, so they leave.

But it's a great pity. And as much as I like *There Goes Rhymin' Simon*, to me, Simon hasn't come up with [a] "Bridge Over Troubled Water" since he's been on his own.

So, there must be something about being together with Garfunkel and as much as I like *Band on the Run* and *Imagine*, not one of the solo Beatles has put out anything that can measure up to *Pepper* or *Abbey Road*, especially the second side.

On the Beatles' Genius

I bought "From Me to You" only for the song. I mean, anything that started the major entering the minor was right there, the melody, the intonation was impeccable.

The guys at that time in Southern California were not into the Beatles when they hit.

I took my *Meet the Beatles* album to school. I was a senior, and brought it around telling people, the guys. They had a contest on KRLA: Who's more popular—the Beach Boys or the Beatles? The Beach Boys won.

I was a big Beach Boys fan—forever—but the Beach Boys won on Southern California radio because the guys were so p——— off at their girls going on about the way the Beatles looked, and the Beach Boys were singing about 409s and "Little Deuce Coupe" and "Surfin'" and everything they dug. Very Californian. The guys were p——— off at a bunch of weird-looking guys from England who could possibly challenge the Beach Boys. Well, I just sat back and listened to them both.

We had some teachers at school who were interested. "The Beatles? I've read a lot about them." And they got the record player out and they played the album right there in the classroom.

The guys went "Boo," and the teacher went "Awful!" And I went: "Awful?" Can't you *hear* the chord progressions there? Can't you *hear* how different this is?

I really got upset. And I said: "These guys are gonna be around a helluva long time." Anybody who can write "From Me to You" and "It Won't Be Long" and "All My Loving," which is a beautiful song with a good line tempo, and "Do You Want to Know a Secret," is gonna be around a helluva long time.

I still get really excited about the Beatles.

Didn't their long hair mean anything to you?

The music, only the music. So our music is just what we do. I mean, I love many different styles of music. I'm a big Zappa fan, been into the Mothers of Invention ever since *Freak Out!*, but that doesn't mean—just because you understand what he's saying in his lyrics and can get into his avant-garde arrangements—that you can do it yourself.

So we do what we can do. But that doesn't mean we are doing music as a statement of what we believe in, as far as lifestyle goes.

Shopping for furniture on a Saturday or apple pie or whatever—that's how we're bracketed. It's NONSENSE!

I look back at some of the pictures, and people didn't know how to deal with a brother and sister act. There's never been one, since Fred and Adele Astaire!

So they stuck our heads together: "Put your cheeks against each other and smile!" And we *did* it! So Karen was 19, I was 21.

"Put your cheeks together. No—closer! Put your arms around her, smile!" And we did it! So really, how can you blame people for the reaction some got? We were told: when you go out to do interviews, don't say anything adverse about anything. Everything is groovy. Everything is terrific.

Don't say anything bad, don't say you dislike anything. You like everything. And we went along with it. We were young. Six years ago. But it's really not what we are.

What do you think of the four ex-Beatles as soloists?

My favorite was always McCartney. Well lately he's been getting incredible acclaim for *Venus and Mars*, when I feel he should have gotten it for *Band on the Run*.

But at any rate, commercially, he's done better than any of them and it's kind of ironic. Ringo's done next best, I think.

The first two albums George did—I mean *All Things Must Pass* and *Living in the Material World*—did real well, but sorta flagged off, and now with "You" he's come back. But Ringo—largely due to the efforts of Richard Perry's commercial ear, Ringo has done real well.

Is commercial success all to you?

No.

But you salute McCartney because he is commercially the most successful. Is that the crucial point to you?

No, no it's not. Having a commercial flair is a talent in itself and people shouldn't be put down for being commercial. Melodically, he is superb. And his arranging and rhythmic mind is incredible.

Six years ago, did you want gold discs and fame and the sort of success you've got now?

Oh, I suppose so. Is it a crime to want to sell a million?

On Karen's Voice

Are you ever critical of Karen's work?

We never get too heavy, because to me, Karen sings so well, that there's good and then there's better. There's nights when she'll play dumb all over the place and she says, "My God, was I awful tonight," because it's her ear.

On top of being at the front of the show and doing all the lead singing, she's listening to every note that's being played by Tony, Bob or me or whatever and she hears every mistake.

And she'll say: "My God, what was the mistake in this song? Why did you make a mistake in that song? What happened to you here?"

Would she be right?

Yes, always, but the same thing will happen in the opposite direction. Karen will overinflect a song, or move too much backward and forward, or something.

I mean it's not something that happens every night, don't you get me wrong. But we do have mistakes, problems.

Do you have disagreements on music or do you have complete empathy on music?

Mostly it's together. Karen did not care for "Superstar" at first. I respected her view, but it's about the best thing for her that's ever been written.

So I had to persuade her for about a week. I figured, if she's not into it, we won't do it, but the more I listened to it, the more I got into it, and I said: "Karen, FOR ME, PLEASE do this one!"

And by the time it was finished she said, "I had no idea it was gonna sound like this because I heard the arrangement and all the 'ooh baby's,' in the back the oboe, and the harp and the strings" and she ended up liking it.

There aren't many out of all the tunes we did that she was against, but there are a couple. "Superstar" is one and "Solitaire" is the other.

She never liked "Solitaire" at all and it really turned out that she, as far as the commercial ear goes, was right—well, it's the worst-selling single we've had since "Ticket to Ride."

So she may, commercially, have been right on that one—not may have, she *was*. It went Top 20, but it's [our] lowest chart position [and] worst sales since 1969.

So she's right, but most of the time we agree. Most everything I pick out she loves. I mean, I can hear something and say, "Hey, Karen's gonna like this."

There's one I wanted to do for a year and a half, a song off Elton John's *Empty Sky* album, "Skyline Pigeon." Love it. Can't get Karen to do it. She won't do it.

But I can hear it and maybe someday we'll do it. She may be right, in that the bulk of our fans might not understand the lyrics. They are subtle lyrics.

So far, all our stuff has been direct. Fans are difficult. When we came out in *Melody Maker* with a thing about Mott the Hoople, we had people quit the fan club.

They just said, "I'm never gonna buy another album by the Carpenters because of what they said about Mott the Hoople." So who knows whether the bulk of the people would or would not understand the lyrics of "Skyline Pigeon"?

Do you sight read?

I don't know the full bag. But with all the things we record, I don't even need the music. I mean, take "Skyline Pigeon"—I just listen and I can hear the chord changes, so I know Karen's range. I'll go to the piano [and] find her range. . . . That's how we work.

So as for music being written, I scratch out like once on a napkin. . . .

Say you're doing "Close To You." You go like this for the bars and you put C 1234, "why do birds suddenly appear 234," on each line is a beat . . . D 234. . . . Like so.

And if you're in a hurry, and a couple of things have been scratched out on napkins in the studio, you never have to fill out a real chart for the musicians.

They read, but you just don't need to do it. And Tony Peluso, our guitarist, doesn't read. The "Goodbye to Love" song I sang him. But the incredible solo in the middle is his.

On Karen's Illness

She called me today and now she's got the flu on top of her sickness. Her resistance is so low that she picks up like just everything that comes along.

She really isn't, at this part of her life, strong. She's just kept up far too tough a schedule for her and really run herself down.

She always wanted to show that she could do just as good as the guys could, and really pushed herself. She would never dream about complaining about work, even if she might've not felt like it, in which case she was prepared to go down and she just took on too much.

And she went on this huge diet and lost a lot of weight. Oh she was working so hard. And when she would eat it'd be salad without dressing and she had everything figured out calorie wise. No starch, nothing except [things] like fish and never with a sauce.

Anyhow, we had a really hectic schedule. I knew eventually that she'd run herself down. I kept talking with her! It did no good.

We did a tour in April and another in May. It was after the one in April that she was flat on her back for several days.

The doctor told her it would happen—start eating! But diet for Karen really became an obsession. She had to lose more weight and so she got well enough to go out and do the main shows, the summer tour.

It really hit the last week in Vegas, and on top of being too thin and not eating enough food to keep up with the schedule, it also lowered her resistance, so that a cold would come along and she just could not shake it off.

We are very nervous. Also, she gets upset very easily. She's a very tough girl, very strong. There's strong, physically strong, and a very strong personality, a very tough person.

When I say tough, I mean [a] resilient and persistent personality. The strength of her personality kept driving her on, saying, "I can do it, I can do it."

Now she's even got nerves thinking about having made the decision to cancel the British tour. It's troubled her all week.

On Overwork

I've never had so much time off as recently. Now I'm starting to wind down, I've never had this much time off since we started and ah, [when] we get home from these tours all I want is to sit and listen to the stereo. . . . [I] like to work on my cars. Cleaning them mostly, instead of having somebody else do it.

I find it very relaxing and I haven't had the time. I would be so exhausted from the tour and recording. I wouldn't have any energy to bring myself to do it.

Now I'm myself, I found I have more energy than in years. I've been outdoors, catching up on albums, and now, I actually want to get to the piano and start playing, both just working with original stuff and also I really want to learn Chopin's single piano concerto.

Our overwork has been the reason there's been so few songs. I mean, John Bettis and I wrote a lot of songs before the success. Not stuff you release commercial-single-wise, but we were at least turning some out, a lot for the albums.

Whereas for a while every song we had written since '72 became a single—I mean I hear it, write it, release it.

First was "Goodbye to Love" and the next was "Top of the World." They were written the same day and then nothing for a year. I couldn't come up with anything.

I just didn't wanna have to go to the piano and when I came home, I wanted to sit by myself.

The next one was "Yesterday Once More" and the one after that was "Only Yesterday" and, ah, then there was one other one—we wrote "Can't Say Goodbye." And then two things on the *Horizon* album.

It was no fun writing between tours. Just real hard work. I mean, that's not really much output. What we did turn out did well, but we were definitely not prolific.

We used to write a couple of songs a day when we were both in college and the energy was high. But we became like machines these past few years. Producing and performing, the business decisions, and foreign tours.

Do you want to make an impact on pop music for posterity?

Absolutely. I guess people will remember Karen more than anything because of her voice. So recognizable. I feel the original success was a great deal to do with Karen's singing more than my arrangements, but I want us remembered in 50 years as the quality, contemporary music duo.

Arrangements play such an important part, though. Without going on and without being cocky or anything, "Close to You" was written in '63 and was out in '63 and wasn't a hit until '70 and ah, my arrangement on it was quite special. Herb Alpert brought it to us, the song had been lying around "They Long to Be Close to You" I thought it was too long, as a title, so we made a single out of it and called it "Close to You."

I found out later that Bacharach wasn't very happy with it, and Hal David and he weren't happy with it being called "Close to You," but I just felt "They Long to Be Close to You" was just too long a title, and I felt kinda good.

A couple of years later, Bacharach put out an album and it was called *Close to You*. Things like that. And then the arrangement, certain tempo, and modulation equal a hit, and for us THE big break.

It was my arrangement, but the public never recognized arrangers. Singers get famous, songwriters get famous. Jim Webb, of course, Bacharach and David, of course, Lennon/McCartney.

But arrangers don't get famous. [Henry] Mancini would never have gotten famous as an arranger, even though he's brilliant. Bacharach would never have gotten famous as arranger, even though he's brilliant as an arranger.

It definitely wouldn't be as a singer that I will be remembered. I am a good background singer, not a solo singer. I sing well for a background singer, in tune and a good lung. But I've got a talent as an arranger and as a producer, I mean all those songs that were hits, every song we've done, I selected them all.

Do you have any reaction to the description of the Carpenters as middle-of-the-road, easy listening? Most people tend to think it's an ineffectual description, as if it's "wallpaper music."

Bland, bland! Easy listening, whatever you wanna call it now, is taking on a much broader aspect. I mean you've got Three Dog Night, Elton John, [David] Bowie, all in the Easy Listening category or charts. The Eagles are on Easy Listening charts [in the US].

The Beatles went to number one in that chart, so it's a lot broader than it used to be. But let's take it for what most people think it is. I sure as hell don't mean to put anybody down, but the Lettermen, Percy Faith, Jerry Vale are REAL easy listening.

Their producers seem to look at the charts and put out new albums about, oh boy, every four to six months and they look [at] what's been on the charts and see if it could possibly be done by their artists and they take all those songs and the albums are thrown together.

Somebody does the selecting, somebody else does the arranging, and the singer comes in and sings it for a couple of days and the album is put out, and it's usually called whatever the biggest covering song of the day is—*Alone Again (Naturally)*, *Rainy Days and Mondays* or *Killing Me Softly* or whatever.

Where I feel that we're different is that we select it all, we arrange it, pick songs that aren't other people's hits, introduce songs and we're a lot more creative. The albums are not thrown together in two or three days, not recorded, like, from August 3 to August 6, 1972.

And we produce them ourselves. It's different. Anyway—for easy listening definition, look at Billboard's easy listening charts. Most of the chart is made of Top 100 songs. Like "Island Girl"—that'll be in the easy listening charts. It may not go to one but it'll be there.

And Jethro Tull, with "Bungle in the Jungle," [*War Child*] is a great middle-of-the-road album! If they put out a hard thing, it won't get played but if they put out "Jungle," all of a sudden Jethro Tull is an easy listening act. No matter who does it, as long as they don't seem offensive, it will be programmed on the radio as easy listening.

The Beatles went on respectable easy listening stations, and got the number one easy listening song in the nation. Olivia Newton-John is not a country singer, but her single and her album are way up in the country charts. And from what I understand, hardcore country fans are dying out.

John Denver is really not a country artist, and yet he just won [several] of the country musical awards, entertainer of the year and songwriter of the year. I don't believe in classification. I don't feel we're rock and yet we're not easy listening, we're simply contemporary. I mean we SELL, which makes us contemporary. So that's about all I can call it. It's soft rock.

But pop rather than rock?

Yes, and that doesn't mean I have anything against rock. I respect rock which is why I don't feel to class any kind of rock is appropriate.

What you're not selling to the public, which is what a lot of bands do sell, is a lifestyle and an identifiable image. Are you trying to project something beyond your music? Are you saying to your audience, which is what a lot of rock stars say, we stand for something?

No. Just listen to the music, enjoy it, and please buy the albums!

On Missed Hits

Several songs have come in that have been very big records—[songs] that I listened to and said could be a hit, but I really didn't like. So what am I going to do with it? There's one right now—"Ain't No Way to Treat a Lady."

It's been Top Ten for several weeks, by Helen Reddy. I like the hook and that's all I like. Heard it a year ago, listened to it and listened to it, and I said good hook, good hook, but I really don't care for the rest of it. And I still don't. "I Don't Know How to Love Her" [from *Jesus Christ Superstar*] was another.

John Bettis writes rather sad lyrics, based really on lost love or depression . . . "Goodbye to Love" was my idea and my title and I wrote the first sound. In England the first time I was there I couldn't get to sleep one night and I heard it just one night. I heard "[I'll] say goodbye to love, no one ever cared . . ." Those were my lyrics, just that much. Then I wrote the rest of the tune and I asked John to come up and I said I want it to be called "Goodbye to Love" and here's what I've got on it.

So the tone of "Goodbye to Love" was actually set by me. And then he followed through on what I had started. The chorus of "Yesterday Once More," lyrics and music, I wrote, and the first sentence, lyrically, I wrote: "When I was young I [listened] to the radio."

Do you not subscribe to the theory that pop represents youth?

Yeah, you're right. Elvis originally appealed to the teenagers, and now it's the Bay City Rollers. But the Beatles—think about it. They should get back [together] again. The other night on NBC-TV, Simon and Garfunkel were back for one show. People went BANANAS! Instant standing ovation.

I'm really a Simon and Garfunkel fan. I looked at that, I looked at them standing up instantaneously, I looked at the applause that wouldn't stop and I'm thinking what would happen if the Beatles got back together, just did one concert. Think about it.

Vintage newspaper photo of the Richard Carpenter Trio with bassist Wes Jacobs, 1966. *Author's Collection*

Carpenters, 1969.
A&M Records

A Drummer Who Sang—on the set of *Make Your Own Kind of Music*, the duo's 1971 summer series. *Photofest*

Richard concertizing from his Wurlitzer, 1971. *Photofest*

Fielding questions from the British press, late 1971. *Photofest*

With President Richard M. Nixon during a visit to the White House, August 1, 1972. *National Archives*

The musical millionairess, age 23. *A&M Records*

Onstage at the Greek Theatre, Los Angeles, August 1972.
Sherry Rayn Barnett

Hollywood Bowl, 1974.
Sherry Rayn Barnett

Photographed by Annie
Leibovitz for *Rolling Stone*,
May 22, 1974.
Author's Collection

...hotographed in their stage wardrobe during a 1976 tour of Great Britain. *Photofest*

...aren, 1977. *Harry Langdon*

Between poses on a 1977 photo session. *Harry Langdon*

On the set of their 1977 ABC-TV special *The Carpenters at Christmas. ABC-TV*

French *Vogue* photographer Claude Mougin captured this glamorous look for the solo album photo sessions, February 2, 1980. *A&M Records*

Together, 1981. *A&M Records*

Alone, 1983. *A&M Records*

Cynthia Gibb and Mitchell Anderson as Karen and Richard in *The Karen Carpenter Story*, the highly acclaimed "Movie of the Week." *CBS-TV*

Todd Haynes' *Superstar: The Karen Carpenter Story*, 1987. *Iced Tea Productions*

Cover art for 1994's alternative rock tribute album. *Author's Collection*

Back in the spotlight—Long Beach, CA, February 1997. *Ambrose Martin*

But perhaps the Beatles are not hungry anymore? Presumably you didn't have the driving force, the hunger for success that the Beatles did as four guys earning peanuts in Liverpool?

I always wanted to be in music and I always wanted to be successful, so I had a goal. As far as starving—never, I was spoiled. Not that I'm saying my family had money, but what money my dad made was immediately spent on Karen and me for drum sets, pianos.

But to a lot of them, the start was hard. To me, the start was not hard but—orderly. But we still did have to wait a long time for good equipment, unlike most of the big rock bands now. Every mic we used when we auditioned was borrowed.

The car, the amps, were borrowed, the electric piano was borrowed, the oil was borrowed. Except for Karen's drum set, and I had a grand piano [as a] music major in college to study classical music. As far as anything to do with our first group, Karen and I, everything was either homemade, borrowed or we did without.

None of this crap with sponsored PAs. We used to pack it ourselves. We used a station wagon. Bruce Springsteen, whom I saw at the Roxy here in Los Angeles, I thought was terrific. I mean none of this new generation stuff, more like a carry on from the Sixties.

You can sense he's genuine. I picked up the modesty thing from Springsteen while he was on stage, and he's approaching it absolutely right. Instead of saying "my album's number three, man, book me in here and I'll sell it out, make you lots of money," you know, he's doing the smaller places and keeping himself special.

You are 29 and very rich—how does this affect your planning when you need never write or sing another note?

Well, I don't want to, let's say, retire at 30. I just love making music. When you are insecure, you tend to do more than you know you want to do. But Terry Ellis, our new manager, has redefined our future by saying: "You're gonna be here a long time, and your health is more important and you'll be more creative if you have some rest."

So I think we have a good future now. It's not a secure business, music, and sometimes you start thinking: "My God, what if I only last three years?" They tell you to invest your money, and you make enough, work enough and you can retire at 30.

I don't want to retire at 30. I don't care if I have millions of dollars. I could be financially secure for the rest of my life—I wouldn't want to retire at 30. I wanna keep doing what I'm doing.

Part III

THERE'S A KIND OF HUSH

IT'S AN OVERDOSE
OF PRETTY

Joel McNally

Milwaukee Journal, 1976

You may have noticed that a kind of hush fell over the world recently. It was a wonderful sight to see. Everyone laid down their arms and joined hands as brothers and sisters. The reason for this somewhat monumental world event was the release of the new album by the Carpenters, the ultimate brother and sister. The album is appropriately titled *A Kind of Hush* (A&M), and at this point it is the odds-on favorite to win the Grammy, the Nobel Peace Prize and the Reader's Digest Sweepstakes.

Why can't more kids these days be like these nice young people? While drug-crazed, libertine musicians are doing the devil's work, Richard and Karen Carpenter have, in their own quiet way, worked to restore faith in such sacred institutions as home, family and Patti Page. Oh, not that they don't have a mischievous streak. They are not old sticks-in-the-mud by any means. They have come up with an absolutely wild, madcap rendition of Wayne King's 1930s hit "Goofus." Talk about flaming youth!

Richard and Karen believe in honoring their father and mother by restoring the Big Band sound to its proper place in the world of music. Oh sure, they take a lot of abuse for it. Rock critics compare them with

Mickey and Minnie Mouse. That's grossly unfair. Karen does not have skinny black legs and knobby knees. And Richard does not have big, black ears. Pillars of character and virtue they are, the Carpenters remain utterly impervious to such vicious attacks. All they ask is that they be able to make their simple music. And sell 30 million singles and albums.

The selections on their new album are an interesting collection of period pieces from a variety of periods. They aren't living entirely in the '30s, you know. They have such modern, with-it material as Neil Sedaka's "Breaking Up Is Hard to Do." Actually, it is sort of interesting that Sedaka is still included because, in fact, they didn't find breaking up with him hard at all. Last year they fired Sedaka from opening their Las Vegas act because he got confused about who the star of the show was. It was the first time in recorded history that the Carpenters have been heard to utter a curse—even if it was only "Grimy Gumdrops."

The title song, "There's a Kind of Hush (All Over the World)," was first immortalized by another extremely hip group, the legendary Herman's Hermits. Many of the other songs are perfectly pretty. That is the problem. With things like their single, "I Need to Be in Love," "Sandy" and "I Have You," Karen's pale white vocals and Richard's overly flawless arrangements make one pretty much as pretty as another—and not terribly distinctive. Even so, one song, "One More Time," stands out as a particularly fine song. The arrangement is simple and Karen's voice and Richard's piano don't get buried under layers of oboes.

There is really nothing wrong with someone who has an appreciation for the more elaborate musical forms of the past. After all, they could be into a lot worse things. Like playing the spoons or running their fingers around the rims of water glasses.

KAREN CARPENTER

NOTHING TO HIDE BEHIND

Charlie Tuna

1976

AUTHOR'S NOTE: Karen Carpenter and I first talked on the phone in 1972. I interviewed her for a radio special on love songs that I was producing at the time. Many more interviews followed after that, including an annual event when I would call her on the air on the morning of her birthday just to wish her "Happy Birthday" and catch up on her latest projects with Richard. Then in 1976 I invited her to come down to the station to "just sit and talk" for an interview that I would play back on the air later that month. She came alone (no record company or public relations people were with her), and she relaxed and talked with me, and seemed to really enjoy herself. What follows is the full interview from October 8, 1976.
                                                    —Charlie Tuna, 2000

What's the TV special? What's the center theme going to be on this?

Well, I think we're just going to call it "The Carpenters' First Television Special." [*Laughs.*]

Has it been more than you anticipated, as far as work and hours?

Oh, it was an absolute kick to do. We worked on it for a long time [and] actually three weeks ahead of taping, just straight through. Boy, that

179

involves a lot. Knock on wood, I really think it came out great and it was *so* much fun. It's a lot of hours, it really is, but that's really fun.

You had some nice guest stars to help you out, too.

Oh, yes, we sure did—a good friend of ours, John Denver, and Victor Borge, who is absolutely out of his mind [. . .] he's so fast. Wow, is he fast. Right down to the make-up men. [He was] falling in their laps. He's nuts, and just an absolute pleasure to work with, as is John. It was really a lot of fun. We did a race that Richard did out at Riverside [. . .] I haven't seen him that happy in a long time. He was just having a ball. We had "Parnelli" Jones, Al Unser. Richard's always been interested in cars, but in the last year he started collection classics—classics to him. I think he's up to 25 or 26 cars. He always been into Chrysler 300s and he's got a Mark II and '69 Jag, a '29 DeSoto that's just beautiful. A '57 Thunderbird. I could go on and on and on. He's just tickled pink.

If you have car trouble, do you take it over to Richard?

See, he's not mechanically inclined, he just is a trivia freak on [. . .] what needs to be restored, how it should be restore, original colors. He's just really into that and he's very good at it. But mechanically, he was never that interested. He couldn't blueprint and engine or anything like that!

You don't live that dangerously, I guess.

Well, I love fast cars. Love 'em. We've got a '65 Plymouth Satellite that was completely rebuilt and blown all over the place by Keith Black, who is one of the originators of redoing the 392 Hemi, the Chrysler. He built the Plymouth engine and it's just unbelievable. We've got a 1970 Barracuda, a 440 6-pack. It gets off its little duff! The car that I drive all the time is a 350 Mercedes, a little black one. It's in impeccable shape and I love it. It's beautiful and it runs like a champ. When I wanna get in a fast car I just walk down to the other end of the garage and go tearing off into the distance. But the race thing was really somethin'

There was a recent People *magazine article which talked about a condominium you're building. Is that right?*

The condominium is in Century City. In fact, it's pretty close to being done. I bought it about two years ago. What I did was I take two complete apartments and gut 'em and start brand new. I've got 3,000 or 3,100 square feet of one big condominium.

Is that the one where one is named "Close to You"?

No, the "Close to You" and "Only Just Begun" [apartments] are two apartment houses. Those are in Downey. We got that idea from Herb Alpert because he's got one called "Tijuana Taxi" and "Lonely Bull." We did that back in 1970, I think. They're really pretty, too. But my condominium is something I've wanted to do for a while.

You're starting a land empire here, too, in Southern California.

I'm gonna put myself in my condominium. It's gonna be a ME empire! [*Laughs.*]

What does your taste run to, as far as decorating?

Well, we've nicknamed it "contemporary/country/French," which doesn't make any sense at all! It's odd 'cause I like country, yet I don't like antiques. [I like] certain antiques, but I don't get into antique furniture. I like big, fluffy couches. When I first met with my decorator, John Cottrell, he said, "Well what do you like?" and I said, "You better sit down." I explained to him I want it to look classy in a funky kinda way. I want it to be top-notch, top class, yet I want people to feel like they can put their feet up on anything. [. . .] He sat down and said, "Oh, dear." But he's doing a really great job and I've got a combination of a lot of different things—a country kitchen, and on the other hand, I've got Lucite and chrome. It's really going to be nice.

As far as the Carpenters' image, I get the impression that that's kind of how you would like the American public to view you, rather than just a rather placid exterior and not really any funky stuff to it.

Yeah. There's so much that Rich and I like that a lot of times people don't or haven't had the chance to see. [. . .] On the [TV] special we've come pretty close to accomplishing part of what we want them to see.

We cover just about every kind of music possible in the special—a lot of different looks, a lot of different feels, [and] a million different attitudes [that] we've always wanted to get into. But it seemed from day one we were accidentally plastered with a certain type of an image.

It was very middle-of-the-road, I guess, from the beginning.

Well, I don't mind that so much because we're just kinda normal. But as far as certain headlines reading all I do is drink milk and eat cookies, that's not really fair, you know?

Richard had the classic comment. He had said you make Pat Boone look dirty.

Right! Yeah! [*Laughs.*] We're normal. We like to do a lot of different things and that's what we'd like people to see. We just like to have a lot of fun.

With the advent of "Close to You," the music during the early '70s began to take on a different trend. It seemed as though people almost considered cocktail rock the "in" thing to do, if that's the label you'd apply to it. You sort of set a trend for what became a taste as far as music in America.

"Close to You" hit July 22, 1970. Not that I remember dates! [*Laughs.*]

What hour was it?

Let me see. When *Billboard* comes. I think it was about four o'clock in the afternoon, actually. But "Close to You" was [number] 1 and the next week "Make It with You" by Bread went #1. About the same time, James Taylor was hitting with "Fire and Rain," and right after that, I think Carole King hit with "It's Too Late." We named it "contemporary pop," [*laughs*] and, then all of a sudden, the whole trend was changing and it stuck—until about a year-and-a-half ago—and then all of a sudden it changed back around. It's not quite as strong right now, but I have a feeling it's gonna to come back. I hope it does.

There's a tremendous surge of nostalgia that's happened over the last couple of years and you've gotten into it yourself with some of the hits.

When we went with "[Please Mr.] Postman," we didn't do that to get into the nostalgia thing. That was something Richard always wanted to cut, for some strange reason. He said, "I love 'Please Mr. Postman.'" And I said, "*What?*" And it's a great song! It has got four chord changes, but what you can do with them. I had more fun cutting that record. With "Goofus," that's forty years old, you know. Gus Kahn wrote it. I thought that might do something and it never really caught on. I was kind of disappointed because it's such a good song. It's a fun kinda thing, you know?

I think since I have known you the past couple of years, you've always had that urge to do "Goofus."

I really love it. Like "I Can Dream, Can't I?" or something like that. There are so many things you can do. In the whole nostalgia thing, we cut the *Now & Then* album, but we never released anything other than "Yesterday Once More." One day, we were driving on the freeway and it was right in the middle of everybody releasing oldies. [Richard] said, "You know, nobody's ever written anything about the surge coming back." I could see the head lighting up right before we got off at Highland. That was it. Five minutes later, out came the tune. We could have pulled "End of the World" or "Johnny Angel," but we never did because [Richard] didn't want to get into that. We left them on the album as a whole, which is still one of my favorite albums. That album was more fun to cut. We couldn't get anything done because we were laughing so hard.

Does Richard really want to be a disc jockey?

He *loves* it. It's a lot of fun. At one point he was talking about buying a station. I said, "Richard, you've only got one body to give for your country!" I mean, for Pete's sake, you can't go in twelve different directions. [. . .] You have a *ball*, don't you?

I do enjoy what I do. The whole premise of the work is that people are too lazy to get up and turn the records over themselves. That's really what it boils down to.

Yeah, I never thought of it that way. But [Richard's] such a record lover, music lover. The collection that he has is just unbelievable.

Who were the people that made the impressions on Karen Carpenter? And the style that you have?

Well, I don't think anybody particularly influenced my vocal style, it just kinda happened. I don't really style myself after anybody. When I opened my mouth, it came out and that was it. [*Laughs.*] As for liking different vocalists, [there are] just a million of them. Harry Nilsson floors me. This could go on for days. I love the Beatles, the Beach Boys, James Taylor, Dionne Warwick, Dusty Springfield, Ella Fitzgerald. I could go on for days. All different types. But I never really *copied* anybody because, like I said, when I started to sing it just kinda developed. It's funny because we were listening a couple of months back to a song that we cut years ago, '67 probably, on Magic Lamp Records. A good friend of ours, Joe Osborn, who is a phenomenal electric bass player around town. He had a studio in his garage and he had a label for about two weeks [*laughs*] and we cut one of Richard's songs called "You'll Love Me." I listened to it and I sounded country. It was very odd. No vibrato. It was in tune, but there was no vibrato and I sung very hard. I sound just like a *country* singer, but you could kinda tell it was me. And then, all of a sudden, I don't know where [the voice] *came* from, to tell you the truth.

I read that you originally started out playing the drums before you even started singing.

It happened pretty close. I was influenced by a kid in high school to play drums. I wanted to get out of gym 'cause I didn't wanna run around a track at 8 o'clock in the morning. [I'm a] musician at heart. You want me to do *what*? *When*? But I didn't do a *thing* at the time. I didn't play. I didn't sing. I'd gotten into the choir 'cause I wanted to get out of geometry. [*Laughs.*] Crafty, aren't I? Geometry went right by me. I have no mind for [it]. So I got into the choir, but I still didn't know I could sing. And I got into band to get out of gym. [. . .] I was absolutely *fascinated* with drums. I don't know why. In my junior year I got real friendly with a kid named Frankie Chavez, who was head of the drum line. All I ever heard—and this is the honest-to-god truth—[was] "girls don't play drums." That is such an overused line, but I started [playing]. It was so true. They said, "Oh, you're out of your tree. You're just not well!" So they gave me a glockenspiel. And this all true. Well, the glockenspiel was just horrendous. [. . .] I held the glockenspiel for about two months and couldn't handle it. I just couldn't take it. So I said, "Let me see if I can play. I know I can play." I went over, I picked up a pair of sticks. It was the most natural feeling thing I've ever done and then that was it. A week later I asked my mom and dad for a set of Ludwig drums. I wanted Ludwigs and Richard said, "Buy 'em. The resale is better." He's nice isn't he? [*Laughs.*] Well, Ludwigs are the best in our opinion so he said, "When you go to sell 'em after she doesn't wanna play 'em in another week you'll get more money." I kept that set for two months. I kept it, but then I wanted a show set. *Two months* and I wanted a show set! I wanted silver sparkle double floor tom-toms, the whole thing. And they bought 'em for me. I was never more at home on a set of drums and within six months I was playing with Rich. In another couple of months we won the Hollywood Bowl Battle of the Bands in '66. I couldn't even pick [the drums] up, they were so heavy. I sang and played kind of at the same time because we started getting gigs on the weekend and they needed somebody to sing. Richard said, "Well, sing 'Yesterday.' " And then, I'd do "Ebb Tide," you know, and all that stuff. But I never stopped playing! I did everything at once.

"Girls don't play drums." But to sing and play drums at the same time is even more difficult.

It was the most *comfortable* thing and I played the entire show for two years. We were out on the road for two years before Richard finally said, "You've got to get up." We had four or five gold records. [. . .] We were way into "Superstar" before I finally had to get up. Petrified. You have no idea. The *fear*! There was nothing to hold onto.

No security blanket.

Nothing to hide behind. My drums, by this time, I had so many of them, all you could see were my bangs. You couldn't see the mouth, you couldn't see the hands, you couldn't see anything. So we're out on the road and we're doing all the hits and the dummy is buried behind a full set of drums. [*Laughs.*] So finally, I started getting up.

Was it awkward because suddenly you didn't have anything to do with your hands?

Oh, sure. It took a little while, but now I can't stand still [with] everywhere I want to run. Now, we have incorporated into the show an entire seven- or eight-minute drum spectacular. It is just drums. I don't sing a note. We end up with twenty-three drums on the stage, which is something you will also see on the [TV] special. I love to play—I *really* do—and I love to sing, but I wouldn't want to give either one of them up.

You've stayed pretty close to your parents all these years. I'm curious if there's a secret behind that. The initial reaction to somebody bringing a whole drum set in the house would be: "Are you really serious about this?"

From day one, they worked like mad to get Richard and [me] anything we wanted. We were a middle-class family, we didn't have any money. My dad worked two gigs, my mom worked. They always somehow managed to get [Richard] a piano. I played flute for a week. I played piano for a week. Accordion, that was a biggie—lasted *two* weeks. When I decided that I wanted drums, they didn't know whether I was becoming detached upstairs, but they went and got brand new set [of drums]. When Richard wanted a grand piano they somehow swung it. The whole setup was set right in the middle of the living room and it stayed there because they knew . . . well, Richard has always been musical since the day he showed up. But I didn't know I could do anything till I was like 16 years old. And then all of a sudden it was just [*snaps*] all there! It was very odd the way it happened. I wish that I had started when I was little. [I] could be that much further along. But they always believed in him and I guess, for some reason, they had a feeling that it was gonna stick. They always got everything we needed; couldn't afford any of it. I think that is one of the reasons that we're so close. And Richard and I have always been *extremely* close. Even when I didn't play or anything, I'd always follow him to the gig just to watch him.

Who makes the decisions—or is it a mutual decision?

It's pretty much mutual because we think identically on 99 percent of the things. We very seldom disagree. If there is something that comes up, we talk it out. If it gets down to who's going to make the decision, if it's a musical decision, he'll make it. But I can't even remember when there was that kind of decision that we disagreed on. Oh, yes, I do! "Superstar." When I think back on it, I can't imagine how. I had heard the tune originally on [Joe Cocker's] *Mad Dogs and Englishmen* and then we heard it again on Johnny Carson when Bette Midler did it as a torch song. [Richard] came running up the stairs and said, "I've found *the tune*." I heard it and I said, "That's nice." And he said, "*Nice?*" But he heard the whole record in his head, needless to say. It didn't knock me out until I recorded it, at which time it just blew me over. That was the only question I ever had.

Somebody said you weren't that enamored with "Solitaire" either. I guess it was the initial impact.

I think I heard that the first time in England. I do stand corrected. I think the versions that I had heard didn't knock me out. I *do* like the song. It's not my favorite, but it's a beautiful song and Richard produced the hell out of it. He really did. I like doing it, but there are others that I am more fond of. I think my favorite *today* is "I Need to Be in Love." That really upsets me when I hear it.

I've had so many ladies call me on the phone and say, "That is my song." So many have the empathy.

It really hits me right at home. Certain nights on the stage, it really upsets me. I sing it and I'm almost putting myself into tears. It's so personal because John Bettis, our lyricist, wrote that. When Rich heard the title he said, "Oh my God, that's beautiful!" Oddly enough, the title had come from Albert Hammond. Just the title. John, Richard and I are kind of sitting in the same boat. We're all looking.

You've always been portrayed as loners.

Well, we're *not* loners, we're just looking for somebody to share our life with and we haven't been lucky enough to find it yet. That's really the easiest way to say it.

What are the requirements you're looking for today, Karen?

Well, I have my list here, but I'll have to stand, just in case it hits the floor! Again, John thinks exactly the way we do. When he wrote the lyrics to that thing, I was just flabbergasted. The first verse of that says, "The hardest thing I've ever done is keep believing there's someone in this crazy world for me / The way that people come and go through temporary lives / My chance could come and I might never know." And I said, "Oh, my God, it's so true!" It's very hard in the position that we are in [. . .] not only to meet people, but to find somebody that's real.

You have to question their motives a little bit. Are they attracted to you simply because you're a star?

It's a terrible thing to say, but it's kinda true. It's hard because we're constantly around somewhat of the same circle of people. I find sometimes with guys, a lot of 'em don't know what to expect. Some of them get upset if we walk into a restaurant and they recognize me and don't recognize him, which puts me away because I don't like to hurt people. A lot of times, *they* don't know how to act. They freeze. I'm saying, "What are you freezing for? It's only me." But they don't realize that we're just human and it's kind of a difficult position to be in. We're always looking for somebody nice, somebody that's real, and has a way with 'em that's going to make me happy for the rest of my life.

Do you see the business—the broad spectrum of entertainment—as being a problem of having a marriage with somebody?

Not if it's somebody that understands, see. That's a definite problem in itself. It's rough because you spend a lot of time on the road. Obviously, I would want to cut down on the work, but you can do everything. You don't have to get married and sit in the house. I *couldn't*. There's no way I would ever stop singing or performing or doing whatever I want to do. But I want to do it with somebody and share it. I want somebody to share my *joy* with! At the same time—whoever it is I find—I want them to be able to feel the same way and to share their accomplishments. There's a lot to do in this world.

What makes you happy? What really entertains Karen Carpenter or puts you on your high for a day?

I'll tell you, one thing that I couldn't have said a year ago is being healthy again. When I got sick it scared the hell out of me. I said, "Whoa!"

You were down to the 90-pound weakling.

Yeah, [I got] right down to the ol' eighty-nine pounds there. That made me stop and think. It really did. Now I have a priority list. Certain things that would have upset me a year ago don't anymore. Trivial things don't shake me as much. [. . .] I enjoy what I do immensely. I love to sing. I love making records, performing. Sooner or later I'd like to look into doing a movie. I'm having an enormous amount of *good* times doing my condominium. I love needlepoint. Most of all, I would like to have some more time to just be with my friends. Now, if somebody calls up and says, "Hey, you want to go out?" I say, "Yes, July 6th is free. Not this July 6th, *next* July 6th!" They say, "Well, when are you leaving?" "Tomorrow morning." "When are you coming back?" "Oh, I'll be back in about six weeks." It's really rough. You say, "Well, listen, I'll call you from Germany—if I can get a line." It's *hard* because every time you set something up you *leave*.

Do you find your friends changed—the friends that you had before you were "The Carpenters" in an international spotlight?

Not my close ones. Friends that show up and say they were friends that I've never heard of, those are a little different. I'll never forget. When we first started, Herb Alpert said to me, "I'm tellin' ya right now, when you 'hit' you're gonna find out you went to high school with 25,000 kids." It's no lie! People say, "Hey! We went to school together!" And I say, "I never lived in that *state*. What do you *mean* 'We went to school together'?" You find out you're related to 73,000 people. It's odd because people always call up and they say I'm their cousin. The ironic part of it is [that] my road manager *is* my cousin. He says, "*You're* not their cousin! *I* know if you're their cousin, 'cause *I'm* their cousin!" They stop dead in their tracks. People come from *all* over the place. But it's natural. And it's kinda funny the way people find ways to pull off things like that. It's *amazing*.

What about the mail you get? I was curious because I think you tried to set the record somewhat straight with the People *magazine article and now with the [TV] special coming up. Did the mail change, as far as the letters and fan mail you would get, or calls, after that article? Was there a different element that suddenly surfaced?*

I wouldn't say *too* much. There were some people that took the article totally wrong. I find that one of the problems that we faced with that article was that certain people just wouldn't accept that we *are* human. And I find that saddening. We are, by no means, I repeat, trying to put down what we are. I am not ashamed of what I am. And neither is Richard, but the fact that he might smoke a cigarette is not an immoral act. It's just not *fair!* We are not drunks. We are not dope addicts. When we said in that article that we would have voted for legalization of marijuana, it does not mean that we smoke the stuff. I wouldn't know it if I tripped over it. I have never touched it, I don't care to touch it, and it never entered my mind to touch it! But I do feel that this is a free country. People can do what they feel like doing. I got a letter that was accusing me of being a dope addict, which is absolutely ridiculous! I have never touched it and I really could care *less!* But I still have a mind of my own and that's what I don't like being deprived of. I do like to be able to speak what I feel. I don't like being cornered and neither does Richard. As for us putting down the milk-and-cookies image, that's not fair either. I think we're pretty straight ahead people. We're honest. We try to be very loyal to our fans. We spend 24 hours a day worrying about whether our product is good enough. We spend an awful lot of time trying to achieve perfection, as close as we can come, and that's not that easy. It's a fulltime job and it's, by far, the foremost thing in both of our minds at all times.

Trying to be a perfectionist is difficult. Some people regard it as something that's impossible. In analyzing your personality, have you ever started to be introspective and figure out what your biggest asset might be and then also, as Shakespeare put it, what your tragic flaw would be, at the same time?

Oh, sure. That's a thought that's always in your mind. It's hard to break it down. You can say, on one hand this is terrific and on the other hand you're a total loser. [*Laughs.*] That's *always* in my mind. And perfection is just about impossible, but we really try. One of the things that we just [finished] was completely doing a whole new show, which is something that we've wanted to do for five years. But we were kept so busy on the road all the time and never getting a minute to do anything that we never got around to doing the show until finally, when I got sick, Richard had a second to get his thoughts together and that was, incidentally, the time he wrote "I Need to Be in Love." We finally got together with a guy named Joe Layton. He did Bette Midler and just did Diana Ross's new act. He did us, now he's working with Olivia Newton-John. He's just a genius. Together with Joe Layton and Ken and Mitzi Welch, who do all the special musical material on "The Carol Burnett Show." We took the show from start to finish. It's brand new. It covers everything you can possibly think of. The joy of doing that finally has uplifted not only Richard and I but the whole group. Now it's not just Karen and Richard with a backup group, it's just one big go-get-'em group. The show is an absolute thrill. [. . .] I love doing it. It's so much fun. [. . .] Richard and I are real proud of it.

Do you ever get tired of doing those tours over and over?

Not if you do them right. I was real tired of them about a year ago and finally my body said, "You're tired, dummy. Lay down!" But now things have all changed. We're doing things right. The [TV] special is going to be terrific. We go out [on tour] for maybe two or three weeks at a time, at the most. We come home for a couple of weeks, we do something else, and if it's handled properly—which it is now—it's *fun.* You go out for just enough time and when it starts to wear off you come home. If you get tired, you come home.

Do you find the trappings of success—that constant demand and the public spotlight that you have to be in—to be something that you regret?

Very seldom. It's one thing when you start out and you say, "I've got to get a hit record." You have no idea what is following. You really can't comprehend, but every now and then, you're really tired out. You just want to sit and not be constantly confronted with something. On the whole, I wouldn't trade it for anything in the world. The funny times or the odd moments are when you're overseas, like in Japan or England. It's just *unbelievable*. You can't go out. You can't go anywhere. The secret ways to get in and out of hotels are very entertaining. You find more ways to do things. But I wouldn't trade it. Ever.

That must be a little unusual to sing to a German or a Japanese audience.

It *is* odd, but they know every word. It's amazing. You're two bars into the tune and they know it. I don't know how but they seem to pick up on the vibe, even when you're talking. The last time we were in Japan I did about half the show—speaking wise—in Japanese. [. . .] I would go to each town and they would give me the different dialects and I would make it a point to tell them that I was sorry that we had to cancel the tour, tell them that I'm all better now. I would say certain things about Richard in Japanese. Onii-chan is "the great brother." They call Richard "the great brother," which just broke me up! [*Laughs.*] If you do things like that, they really appreciate it.

How do you recycle yourself to be fresh each evening for a concert when you're performing like that on the road? Are there any mental gymnastics you go through or is it just the audience that does it for you?

It's funny because people say, "What do you do to warm up and get ready to sing?" Well, I walk about ten steps from the dressing room right before they say, "Ladies and gentlemen, the Carpenters." Then, when they do say that, I walk on and that's it!

You don't any ritual or superstitious stuff?

Nah. You walk out and you do it. [. . .] I warm up right there. I open my mouth and out it comes!

Are there any unseen influences in your lives? People today are talking about EST and astrology. Is there anything else that goes [on] behind the scenes. What's Karen Carpenter really influenced by?

I don't know. I've got a lot of friends that have done this EST route. [. . .] I just really don't know whether I'm ready to swallow that yet. I *might* go. Again, I haven't had the time to get two full weekends. See, that's the problem! It seems that most of the time I can straighten out anything inside my own head. Whether I'm happy or unhappy about something I figure it out. Fix it. That's basically where I'm at. This EST thing. Every time I get together with certain people that have done it, it gets my interest for the moment, but then I go on and do other things. I don't know what to say about that. If I go I'll let you know! [*Laughs.*]

How do you unwind? Is it the needlepoint that does it for you?

That helps. I like to listen to music. I like to ride my bicycle, my motorcycle. [*Laughs.*] I love to cook and as soon as I get into my condominium, I'll be doing *much* more of that.

What's your gourmet recipe? Say you found that special person and you're preparing a dinner that night. Have you got a specialty you'd fix right now?

I love French food. Of course, you can't beat a good plate of spaghetti! [*Laughs.*] Oh, there's a whole bunch of things I like to do. It's a toss-up at this point.

It's funny because it sort of comes full circle. You play a good game of softball. I can vouch for that having popped up to Karen Carpenter [and] trying to hit your pitches. You're fairly athletic on the outside, even though that was the thing that got you into music in the first place, trying to get out of gym.

Yeah, well they didn't let you play. They wanted me to run around a track and get in a swimming pool at eight o'clock in the morning. I just couldn't see that. I've never been one that likes being told what to do. If it's somethin' I really don't wanna do, I really don't wanna do it. I'm kinda hard-headed about things like that, so I find other routes. I'm glad, though, you know, 'cause it turned out much better this way. I'm glad the way everything turned out. I really am.

We'll wrap it up with the obvious question—you expressed an interest in maybe doing movies in the future. Any other things you'd like to do?

Speaking of movies, which would you see yourself in—a dramatic or comedy role?

I'd kinda like to do some kind of a comedy-musical. My favorites have always been, well, Carol Burnett just slays me. I think she's so talented. Lucy, I've been wild about the old *I Love Lucy* shows for years. Streisand just floors me. She's so good. I would like to do something like that, I really would, but I don't know what's going to pop up or what I would do first. I really couldn't say. But I'd like to do a movie.

We'll look for the [television] special is a start, right?

Yeah! That sure was fun. An enormous amount of fun.

Thank you, Karen Carpenter.

Thank you.

CARPENTERS ÜBER ALLES!

Ray Coleman

Melody Maker, 1976

There's a moment in the astonishing new Carpenters stage show in which Karen and Richard hold hands. During their classic hit "We've Only Just Begun," they pretend for a split second to be lovers, looking straight into each other's eyes—a rarely seen moment of near passion from a brother-sister act not noted for warmth, in spite of the romantic beauty of their songs.

Even the most ardent Carpenters fan might be forgiven a groan of embarrassment. There they are now, compounding the appalling Mickey Mouse, "squeaky clean, apple pie" image which has plagued them for two years.

Speaking as a fully paid-up Carpenters music follower for six years, I felt the flesh creep uncomfortably at the sight of grown-up brother and sister acting out this slightly incestuous scene as just "part of the act." But that's precisely what it is. "We've never been a touching or kissing family, [we were] not raised that way," Richard says.

"And now, when we're thinking about it, it seems natural and normal," says Karen. "People who came to see the show, close friends and managers, said it was ridiculous that we didn't touch each other through-out," says Richard. "So we put it in."

Right now, after a couple of inferior albums and a failed battle to wipe out their antiseptic image, they are at a crossroads, prepared to be adventurous, even dangerous.

Karen says holding hands felt uneasy for a while; Richard, too, fought off the idea on the grounds that they were "not in love that way." And then, in the context of a violent change in their stage act, they agreed to get closer to each other.

This strange episode in the evolution of the Carpenters, the band that has made it almost hip to like middle-of-the-road music, charac-terizes as well as anything the convolutions of their appearances, both public and private.

They are currently at a tricky stage of their career. Wealth has been achieved, musical credibility established. Yet there's this nagging feeling that they are marking time, and with Karen's serious illness of last year still lingering as a memory, there seems a desperate need to plow into a new direction, make some noise, raise the roof!

AND SO IT came to pass that the Carpenters caravan of 20 rattled into Germany last week for a pre-British whistle-stop tour, to show off their daring 1976 look. And to be sure, the old act has been shaken, rattled and rolled into a frantic production routine which projects the Carpenters As You've Never Seen Them Before, a show reversing the emphasis on Karen's voice into a slick two-hour whizzo of entertainment.

Richard no longer sits sternly at the piano—he roars on stage on a motorcycle at one point during a spoof of the Fifties—and Karen has abandoned that forlorn stance in a sad little red dress which so helped to dent their reputation last time.

Now, she tears at three sets of drums and a battery of congas, looks kookie in jeans, changes from sharp culotte suit to beautiful ball gown, and acts neatly while dressed as a Fifties tart during the motorbike sequence.

It's an amazing transformation, conceived because the producer, Joe Layton (who worked similarly devastating tricks for Diana Ross's show), believes the Carpenters' millions of record buyers want to see Richard and Karen DO something, beyond stand up there and sing. After all, he reasons, fans have the records at home—who needs a replica of that?

The positive view of the mindboggling new Carpenters stage show would be that they have planted the kiss of life on a two-year-old corpse, and that their audacity has won. Their 1974 show was boring. The 1976 show is overambitious.

The uncharitable could say that they have snatched catastrophe from the jaws of disaster. The truth lies somewhere between those extremes. Like it or not, the new show forces a reaction. Nobody sleeps during this concert. The Carpenters are alive and well—and working hard, as always.

They know no other way. Richard and Karen are hardly pop stars in the accepted sense (he adopts the classic paranoid stance of wanting to be noticed but resenting intrusion into privacy; Karen is too lacking in visible neuroses to be considered a star).

Above all, the Carpenters and their five regular accompanists are musicians. Troupers in the grand tradition. It's not rock 'n' roll, too musically innovative and melodic to be considered crass showbiz.

The standard of musicianship is very high, and they do, after all, have the strength of the most delectable female voice in its field since, say, Sarah Vaughan or Peggy Lee.

The Carpenters are something special, as their German fans loudly affirmed last week; like their British dates, there were sell-out concerts all the way across Europe, from the Deutsches Museum in Munich to the Dusseldorf Philipshalle to the Hamburg Congress Centrum.

THE CARPENTERS ARE important because they are exemplary craftsmen. And they touch people. "In a way," says their quietly canny electric bassist, Danny Woodhams, "Rich and Karen HAVE changed the course of popular music in the past six years.

"It's become respectable for a musician like me to say: I play with the Carpenters. Without them, it would have still been acid rock and

Motown. It's a testing time right now, but that track record of work between Richard and John Bettis (lyric writer) is amazing, and Karen's voice—well, it's just lovely."

Richard, however, seems bothered that when the history of popular music has to be written, the Carpenters will not merit a chapter. "Beatles, Beach Boys, Dylan—they'll get chapters," he said.

"Not the Carpenters. They'll bracket us with a load of others as bland, easy-listening, middle-road. We've gotta change all this, and it's gonna take time."

Still, he was encouraged by the admiration of artistically lesser breeds; he points out that Alice Cooper had gone on record as admiring the Carpenters, and Karen said: "Kiss like us, you know." She raised her eyebrows in mock disbelief.

"As far back as 1971," said Richard, "I've been concerned that we've not been accepted as well in concert as on record. It's sure not the fault of Karen's voice, because she sings the same anywhere, everywhere, in the studio or on stage. The same. The group's usually been clean and tight. No, some magic was missing.

"For five years now it's been worrying me. I'd get home from shows and say: no, we're not getting the same thing going on stage that we do in the studio. Charisma. That's been missing. Guess we're now trying to graft charisma onto our act. Well, it sure is not before time. . . .

"There's people who don't sing as well as we do, haven't had our amount of hits, who aren't a fraction as well-known as us, getting the audiences going. Thus far, we've failed in that direction. And yet, I know we're a good group. Not perfect, but good.

"When you know you're doing a good concert and not pulling in a response from the audience, it's demoralizing.

"To some extent, it's the people. They're an older crowd and they don't go 'Whoooooooohoooo' when we do our hits. On the other hand, the nice part is they don't go talking all the way through the songs, either.

"Well, I'd worry myself sick about all this. I'd go home with Karen after a show and say, for an act that's sold so many records and doesn't get something better going on stage, there's something wrong.

"But our manager said: 'Don't worry, those people who came to see your concert will be back.' And they came back, we kept selling out.

"So I said, maybe we're just selling records to quiet people! Anyway, it built up in my mind and nagged away. So here we are, with this radical change. Joe [Layton], the director of the show, says we've all been playing the role of good musicians for too long.

"He says we're too good—people don't want to concentrate on music so much, if they want the Carpenters sound they'll stay home with the stereo. I'm not sure. We'll see on the next tour whether they come back. It's a test."

Karen: "We're hams. We enjoy dressing up and the production. Have we gone over the top? Well, the answer's in the audience; it's been received well everywhere so far. Ask me next year."

SHE'S LEAVING HOME: Very soon, Karen will depart the house she and Richard live in with their parents, and set up her own Los Angeles home. She's 26, Richard 30.

They get along well, but Karen feels the need to build a house as some kind of personal statement. Richard has encouraged the move. Together, they scarcely seem to look at each other; yet there's a natural bond, and at a Munich press conference last week, answering outstandingly banal questions, they unitedly stonewalled with impressive brevity.

Later that night, when I asked both together to name the other's most irritating characteristic, Richard bridled slightly while Karen came straight out with it: "He'll always stall when we're due to go in the studios, and not let me know the title or nature of the song until we get there.

"I keep saying, for days before: 'What's the song?' And he keeps saying: 'Oh, you'll be OK. It's easy for you.' He doesn't let me know what my work is till we get inside the studio. I hate that about him."

Richard thought deeply before being pushed to this reply: "If I'm with a girl Karen doesn't like, she gets in her three cents' worth, and then doesn't leave it at that. And after a while it starts to get on my nerves, and we argue. It's usually not musical.

"I wish Karen wouldn't act, sometimes, like a 26-year-old Jewish momma, and interfere so much in my personal affairs."

Did Richard interfere with her private life, or did Karen accept his role as big brother? "Not a lot—sometimes I'll offer a view, but I'd never tell her not to date this guy or that. I figure that'd be impertinent. However, Karen seems to see it as her duty to give me advice. I don't like that."

What were their joint worries? "Staying where we are," they answered in unison. "Maintaining. Very difficult in the American pop market," Richard said.

"Y'know, it seems that if you're in country-and-western and you make a coupla hit singles, you're there for life. Not in pop. We can go down as quickly as we came up, if our records stop selling."

And how vital was it to him and Karen to keep on keeping on, achieving massive record sales? More important than their private lives now?

Karen answered that if it came to a choice between privacy and fame, hers would be fame rather than privacy. Her career meant everything to her: "I gotta sing. I love that crowd . . ."

Richard was more equivocal. "Sometimes I think [it's] wrong that we aren't famous enough in person, considering the millions of records we've sold. Sometimes, we are not noticed in the street and that gets to me. Other times, I get hassled in a restaurant and don't like that either."

Yes, he agreed, he wanted it both ways. John Denver belonged to the same management stable as the Carpenters, and Richard couldn't stand the prospect of that lack of private life.

On the other hand, he envied Denver the ego satisfaction. In the end, Richard wanted to go to the grave having been regarded primarily as a musician rather than pop star. "You can be a pop star for a week," he said thoughtfully. "I'm gonna be a musician forever."

Talking of death, he wanted to die in his sleep. Karen, too. Both are certain that whatever else they record, the song "We've Only Just Begun" will be their musical epitaph.

"Huge though 'Close to You' was," said Karen, "it didn't have the impact of 'Begun,' and no one song has been so associated with an act so much for a long, long time as that with us."

Richard said college music students were even writing essays on the theme of that one song, and [he] and Karen were consistently being questioned about it. "Yep, that's the song that's going to remain with us and if you ask me what song I'll take to the grave, that's the one."

IF THE CARPENTERS are refreshingly uncloying when they sit together, they lead different lives, and have separate worldly views, when they're apart.

In Germany, apart from a chilling trip together to Dachau concentration camp and a visit to a Charles Aznavour concert, they went largely separate ways, partly because Richard has brought to Europe his girlfriend, Mary [Rudolph].

During the day, both keep an extremely low profile, the very opposite of the traditional boisterous traveling circus which so many seven-piece acts offer as a sideshow to the passing observer.

Richard, a piano fanatic, made a point of checking out the Steinway manufacturing house because he believed pianos made in Germany were of better quality than those made elsewhere; Karen did a sharp look round Dusseldorf to establish that it was a vital city. They have separate identities, go their own ways.

But in the evening, she's the singer in the band, and while the more brooding Richard is a razor-sharp, gifted musician confronting his gaunt and wasted look with musical masterpieces, Karen's vocals are so stunningly warm as to defy comparison. The lady seems incapable of singing out of tune.

Their band is the same as that which came for the plastic show which graced our stages in 1974, and their unashamed loyalty to Richard and Karen is something they freely admit: Danny Woodhams (electric bass, vocals), Bob Messenger (keyboards, bass, flute and tenor sax), Doug Strawn (vocals, keyboards, and electric clarinet), Cubby O'Brien (drums), and the dazzling guitarist Tony Peluso, whose love of the Carpenters was such that he turned down an offer from Paul McCartney to join Wings.

Peluso's legendary solo on "Goodbye to Love" is now more heavily into feedback, but its melodic strength is intact, and it's still a killing show-stopper.

The new show begins with an immaculately suited Richard walking out to bow to the audience, a bow which emphasizes his great height. When Karen emerges for a jazzed-up version of "There's a Kind of Hush

[(All over the World)]" and "Top of the World" looking more attractive than in recent years and dressed in a culotte suit, it's immediately apparent that they've acquired a presence missing in any show they've done before.

And when strings sweep them into the glorious ballad "I Need to Be in Love," the hallmark of the Carpenters' beauty—haunting melody plus tasteful arrangement plus that voice—is rammed home with some force.

Karen sings that line: ". . . It took a while for me to learn/that nothing comes for free / The price [I've paid] is high enough for me . . ." with a conviction that could strike a chord in many a broken heart, so meaningful is her voice.

There follows a "[Spike Jones and His] City Slickers" segment which marks the ruination of "Close to You" as a song—it's speeded up to two or three times its recorded tempo, with lead vocal by Richard and the rest of the band spoofing it up with kazoos and hooters à la Temperance Seven.

It's awful, but Karen reappears quickly enough to repair the damage. She has changed dresses again, and looks splendid (she has recently acquired the services of the same clothes designer as Olivia Newton-John, one of Karen's friends).

"Sing" calls for audience involvement, Karen moving among the front rows for a volunteer to join her. (A fundamental mistake, for it diminishes their role as stars who should keep a distance from the audience.)

"Mr. [Guder]" and the glorious "Yesterday Once More" come before Tony Peluso's breathless spoken introduction of the Fifties sketch. This is spirited stuff, with Richard riding a motorcycle on stage (Karen acting the role of his girlfriend with genuine acting flair), band joining in with a doo-wop vocal parody and Karen looking every exaggerated inch the Fifties tart, complete with gigantic bouffant wig.

She follows this with a splendid attack on the drums (three kits and congas) during a mini-biographical sketch on the Carpenters' career story, narrated by Richard and Karen alternately.

A filmed backdrop provides a good glimpse into their growing-up years.

Richard's piano peaks are scaled with a fine, serious "Warsaw Concerto," before the hits start rolling: "For All We Know," "Ticket to Ride," "Only Yesterday," "Please Mr. Postman," "Superstar," and a wretched encore with two improbable songs for the Carpenters: "Good Vibrations" and—horror of horrors—"Comin' Through the Rye."

There's an air of desperation about the show—but at least it's a positive effort to blitz the audience with something beyond Carpenters music. The big question for their crucial British season, starting this week, is whether they've reversed too far, and skated too thinly over their real strengths, the songs. Clearly, they had to do something, and they can't he accused of being stagnant.

More than anything, I think the new Carpenters show qualifies them for bravery medals. Less bold stars with 30 million record sales would have sat tight.

And when all's said and done, the Carpenters are not disco, and they represent standards. In these often dark days, they are a beacon of light, a good force in popular music. This week in Britain, they'll send 46,000 people out of the theaters with a happy smile.

That's something.

CONCERT REVIEW

LONDON PALLADIUM, NOVEMBER 25, 1976

Variety, 1976

To say the Carpenters use every conceivable device, from pots and pans to a motorcycle, as part of their impressive new show, in for a week at the London Palladium, is only slight exaggeration.

Just when the large stage seems crammed to overflowing—with Karen Carpenter's four drum kits and nine visible mics, brother Richard, five band members, assorted keyboards, electric flutes, clarinets, guitars and tape recorders—the backdrop vanishes to reveal a 42-piece orchestra.

Messy as it sounds, this is slick staging by Broadway producer Joe Layton, and the production as a whole is value-for-money entertainment.

The Carpenters, six years on, are in fine form.

From a slightly raised platform, fringed with red streamers like a giant Christmas cake, they provide their own potted discography beneath an assortment of some 60 spotlights.

Razzle-dazzle effect of the act is enhanced when they leave the stage to enlist audience support for a mad arrangement of "Close to You."

A wheel-on percussion table, which boasts pots and pans, klaxon horns, tin whistles, etc., provides a fun number and Karen Carpenter displays boundless energy and flair with her lengthy drum solo.

Endorsing their pre-publicized changed-from-clean image, they launch into a college skit with bobby socks, false busts, a rude song about Sandra Dee and a noisy climax by Richard driving a motorcycle on stage covering the first 10 rows with fumes.

In a more serious vein, Richard gives a virtuoso piano rendering of the "Warsaw Concerto" backed by the Dick Palombi Orchestra and reflected in a huge suspended mirror.

The femme Carpenter takes her turn with a "studio session" singing a medley of the duo's disk hits such as "Top of the World" and "For All We Know" etc. She seems to be on stage during the entire show yet somehow manages five costume changes.

The boys in the band have their own highlight with "[Goodbye] to Love" and an exceptional guitar duet by Tony Peluso and Bob Messenger.

Audience loved it all. Seventy-five minutes of entertainment bristling with vitality. [. . .]

"SURPRISE" BY THE CARPENTERS

Ed Harrison

Billboard, 1977

LOS ANGELES—Karen and Richard Carpenter may well surprise a lot of people with the release of their new A&M album *Passage*.

The duo concedes that it's their most diverse album yet, touching all bases of the musical spectrum from the reggae-sounding "Man Smart (Woman Smarter)" to the orchestral "Don't Cry for Me Argentina" from the rock opera *Evita*.

Says Richard Carpenter: "On this album we let the musicians stretch out more on the solos. We usually build an album from the bass, piano and drums, but are now incorporating brass, percussion and congas. We used more musicians to get a better feel."

The most elaborate undertaking on the album is "On the Balcony of the Casa Rosada/Don't Cry For Me Argentina," which includes the services of the entire Los Angeles Philharmonic Orchestra and the Gregg Smith Singers. By the time the tracks were ready to be laid down, 162 performers had assembled on the A&M soundstage.

"When we brought in all these pieces we didn't know if it would work," says Richard. "But we wanted to do it in a big way. And we wanted an orchestra which plays all the time rather than studio musicians."

Other tunes covered include such diverse material as Michael Franks' ["B'wana She No Home,"] Klaatu's spacey "Calling Occupants of Interplanetary Craft" and "I Just Fall in Love Again," another big orchestra production.

Other luminaries contributing include Leon Russell on piano, saxophonist Tom Scott and King Errisson on congas.

"Because of the arrangements," says Richard, "there is a more sophisticated sound. I feel that little has actually changed except maybe compared with some of the older albums."

Adds Karen: "When choosing a song, the melody must fit me first although the lyrics are also important."

Karen, since the past two albums, has ceased playing drums to allow her to concentrate on singing. "Richard wanted a stronger sound," she says, "and I no longer have the strength."

Karen's singing has also taken on an air of refinement since the earlier albums. "I used to oversing," says Karen. "I was too loud. I'm able to feel a song now."

Under the guidance of manager Jerry Weintraub, the Carpenters will begin making selective television appearances. They will have their own Christmas special this year and contemplate one or two specials every year.

"Jerry got us the TV deals," says Karen. "He's thinking more long-range. Before, we would just record and tour. Now TV is locking up a lot of time."

The Carpenters, however, are shying away from what some call the traps of a possible weekly variety show of their own. "We don't want to overexpose or exhaust ourselves. It would be impossible doing a weekly. If we did we'd have to sacrifice everything else," says Richard.

"TV might cause a brief spurt in album sales, but our own show would have to be done right," he adds.

Both Karen and Richard concede that their somewhat wholesome image has made for "closet Carpenter freaks."

"There are a lot of fans who kind of hide the fact they like the Carpenters," says Karen. Nevertheless, they receive stacks of mail from young people thanking them for straightening out their lives and giving encouragement through such songs as "Top of the World" and "We've Only Just Begun."

"We like appealing to all ages," Karen says. "Everyone from young kids to their grandparents come to our shows."

What lies ahead for the Carpenters? Karen says she would like to do a film musical while Richard is eyeing other acts to produce.

CONCERT REVIEW

HARRAH'S, TAHOE, AUGUST 4, 1977

Variety, 1977

The Carpenters are sticking to a winning combination for a second year as the South Shore Room date is nearly the same as last season's Sahara Tahoe fortnight. It's the formula that finally made the personable siblings into a viable nightclub act, a mix of gag outings, mellow music, and visuals.

Only new addition is Karen's warbling of [Tim] Rice & [Andrew Lloyd] Webber's "Don't Cry for Me Argentina," an excellent vocal, introduced by a routine wherein she begs for accomp, but rhythmers leave the stage, brother Richard cuts out, and the orchestra begins thumbing through newspapers, so she opts for the tape deck, which provides the sounds as the curtain shuts off all distractions behind her.

The '50s revival is more fun on second viewing. Richard's playing of "Warsaw Concerto" still has impact, although this one has been around three years now; the hit medley blessedly compresses all the similar Carpenter tunes into one; and the use of the tape deck to play back audience sing-alongs adds a dimension which will work only some night when the kids have hit it lucky with participants.

Dan Woodhams is on bass, Cubby O'Brien on drums, Bob Messenger on flute, Tony Peluso on lead guitar, and Doug Strawn on clarinet. Dick Palombi cues the Brian Farnon Orchestra.

THE UNWHOLESOME CARPENTERS

Joel McNally

Milwaukee Journal, 1977

K aren and Richard Carpenter would seem to have everything, right? They make a good living. They have the thanks of the nation's grateful Patti Page freaks. And they've got each other.

But are they happy? Oh, no. They want more. They want people to take them seriously.

Every time Karen and Richard are interviewed, they complain about cynical old music critics who put them down for being wholesome and clean. Sometimes, they get so worked up on the subject that they let out with something like, "Gosh darn those old smarty-pantses, anyway."

You see, in the music business, wholesome and clean are considered lightweight. Getting scuffed up a little is believed to lead to meaningful musical insights. It is a questionable theory. Following that logic, laying in a doorway swigging Vitalis is excellent training for superstardom.

This obsession that the Carpenters have with wanting to be considered heavy has lead to the recording of something like their new album, *Passage*.

Personally, I found their 1975 recording of "Please Mr. Postman" to be a deeply significant song. You had to listen closely to the lyrics, but that was obviously not enough for two musicians as heavily into grooviness as Karen and Richard.

Like, would you believe a song which features Karen Carpenter and Che Guevara? (Wouldn't that just look terrif on a marquee in Vegas?) The song is "Don't Cry for Me Argentina" from the revolutionary rock opera *Evita*.

The song includes a lengthy, dramatic introduction [featuring] a cast of tens. More than a hundred members of the Los Angeles Philharmonic also were brought in to support Karen's rendition of one of communism's most musical moments.

Showing their upfront tolerance of other systems of government as well is another intended blockbuster, the Carpenters' version of "Calling Occupants of Interplanetary Craft." That's the interplanetary peace song that was originally done by Klaatu.

The song calls up the image of sending Karen and Richard out to greet any other life forms that attempt to contact earth. You know, to tell them about how aliens have to register at the post office and [stuff] like that. Of course, there is always the possibility that the visitors will take over the bodies of Richard and Karen, but that is a chance we will just have to take.

At least two other wildly divergent songs for the Carpenters are included, "B'wana She No Home" and "Man Smart (Woman Smarter)." Apparently Karen is trying to answer criticism that she is so white she is invisible. Both songs have calypso roots, but they have been repotted and put on a coffee table.

A little more standard Carpenter fare is "All You Get from Love is a Love Song," in which an affair which shatters someone's life is "a dirty old shame."

You get this image of Richard (who chooses and arranges this wide variety of material) searching frantically for the most unlikely stuff to do, and then, Karen singing it just like Karen Carpenter. On "Two Sides," Karen laments that "there is another side of me." It is her left side and it looks quite a bit like the right side.

So, you know, as bizarre as some of the material is, Carpenters fans will be pleased with the result. The cynical music critics still won't take them seriously. If I thought it would make them feel better, though, I would call them "unwholesome."

THE CARPENTERS GO COUNTRY?

Nancy Naglin

Country Music, 1978

AUTHOR'S NOTE: When I interviewed Karen and Richard Carpenter in 1978, I was struck by Karen's fragility, the impossible and alluring slenderness of her body and, most especially, the translucent quality of her skin. She was an enigmatic personality who welcomed the attention but disclosed personal information with sweet regret—or was it resignation? My curiosity piqued, I tried to get beneath the surface and so asked about her charm bracelet, an odd and clunky piece of jewelry for the '70s. Each charm meant something—a personal milestone. Dutifully enumerating them, she sounded like an emissary from a private world.

I talked with friends about the impact Karen Carpenter had on me. I wanted to describe her peculiar detachment in the article; however, I believed my speculations were inappropriate. Her unnerving ethereal presence haunted me then and over the years. I had never seen anyone starving to death before.

—Nancy Naglin, 2000

◆

"Sweet, Sweet Smile" by Karen and Richard Carpenter has been on the charts for 15 weeks. After ten years at the top of the squeaky-clean pop music field, after millions of records sold, this is their first country hit. They seem a little surprised and confused. Yes, they are happy with the hit, but don't seem to know what's next.

The Carpenters' hometown—New Haven, Connecticut—with its church spires poking through the drizzle and the gulls huddled in the reeds alongside the railroad tracks—is a long, cold way from sunny L.A. Years of back-to-back touring, inhuman schedules and an obsessive attention to detail, sometimes bordering on the neurotic, have brought them light years away from their humble New England beginnings. But even comfortably at home in their A&M Records office, sister Karen and brother Richard, basking in the deflected glow of their 18 gold records, are sunstroked yet with the sudden success of "Sweet, Sweet Smile" from their *Passage* album.

"I knew it was off the wall," says Karen, absolutely mystified by the tune's success. She has just come from an all-night session, putting the finishing touches on a TV special and although exhausted, she is still revved up. "A true workaholic." Richard's word to describe them both.

"Ever since 'Top of the World' happened with Lynn Anderson, people always ask us how come we didn't have a hit on it in the country field." She turns to brother Rich—partner, arranger and companion—and shrugs. He opens his mouth to answer; she blithely reads his mind.

"It's because we released ours as a single pop after she had the [country] hit. Ever since then we always thought it would be possible but we never did anything." Rich nods agreement.

The Carpenters, for years the darlings of the squeaky-clean, middle of the road, easy listening sound, with their TV specials and Vegas shows, have wandered across the charts into Opryland and they're not quite sure how it happened.

"We're kind of soft, easygoing country," Richard concedes, groping for the words to properly describe his sound.

"We always try to get one country song on our albums," adds Karen. "Not for any specific purpose but because we like it. We don't go in and say we got to record a song that will get on the country charts. We always just go in with what we like." Then she flashes her famous down-home smile, bright with the reassurance of a flight attendant's welcome.

For although the Carpenters, versatile survivors of a dozen years and almost as many music trends, are bewildered by their tune's success, they are genuinely delighted in finally finding a country audience. In the hard rock days of the late '60s, they nearly got left behind before they really started. Then James Taylor floated in with the easier sound of the '70s, and they felt redeemed. Through it all, the Carpenters have remained a self-sufficient, inward-looking team who select, arrange and produce their music without ever going beyond the family circle. "Yeah, it's always been that way," says Richard. "It seems like if you ask five different people, you get five different answers."

"It was like when we first got started and we were mixing 'Ticket to Ride,'" recalls Karen. "It finally got around to where we were asking so many people that it seemed that the next person we were going to ask was . . ."

"The security man," says Richard, his voice coming in on top of hers.

If their music now has a country flavor it's because, self-consciously or not, the sound has filtered through Richard's ear. According to Karen, when album time rolls around, Richard goes home with a carload of material and begins "the ever-long search through the piles of things that come in."

"No, I don't write. It's sad, isn't it?" she says brightly, as Rich stares at the floor. "Nothin' ever came out."

By chance, Karen was visiting a friend who played a tape of "Sweet, Sweet Smile," written by singer-songwriter Juice Newton. She brought it home to Rich, and as soon as he heard it, he wanted to add a few things— like a banjo.

"When I hear country, all of it sticks," he says, tilting his head to the side as if he's reading off a sheet of imaginary sheet music. When he was a kid, his father was a big fan of Spade Cooley, and Richard spent hours listening to 10-inch LPs recorded in the early '50s. Cooley's sound was smooth with full brass and reed sections. "Then there was the steel guitar. See, I remembered it," he says tapping the side of his head.

"And it's not like we didn't do country before," explains Karen, mentioning "End of the World" on the *Now & Then* album (1973) and "(I'm

Caught Between) Goodbye and I Love You." Like Kenny Rogers with "Lucille" and Olivia Newton-John, they've crossed into country, but whether they have the intention or desire to stay is still in question.

"We were very excited when this thing started," says Karen cautiously, as if still not believing the charts.

"But if we were going to go in and snap out a country single, well, that wouldn't happen at this point," says Richard definitely. "Of course, it would be great if it happened again."

"To this day people say who did I style myself after? Who influenced me, and to that I say nobody. But when I first began I sounded very country," says Karen. "You got a country streak in you," she proudly remembers electric bass guitarist Joe Osborn saying when he recorded their demo tape in his [North Hollywood] garage back in 1968.

They have discussed going to Nashville. "For the players," says Richard, his eyes gleaming. He's an obsessive-compulsive perfectionist who once flew to Nashville to record exactly two bars of music for the "Desperado" cut on the *Horizon* album. But as much as Nashville studio musicians entice him, he's true to the sound he hears in his head. The only way they'll make a Nashville album is if the album warrants Nashville talent, and judging by the way their albums get put together, when—or if—that happens is anybody's guess.

"It's nice to be able to pick your own stuff, have total control," says Richard. "The thing is, you're responsible for it if it hits or if it flops."

His bottom line is the artistic quality. He started playing piano when he was 12, and knew that one way or another music was his world. Karen "kind of followed him around," starting to sing when she was about 16, and then getting them both kicked out of clubs because she was too young to drink. That led to an early recording career, and both claim that over the years their ears have sharpened. Rich just about shudders remembering the creaking of a closing door that made it on to one of his albums.

Then followed years of hectic touring until Karen collapsed in 1975. "We realized then that we didn't need to run all over the world like maniacs," says Richard, and instead they developed a Vegas act. "If it costs, it costs," says Richard, "because it's got to be what I hear."

Since "Sweet, Sweet Smile," there's been talk of the Grand Ole Opry. Karen is especially intrigued by the possibility of a new audience. There are the TV specials and the Vegas show that needs to be overhauled, but she's looking for something new—even considering TV roles.

"We pride ourselves in being trendsetters for the easier listening sound." She speaks slowly, as if oppressed with the role. "When we started we were knocked for being dressed cleanly, for taking a bath. We were titled sweet and clean," and when she says, "Goody four shoes," Richard laughs and shakes his head.

Now he wants to produce other artists. Both of them, too, would like to marry and set up private lives.

"But schedules make it difficult to meet people and date," says Karen wistfully. "We always worked together," she says, looking back over eight albums, her hand resting beneath a gold charm in the shape of a record, a Christmas gift from a grateful record company. "I'm hoping—but I—neither one of us—have found anybody we'd want to get married to. We have so much to give and we've accomplished a lot on our own. It would be nice to share it with somebody [but] at this point, we're just sharing it with each other."

"The group, too, has been together for 10 years," says Richard about the guys in the band who are like an extended family.

And if they cut another surprise country hit or if they took up the invitation to the Grand Ole Opry?

"We'd have to go just the way we are," says Richard unhesitatingly. And doing things in their own sweet time, living like cactus in the desert of L.A., off their own juices, the Carpenters may be just a little more country than they think.

CONCERT REVIEW

MGM GRAND, LAS VEGAS, MARCH 7, 1978

Variety, 1978

R ichard and Karen Carpenter followed no trend or succumbed to rock critics' irascible putdowns of their music when they came upon the scene about 10 years ago. It was the softest of sounds on the contemporary scene lumped under rock 'n' roll, but the Carpenters really made their own kind of sound and music then and now. If it was said to be dated then, it is dated now. But it is not. It is directly in the melodic pops mainstream currently enjoying high popularity.

Neither Karen in her singular style and timbre of song projection, nor her brother Richard as the songwriter-performer-leader had or have any deep emotional, heavy-laden statements or profundities in their music. They are pop tunes, pure and simple, and the audiences at the Grand respond strongly to their messages of entertainment. The act itself has held on to the same format for some time and it's a slick one showcasing the leads as well as the excellent quintet that helped create the indigenous Carpenter sound and kept it that way. The new direction, possibly, could follow or coordinate with their latest spacey record album, but certainly the solid hit parade built up over the years would be a mandatory inclusion. [. . .]

"IF SOMEBODY WOULD JUST LET US KNOW WHAT THE PROBLEM IS . . ."

Bill Moran

Claude Hall's International Radio Report, 1978

It's been almost 10 years since your first chart record. You've sold millions of records around the world, 30 million in the U.S. alone. Is it still fun?

Karen Carpenter: Yes, very much so. In fact we just returned from Germany about a day ago. So we're kind of just getting readjusted. We went over to do a television show called *Star Parade*. It's an hour-and-a-half variety show that is done live six times a year. It goes out to a minimum of 30 million people. It's amazing that at any given time during the hour and a half it's covered on 56 percent of the TVs in Germany.

Richard Carpenter: The show was even seen in Sweden and in Holland.

Karen: It's really wild. ABBA was the only other group that we knew. There were people from everywhere. There was one group from Israel, and there were groups from France and England.

Is the international market as big as it's always been for the Carpenters?

Karen: Yes, very big. "Calling Occupants of Interplanetary Craft" was a gigantic hit. "[Calling] Occupants [of Interplanetary Craft]" was the number one most-played album in Japan and "Sweet, Sweet Smile" is coming on like gangbusters in Germany. What we really want to do is get our market back in the United States.

Are you saying that Top 40 radio is resisting your music here?

Karen: We've been asking ourselves that question for almost three years. The last three years there has been a definite resistance to our product and I don't know why. We've been doing our best to turn out the finest product we can. Richard keeps changing direction. We've covered practically every aspect that is capable of being put to disc with the exception of classical. We haven't done that yet but . . .

"[Calling] Occupants [of Interplanetary Craft]" was certainly a change of direction, wasn't it?

Karen: You could say that and as far as being timely, it was ahead of the game because we cut that before *Star Wars* hit the market.

Then what's the answer to this dilemma?

Karen: It's a very touchy question to us at this point. We just don't know what Top 40 radio is looking for. One minute they say they're looking for a traditional Carpenters record. We give them one of those and they don't want it. They say they want something different, so we give them "Occupants" and they don't want that either. We give them country and Top 40 again resists. If somebody would just let us know what the problem is, then we could take it from there. Everybody has a different answer.

What are some of the answers you're getting and what are some of the Top 40 guys telling you?

Karen: We talked to Paul Drew. He said come with a three-minute record. We did that and nothing happened on Top 40 radio. He mentioned things we should do and we did them. And still Top 40 radio didn't respond. It's the weirdest damn thing. They just turn it back at us. We're trying. That's what's frustrating.

Richard: We've had a change of direction which I wanted to do anyway. Not a total turnaround, but just a couple of things were different. Then they said that "Occupants" was just a little too far out. They didn't like the guitar solo in the middle. We said there was a guitar solo in the middle of "We're All Alone."

I guess it doesn't matter what they say, does it?

Richard: Well, you can't have anything over 3:15. So we come out with "Sweet, Sweet Smile," which is three minutes and Top 40 doesn't play it. I think you have to do what you want to do. You have to do something you're most comfortable doing . . . something that doesn't sound contrived.

Is your image hurting you as far as Top 40?

Karen: I couldn't answer that. I'm getting sick and tired of this image thing. What is the matter with a brother and sister team who happen to be the first ones who just record and enjoy life?

Are artists forced to stay in a mold?

Richard: There are some that I think have to keep changing and want to change and there are others that I don't think will ever change. I don't think one thing applies to all artists.

Does it get to the point where radio says to an Elton John, a John Denver, and the Carpenters that enough is enough?

Richard: The American people are fickle. They go from one extreme to another with an artist. And I think radio wants to cater to them. If an act gets hot then people can't get enough of it. I'm relating your question now to records, artists, and radio.

Like what the Bee Gees are into right now?

Richard: I love the Bee Gees. I thought they were turning out great product all along. I was into them starting with "New York Mining Disaster 1941." They went on for years without anything happening. Now it's Bee Gees, Bee Gees, Bee Gees.

Is it almost a burnout problem?

Richard: I think that is what is going to happen. It happened with Elton John.

It may have happened to the Carpenters.

Richard: I was just going to bring that up. It did happen to us. And the same thing happened to John Denver and the Captain and Tennille.

Relative to the Carpenters, how do you counter the burnout thing? Was there a saturation of Carpenters product?

Richard: It wasn't a matter of too much product. What happened was that our sound was new. We've got a lot of people borrowing the sound. On top of our own records, there were other records coming out. It's about time that people stopped trying to imitate us. This one particular riff is still being used and used and used from the beginning of "Close to You." I still hear it. We set a trend and everybody jumped on it.

Are you looking for outside material?

Karen: Sure, all the time. Especially from Richard.

Were you the first to do "Can't Smile Without You?"

Richard: Yes, we introduced it two years ago. We did the whistling and the whole thing.

In other words, it's all in the timing.

Richard: Yes, and Barry Manilow is hot.

Do you feel there is any creativity left in Top 40 radio?

Richard: I feel the playlists are a little too tight and the records get played more than they ever did. But there are some nice records out now and some are getting played.

What have your experiences been when you have visited radio stations?

Karen: There is so much going on in the studio, especially with all the TV things. We spent an awful lot of time on the TV special. That took about three months. Unfortunately, it does not give us much time to visit radio stations.

Richard: Karen and I really get off on doing interviews. We enjoy doing them and you can't get away from them.

You mentioned all the time it takes to do TV and personal appearances. Does that take away from the real bread and butter, the making of records? Or is recording no longer the real bread and butter?

Karen: We still feel it is. We don't spend as much time as we would like to in the studio even though we spend an enormous amount. We haven't really been on the road in a long time. We should go back out. That is an area where we are sorely missed. We feel it's our fault too. You just start to get into a pattern and all of a sudden things start weaving.

Have you ever given any thought to using an outside producer, particularly during the last couple of years?

Richard: No.

Karen, have you ever given any thought to doing solo things?

Karen: We've thought about it. There were things I've done that were just the lead vocal, songs like "I Just Fall in Love Again," "I Can Dream, Can't I," "Sometimes," etc. This brings us back to the fact that we want to get back to that big vocal sound again . . . more so than in the last couple of years. We were just checking out other areas.

Are there any producers who can guarantee you a hit?

Richard: No, not Mike Curb, not Richard Perry. Right now Barry Gibb is red hot. And everybody wants to be produced by Barry Gibb. But how long will that last?

Richard, you wrote a country song, "Top of the World," that was a number one record on Top 40. Country radio didn't play your version, but went on a version by Lynn Anderson. That is understandable because country radio didn't look at you as a country artist. Why all of a sudden have they accepted "Sweet, Sweet Smile"? That has to be a weird experience for you.

Richard: It was really quite exciting.

Karen: Since "Top of the World" we always try and get maybe one or two country things on an album because we like them, but having one come out as a single and [doing] that without really even thinking about it is really a welcome surprise.

Is that your song?

Richard: No, that's Juice Newton and Otha Young who wrote it.

So you were not openly romancing the country stations?

Richard: No, not really. We always put a couple of country-flavored things on each album. We just did that on "Sweet, Sweet Smile" because we liked it that way. I felt it also needed a fiddle and a banjo and it started to come on the country charts.

Why did country radio go on this record as dramatically as they did? Wasn't there a country cover version they could have played by an established country act?

Karen: No. In fact, when we heard the tune, it was on a cassette run-off from Juice's album and it was the only one tune in the album that was hers and really appealed to us. So when we decided we wanted to do it, she held it off her album. So really nobody knew about the tune, and out it came.

And it really made it in the country area. Have country radio stations called you for interviews?

Richard: We did one with Bob Mitchell up in San Bernardino, KCKC.

Has A&M Records done anything specifically to push the country market since the success of this single as far as your careers are concerned?

Richard: Well, I think they hired some outside promoters for "Sweet, Sweet Smile."

Do you see yourself going more into country music as a result of your problems with Top 40?

Karen: We wanted to cut something else country. We discussed it with the company. They said that would be terrific, but then all of a sudden everybody leaned on us for a country album, at which point Jerry Moss almost lost his hair. I mean, let's face it. Our first priority has to be to get a pop album. That is the most important, but we definitely want to try country again. We love and enjoy doing country music.

Hollywood has discovered the recording industry. Do you see yourself getting involved in motion pictures?

Karen: Yes, we're looking for a script. We have been for about a year. It's something I would really like to do. I love to act and sing. I'm not sure how or when it's going to come down, but I'd like to do a musical. Our all-time love is to do a college musical. It would be set in the 1970s. It would have to have modern technology plus a classic serial sci-fi approach.

Do you also want to act, Richard?

Richard: I wouldn't mind it, but [I don't want to] as much as Karen. My first love is the recording studio.

Karen: I want to do some television acting, too. There has been a couple of scripts that were submitted, but I didn't have time to do them.

Do you think the record industry is qualified to make movies today?

Karen: I think the record industry can handle anything that is put in front of them. They don't fall short of anything. This business is confronted with new things every hour.

THE VOICE
OF CHRISTMAS

KAREN CARPENTER

Ted Naron

A Blog of My Own, 2010

K aren Carpenter was the Great American Songbook singer who wasn't. On most Carpenters albums, her material, with some exceptions—"I Can Dream, Can't I," "When I Fall in Love," and "Little Girl Blue"—while superior, was of the 1970s and not the Golden Age. There is, however, an album containing many examples of Karen Carpenter assaying the Great American Songbook; it is the LP the Carpenters released on A&M Records in 1978, *Christmas Portrait*. [. . .] She had the talent, the affinity for the material, and the wide contemporary appeal to have kept the Great American Songbook flame burning into our present time and beyond. [. . .]

Richard Carpenter here surrounds his sister with orchestral and choral-group arrangements comparable to those one might hear in the glory days of MGM musicals, when Conrad Salinger, Hugh Martin and Kay Thompson worked in that studio's music department. The material demonstrates how Christmas brought out the best in our songwriters. Fourteen songs on this set are Great American Songbook entries, several of them uncommon (e.g., "The First Snowfall" by Sonny Burke and Paul Francis Webster, "Sleep Well, Little Children" by Leon Klatzkin and Alan Bergman, and "It's Christmas Time" by Victor Young and Al Stillman). Various instrumental medleys feature Richard at the piano. As for the vocals, the spotlight is Karen's. With her dark, melancholy alto, the way she subtly scoops up to her notes, the texture in her voice as it ever-so-softly cracks, and her empathic understanding of lyrics, she fashions a style that feels less like a style than the sound of a human heart breaking.

Take "I'll Be Home for Christmas." The song is a story with a killer twist of a last line, one that reveals the singer's promises of returning home for Christmas are lies, mere fantasy—that the only way the singer is going anywhere, alas, is in her dreams. The pain in that line is nowhere to be found in most renditions. When Karen sings "if only in my dreams," the pain is more than palpable, it's exquisite.

If it's a truism that only one who knows despair can know joy, Karen proves it on the happier material. You can feel the winter air on her "Sleigh Ride," you can breathe in the roasting chestnuts in her "Christmas Song." [Karen Carpenter] takes songs you thought you never needed to hear again and makes you hear the greatness in them. [*Christmas Portrait*] is the best Christmas album ever made. For those who have it, it wouldn't be Christmas without it. [. . .]

MADE IN AMERICA

A&M Records Press Release, 1981

F or Richard Carpenter, it was a day of triumph only a hard-core life-
long musician could appreciate.

After nearly a year of "listening, literally, to hundreds and hundreds
of songs, my own writing, arranging, orchestrating; doing background
vocals and piano, and mixing," the master tape of the new Carpenters
album, their first in three years, had finally been put to bed and sent off
to the manufacturing plants to become *Made in America.*

The title itself was revealing on a number of levels. It had turned up
in one of those offhand, serendipitous flashes that seem to come from
nowhere yet are right on the money. "We were playing around with any
number of possible titles for the album," said Richard, "when Karen
came into the studio one day wearing a running suit with a tag on it that
read MADE IN AMERICA, and I said, 'That's it!' "

Karen and Richard Carpenter were born in New Haven, Connecticut, but grew up in Downey, California. From *Ticket to Ride,* their first
album, onward, the Carpenters have always been a quintessentially
American phenomenon, though a significant portion of their 55 million
or so record sales were racked up abroad—in England, Europe, Japan,
Australia, Canada, and just about every other record-selling nation on
earth. Something in their music—its melodic sweep, the flawless arrangements, the bell-like perfection of Karen's vocals—touched a responsive

chord that leapt all boundaries and borders and made the Carpenters international ambassadors of that intangible something that was once referred to as "the American way."

Regarding *Made in America*, Richard says: "It's a very American sound—even more so, a California sound. We've been classified as a classic California sound. I have to agree with that." And in spite of recent shifts and trends in popular music, he feels that "things really aren't that different than they have been. There are a couple of things that have a little twist that I enjoy, like the Police, but nothing really that radically different."

And if *Made in America* is not "radically different"—refusing to pay homage to the weirder pop trends that come and go like summer lightning—it clearly documents the depth, growth, and striving for perfection that characterizes all of the best of the Carpenters' work. Richard sums it up simply: "I select songs that hit me at the gut level and fit our style."

The album includes two new songs by Richard Carpenter and John Bettis: "Those Good Old Dreams," a tune Richard suggests "has the flavor of 'Top of the World,'" and "Because We Are in Love," which they wrote expressly for Karen's wedding last year to Tom Burris.

[The Carpenters' current hit single, "Touch Me When We're Dancing," was one of several tunes selected for *Made in America* penned by outside writers.] Burt Bacharach contributed "Somebody's Been Lyin'," with lyrics by Carole Bayer Sager, and Richard believes "it's one of the best things Bacharach has written in years." Also included: a new Roger Nichols/Bill Lane song, "When You've Got What It Takes," that sounds like an instant classic. The remainder of the tunes (with the exception of the old Marvelettes' hit "Beechwood 4-5789") were written by various relatively new writers: "Strength of a Woman," by Phyllis Brown and Juanita Curiel, and a lovely new country/pop ballad, "When It's Gone (It's Just Gone)," with words and music by Randy Handley.

As has always been the case, the Carpenters' music is eloquent, and above all, has *style*. As a matter of fact, *style* may be the key word in understanding the stunning success of a young man and his sister who felt they had something special to say, who have paid their dues in triplicate ("There were many times," Karen recalls, "when we'd spend four or five months in the studio working day and night on a new album, rush out to the airport the day it was finished to start a two-month tour of back-to-back dates. It was unbelievable"), and who triumphed beyond their most extravagant fantasies.

Of *Made in America*, Richard says: "Karen and I think it's the best thing we've ever done. It's the combination of production, performance, engineering and material. It's just that you grow, you hear more things, you grow in your arranging, and Karen, of course, grows in her interpretation. You just grow. . . ."

It took a year of work, it's been three years since we've heard from the Carpenters, but it's here.

Made in America. Created by the Carpenters: A matchless achievement.

Part IV

RAINY DAYS
AND MONDAYS

KAREN CARPENTER DIES IN DOWNEY

Pat McGreevy

Downey Herald-American, 1983

Singer Karen Carpenter, who joined brother Richard for a string of musical hits in the '70s, died suddenly of a heart attack Friday morning while visiting her parents at the Downey home she and her brother built for them.

The sudden death of the popular musician, at 32 years of age, was a shock to her fans and friends, many of whom grew up with her in Downey.

Downey Police Department Detective Gary Morrow, who was present during the autopsy Friday, said the preliminary determination of cause of death was pulmonary edema, the medical term for the sudden stoppage of breathing and heartbeat.

He said Carpenter had recently been treated for anorexia nervosa, an extreme weight loss condition where the person does not eat properly to force the loss of weight.

The autopsy found her to be five-feet, four-inches tall and 108 pounds.

Although Carpenter had eaten regularly the week before her death, Morrow said an investigation is continuing as to the cause of her death, focusing both on the anorexia and the presence of prescription medicine found in her bloodstream.

Her Downey physician, Dr. G. A. Monnet, had no comment on Carpenter's death. [. . .]

Carpenter had arrived in Downey at the Newville Avenue house of her parents, Agnes and Harold Carpenter on Thursday for a short overnight visit, according to her agent Paul Bloch. [. . .]

Ms. Carpenter awoke in the second floor bedroom of the large Downey house at approximately 8:10 a.m. Friday but collapsed approximately 30 minutes later on the floor in a closet of the bedroom where her parents found her minutes later, according to Downey police and fire department officials.

The Downey fire department received the call from her parents at 8:51 a.m. and sent Engine Company No. 64 and a paramedics unit to the house near the San Gabriel River.

Paramedics and an Adams Ambulance crew found Carpenter unconscious but with a slight pulse and began performing cardiopulmonary resuscitation [CPR] before transporting her and her concerned mother, with full lights and siren, to the Downey Community Hospital emergency room.

A hospital spokesman said that when Carpenter arrived at the hospital at 9:23 a.m. she was in full cardiac arrest, not breathing and without a heartbeat. A medical team worked on her for 28 minutes but at 9:51 a.m. she was pronounced dead.

Her body was turned over to the county coroner's office for an autopsy Friday [and later released to Utter-McKinley Funeral Home in Downey. The family had not released the details of funeral arrangements as of Friday night.]

Carpenter's sudden death was a complete shock to friends and business associates.

"She was so young and healthy and had everything to look forward to," said Joan Jaffe, a spokeswoman for Carpenter's agent.

Her agent said that Carpenter had been treated for anorexia last year and that in 1975, the Carpenters had to cancel a concert tour [. . .] because Ms. Carpenter suffered from physical and emotional exhaustion, for which she was hospitalized for several weeks.

Jaffe said Karen and Richard Carpenter were planning to go into the studio at A&M Records next month to begin recording a new album which was to be followed by a tour of the United States this summer.

"I was totally taken by surprise," said Carpenter's agent of 12 years, Bloch. "She was young and healthy. She was squeaky clean as anybody who would do milk commercials."

Although her agent said she had not had a history of heart ailments, acquaintances said she had recently returned from New York where she had undergone treatment for anorexia.

"She wanted to keep it quiet," said one acquaintance. [. . .]

Carpenter had also [recently separated from] Los Angeles business-man Thomas Burris, Jaffe said.

Those who saw her in Downey in recent months said she was in good spirits.

In fact, last year Ms. Carpenter recorded a solo album at A&M Records which mysteriously was never released. Her agent would not say what the plans were for that album.

Like several other young musicians of the late '60s and early '70s, Karen and Richard Carpenter rose meteorically to success from their teenage years with the Downey High School Band to their big break in 1969 after Ms. Carpenter had gone on to Long Beach State to study music.

Since 1969, the Carpenters put their sweet "clean-cut" sound on [ten] albums, eight of which were gold albums selling over 500,000 copies each.

In [1970] the Carpenters had their biggest success, "Close to You."

Karen Carpenter played drums and sang for the duo while her brother sang and played the piano.

Their albums continued to sell well into the mid '70s.

Jaffe said Karen and Richard Carpenter were confident that their new album would do well.

"She was always positive and cheerful. She was looking forward to her new start," her agent said.

LOCAL FRIENDS, SAD, SHOCKED

The sudden death of Karen Carpenter [from heart failure] at age 32 stunned not only the musical industry and her many fans, but also the many friends and acquaintances she made during her Downey childhood.

Whether it was her enthusiasm [in] the Downey High School Band, or her close relationship with her family, recollections of Carpenter's youth in Downey by friends painted the picture of a bright, happy woman with a gift for music.

When Harold and Agnes Carpenter moved to Downey from Connecticut with their children Richard and Karen in [1963], they settled in a cozy house near Rockwell International, according to friends.

Karen was enrolled as a ninth grader at South Junior High School while her brother went to Downey High School, recalled Bruce Gifford, a longtime music teacher at Downey High School who coached both Carpenters while they played in the school's band.

They were both influenced by their father's record collection.

"[Richard] originally wanted to play the trumpet but he was such a fine pianist that he stayed with that instrument. When she came to Downey (high school), she wanted to be in the band like her brother," Gifford recalled.

Karen Carpenter played the bells her first year in the band and then went on to play the drums, Gifford said.

"She was the typical student but she didn't smoke or drink," he recalled. "She didn't strike me as musically talented at first but then I've learned to give people time before judging their talent. And you know what happened to them."

Gifford said the striking thing about Karen Carpenter was the close family relationship she enjoyed.

In the many times he had dinner with the Carpenters, he saw an unusual closeness in the family which he says few kids enjoy.

During their teen years, Karen and Richard Carpenter formed several jazz bands on their own, one of which won a battle of the bands contest at the Hollywood Bowl seen by record executives who later signed them.

Karen Carpenter graduated from Downey High School in 1967 and went on to Long Beach State where she and her brother put together the band with which they received their lucky break.

Because the Carpenters were popular during [the] late '60s and early '70s, many of today's Downey High School students hadn't heard of her before her death. Those that had were stunned by her death at such a young age.

The Carpenters' success and the resulting wealth didn't keep Karen and Richard from their friends and family in Downey.

On December 7, 1971, Karen and Richard Carpenter presented the city of Downey with the gold record "Close to You" which is still on display in the trophy case at City Hall.

The two musicians were grand marshals in the Downey Christmas Parade that year.

With the money they made from that million-seller, the Carpenters bought two apartment buildings on Fifth Street between Downey and Brookshire Avenues which they named "Close to You" and ["Only Just Begun."]

They also used a portion of their newfound wealth to build a magnificent house for their parents on Newville Avenue next to the San Gabriel River in Downey.

The large house was equipped with state of the art musical recording and listening equipment and a garage to contain Richard's antique automobile collection. [. . .]

"I couldn't believe it. She was in here a week and a half ago looking as healthy as ever," said Jim Ayres, the owner of Foxy's Restaurant on Paramount Boulevard in Downey.

"I talked to her then and she said she was fine," Ayres said. "She was in with her mother. They always came here for breakfast."

Ayres described her as "bouncy, very energetic."

"She would talk to anybody. She was real friendly," he said. "Her death at such a young age really upsets me."

Downey optometrist Art Fry was also shocked by Carpenter's death. He has known the Carpenter kids for 18 years and had just fitted Karen Carpenter with glasses last month.

"She was a real nice kid," Fry said. "They kept to themselves and never drank or smoked. They would always be home here for the holidays and every other important family occasion."

The family has not yet announced the arrangements for the funeral.

HUNDREDS ATTEND KAREN CARPENTER RITES

Southeast News, 1983

K aren Carpenter, who sang with her brother as one of America's top pop music acts in the 1970s, was remembered at her funeral in Downey Tuesday as "one of God's most gifted and talented creations."

About 700 friends, family members and fans—among them some of the greatest names in the recording industry—packed the Downey United Methodist Church on Downey Avenue just blocks from the house where Miss Carpenter once lived. Hundreds of other fans stood outside behind police barricades.

Following the service, a small contingent of family members traveled by cortege to Forest Lawn Memorial Park for a brief private ceremony before entombment. [. . .]

Present at the [1:00] p.m. services for Miss Carpenter were such singing and songwriting stars as Olivia Newton-John, Burt Bacharach, Dionne Warwick, John Bettis and John Davidson.

Record industry executives like Jerry Weintraub, [bandleader and] A&M Records cofounder Herb Alpert, A&M president Gil Friesen and Mike Curb also were in attendance. Other friends of the Carpenters in attendance were ice skating star Dorothy Hamill and drummer and former Mousketeer Cubby O'Brien.

Richard Carpenter, [36], accompanied his mother, Agnes, and father, Harold, into the church's main sanctuary while adjacent rooms and a courtyard—all equipped with speakers broadcasting the service—were filled with approximately 500 fans who wanted to pay their last respects.

"What Karen loved she did resemble, until Karen herself became a song to the world—a beautiful song to the world," said the Rev. Charles Neal, Miss Carpenter's childhood minister in New Haven, Conn., during his eulogy.

"In the words of (songwriter) John Bettis, 'Too soon and too young our Karen is still, but her echo will linger forever.'

"One of God's most gifted and talented creations is gone. The world weeps because Karen's story graced this world.

"She has captured the hearts of the world with friendship, love and joy. Karen stood for an integrity, a quality of life that is so refreshing.

"She has graced all of our lives with love and song and there is no place on Earth where Karen is not singing."

Neal recalled [that] he first met Karen Carpenter when she and her brother were part of the Methodist Youth Ministry that welcomed him to his new church in New Haven, where she was born.

He said Miss Carpenter's childhood was "a balance of blue jeans, baseballs and ballet," and that when the family got together in the basement of their New Haven home, there would be "Ping-Pong sets, hi-fi sets, baseballs and more records than I've ever seen in my life."

At one point Neal looked at her white metal casket, covered with red and white roses, and quoted the lyrics of one of the Carpenters' greatest hits, "Close to You": "On the day that you were born, the angels got together and decided to create a dream come true." The minister also recited the words to "We've Only Just Begun."

"She graced this world with a new song," Neal said. "Suddenly in the midst of the rock era, she brought a new song, a new sound of joy, happiness and meaning."

Rev. Michael Winstead, minister of the Downey United Methodist Church, also spoke at the service. He delivered the invocation and read several Bible passages, including Psalm 100, which begins "Make a joyful noise unto the Lord," and a section of Romans including the promise that "nothing shall be able to separate us from the love of God."

The choir from Cal State–Long Beach, Miss Carpenter's alma mater, sang "Adoramus Te" by Corsi and a soloist sang "Ave Maria" by Bach.

Tuesday's service was preceded by an instrumental rendering of a medley of Carpenters songs including, "Rainy Days and Mondays," "Close to You," and "We've Only Just Begun."

Pallbearers at the service included bandleader and A&M Records executive Herb Alpert, who signed a contract with the Carpenters at the beginning of their music career, and songwriter John Bettis, who wrote the lyrics for many of the Carpenters' songs. Other pallbearers included Steven Alpert, [Werner] Wolfen (Carpenter's attorney), Gary Sims, Eddie Sulzer [the duo's first manager], David Alley and Ed Leffler.

Honorary pallbearers included Miss Newton-John, Bacharach, former California Lt. Gov. Curb, Hamill and O'Brien.

Many of the hundreds of mourners who attended the service or stood outside were fans in their 20s and 30s who remembered Miss Carpenter from their youth. Many carried rose bouquets.

"When I was growing up she kind of understood what I was going through in her songs," explained one fan, Mary Grouch.

Another, Earl Storm, said he attended the funeral "just to thank her for the beauty she gave to my life." [. . .]

A LESSON IN ART
OF EMOTION

KAREN CARPENTER'S INTIMATE
VOCALS DISARM A CRITIC

Robert Hilburn

Los Angeles Times, 1983

EDITOR'S NOTE: Calling their product "audio wallpaper," *Los Angeles Times* critic Robert Hilburn dismissed the Carpenters' recordings and live performances time after time during their heyday. "There is a lack of challenge, lack of discovery and surprise in [their] music," he wrote in a review of the duo's 1972 concert at the Greek Theatre in Los Angeles. "It would be hard to imagine the group has sold more than 16 million records and filled concert halls around the world. It just goes to show, I suppose, how susceptible we all are to a pretty tune."

It was with heavy sarcasm that Karen spoke of Robert Hilburn in a 1978 interview with Gary Theroux for *L.A. Music & Art Review.* "Oh, he loves us. Right!" she said. "Olivia, John Denver, Helen Reddy, Simon and Garfunkel, Bread. . . . We've all been ripped apart by Mr. Hilburn and I don't know why. He has his opinion and that's fine with us. Everybody has their own taste. But it doesn't make sense to go after our clothes, our hair, or the people we draw, just because some come in a suit and tie. . . . I'll tell you one thing: I like to go home at night and look at gold records all over the place. I like to know that our music is loved and appreciated by people all over the world."

It wasn't until learning of Karen's passing that Hilburn stopped and took a closer look at the Carpenters' work. This essay—a sensitive retraction of sorts—is his response.

◆

I understood my sadness when Elvis Presley and John Lennon died. Along with Bob Dylan, they were my biggest pop heroes in the '50s and '60s. In their best moments, they not only lived up to the standards that I applied as a critic to pop acts, they defined them. I still listened regularly to their records and I had met them: Presley briefly backstage during one of his Las Vegas engagements and Lennon on several occasions.

But I was unsettled last week by my sadness when I learned about Karen Carpenter's death on February 4. It wasn't just the flash of sympathy that invariably follows someone's death.

On a professional level, I try to resist the type of sentimentality that leads you to praise a lot of mediocre artists just because they've died. Such praise reduces all artists to a meaningless common denominator.

My sense of loss after Karen's death was genuine. The reason I was surprised by the reaction was that I wasn't, as a critic, someone you could even remotely list as a supporter of the Carpenters.

So why was I touched?

I dug out some Carpenters albums and listened to them again. In the process, I began reflecting on the differences between the demands made upon artists by a critic (who examines pop achievement) and regular listeners (who simply want to be entertained).

Critics want artists to challenge traditions so that we can gain insights or be inspired. It isn't enough merely to be handed already familiar emotions and techniques.

That's generally why the Carpenters' records were downgraded by critics. Sweet and understated, the music usually lacked the boldness or social examination that critics prize. Except when reviewing their new releases, I rarely played their albums.

After Karen's death, however, I found myself thinking about her voice, even recalling the first time I heard it on the radio in a [1969] version of "Ticket to Ride." Unlike the Beatles' uptempo rendition, this one had the softer, plaintive quality of many a Mamas and Papas ballad.

The attraction for me was the intimacy and warmth of Karen's singing: a strange, but seductive blend of innocence and melancholia. But "Close to You," the record that launched the Carpenters' Top 10 reign [the following] year, wasn't nearly as convincing. It had a timid, almost bloodless quality that was all too characteristic of the duo's recordings. After a while, I gave up on them.

But you really couldn't escape the Carpenters' sound because their records were all over the radio dial. Some tunes seemed catchy: the upbeat country tone of "Top of the World" and the lazy disappointment of "Rainy Days and Mondays."

It wasn't until the *Passage* album in 1977, however, that I was really impressed by what Richard and Karen had done. Though it wasn't their biggest seller, the album contained some experimental touches that added refreshing character to their musical foundation.

On their version of "Don't Cry for Me Argentina" from that album, there's a maturity to Karen's vocal that was far beyond anything in the early years. Even the song's lyrics have a chilling quality when considered in light of what we've learned about her in recent days.

I'm referring here to the move from a Southern California sheltered life to New York, where she battled for independence while struggling against post-marriage depression and anorexia nervosa, the dieting compulsion that caused her to drop from her normal 110-pound range to less than 85 pounds. [. . .]

But that's not the song pointed out last weekend by John Bettis, who co-wrote many of the Carpenters' hits. When asked which of Karen's vocals was the most personal, he mentioned "I Need to Be in Love," a modest hit from 1976.

He said it was written at a time when the Carpenters were established as one of the biggest-selling pop groups ever, but that he, Richard and Karen all felt an emptiness. [. . .]

On these records, her voice conveys a heartwarming cry for understanding and love, a cry that struck a chord in millions of listeners who were unburdened by any sense of critical responsibility.

Though the moment didn't invalidate for me the need to seek out artists who challenge tradition and redirect our thinking, it did remind me that purity of emotion also is powerful.

Karen's voice may not have challenged pop tradition the way the critic in me would have preferred, but the loveliness of her best vocals did enrich us. The loss is real. It's also instructive: The heart of pop music is emotion and you can never measure emotion by critical standards alone.

THIRTY MINUTES WITH RICHARD CARPENTER

Pat McGreevy

Southeast News, 1983

A s Richard Carpenter climbed onto a plane bound for England recently for a stint to promote the Carpenters' latest and last album, it suddenly struck him—this was the first time his sister Karen was not going along on a promotional or concert tour.

"That's when it really stuck me," the singer said during an interview at his Downey home late last week. "It was tough . . . It really was.

"Once I had to go to England and Japan alone for press conferences in 1975 when Karen got ill, and we had to cancel or postpone two major tours. But that was different. This was actually going out with a new album.

"We've worked together and we've always been close for [the] past 17 [or] 18 years, so it was rough. Karen and I were always the best of friends, as well as family."

PROMOTING THEIR LAST ALBUM

Immediately after the interview, Carpenter had dinner with his parents Harold and Agnes Carpenter, and then climbed aboard a plane for a promotional tour of Japan.

"It's Japan, and then Australia, then home for a day and off to New York," Richard said. On the den wall above where he sat was a large framed assemblage of the group's gold records.

Carpenter was at home for only five days last week between promotional tours. One of those days was proclaimed "Carpenters Day" by the Los Angeles City Council. That day, Wednesday, Carpenter accepted a star dedicated to him and his sister on Hollywood Boulevard's Walk of Fame.

"It was really special, although it was also sad with Karen not there," he said.

Richard's globe-hopping is to promote the [final] Carpenters album, *Voice of the Heart*, soon [to be] released in the United States. In England the album debuted two weeks ago at number 11 on that country's album chart.

Karen had completed recording the voice tracks on the album just before her death. Her brother went back to the studio after his sister's death and arranged, produced and recorded the instrumental and backup vocal tracks. Richard wrote three of the songs on the new album and arranged nine of them.

"It would have been a crime to let it sit on a shelf," he said. "Karen had some wonderful vocals. A lot of people were looking forward to the new album."

The pop performer said that while "the Carpenters" are now a fond memory, he has no intention of retiring. He plans to continue playing solo concerts with orchestras, performing pop and light classical music and writing songs as well as arranging and producing records for himself and other artists.

He even plans to explore the possibility of performing on television specials and composing musical scores for films. [. . .]

"MAINSTREAM POP"

"Mainstream pop" is how Richard describes the sound of Karen's drums and vocals and his piano, vocals and string arrangements.

"Call it whatever you want. I call it (the Carpenters' sound) mainstream pop," he said.

"It was never earthshakingly new. It did have a different sound, but it was still in an established genre. It's not progressive—it's traditional pop.

"I like that. I'm proud of that kind of music. It's a lasting art form. Look at Air Supply. They really sound Carpenteresque."

Richard said the music of the Carpenters strikes a familiar chord in the hearts of people worldwide. "It's the ballads and love songs that have been sung over the ages," he said. Even in countries like Japan, audiences enjoyed the Carpenters' concerts and albums, he said.

"There's something in the music that ties it together. Like they say, music is the universal language."

"I'M A HOMEBODY"

When success came, however, Richard kept his ties to his family and friends and stayed in Downey, although he moved into a larger home.

He still collects vintage automobiles, a hobby he has enjoyed for years.

"I am a homebody, and I'm very comfortable in this town (Downey)," he said.

"It's peaceful here. It's nice to come out of it all into a quiet community. So when things broke loose, I didn't want to move to Beverly Hills.

"We're a close family and it's nice to be near my parents."

AN "INSIDIOUS" DISEASE

Miss Carpenter had come home for a regular visit from New York in February when she collapsed from heart failure in an upstairs bedroom.

"I was stunned. . . . A 32-year-old woman falling over with heart failure—especially since she had never smoked or drank or used drugs. It was baffling," Richard said.

He said he and his parents had worried over his sister's long struggle with anorexia nervosa—an illness she was struggling over even when the pair's career was skyrocketing.

"It's insidious and perplexing," Richard said of the illness. "The researchers are trying, and they're learning new things."

Toward that end, the family set up the Karen Carpenter Memorial Foundation, which has been receiving contributions toward musical scholarships at Long Beach State and for research into the cause of anorexia nervosa.

Richard said the family received several letters from the families of anorexic persons after Miss Carpenter's death. "Her death drew world attention to the disorder," he said.

Carpenter said the nature of art has helped him live with his sister's death.

"Karen's death was a tragedy. But the least I can say is that we had been fortunate to have the opportunity to record.

"As a result of that, it's there—it's there forever. That's terrific.

"In one way, Karen goes on."

SHE'D ONLY JUST BEGUN

FINE CBS MOVIE TELLS SAD STORY OF KAREN CARPENTER

Ron Miller

San Jose Mercury News, 1989

The death of singer Karen Carpenter in 1983 from complications of an eating disorder remains one of the saddest and most bewildering episodes in pop-music history.

Carpenter had one of the richest, most beautiful voices of her time, and today, nearly six years after her death, she's still heard on the nation's easy-listening stations, where her many hits are evergreen standards.

It's hard to associate that serene sound with the troubled soul behind it. On Feb. 4, 1983, she was so weak and physically ruined that her heart simply stopped beating. Why would a rich, good-looking and phenomenally successful 32-year-old starve herself in a manic quest for thinness? What went wrong?

That's the question posed by tonight's CBS movie, *The Karen Carpenter Story*, a moving film biography of Carpenter that comes up with a number of possible explanations—most of them credible, all of them tragic.

Though the film was produced by Carpenter's brother, Richard, her creative partner in their immensely popular recording duo, the Carpenters, it seems to pull few punches.

It deals with Richard's addiction to Quaaludes as well as Karen's illness, anorexia nervosa, a psychologically motivated form of self-starvation peculiar to young women. It's also hard on their parents, Agnes and Harold Carpenter, who dominated their lives well into adulthood.

In many ways, the teleplay by Barry Morrow suggests that neither Richard nor Karen were very mature when their music thrust them into the spotlight, leaving them ill-prepared to cope with the stresses of superstardom and the strain of long road tours.

It shows us a childishly insecure Karen, failing at marriage while abusing herself with severe dieting, diuretics, laxatives and endless exercise in what may have been a subconscious attempt to prove herself the master of at least one thing in an overly controlled life: her own body.

Along the way, it also hints that the older brother and younger sister were so psychologically dependent upon each other that they were unable to relate normally to others.

If there's an arch-villain of the story, it's probably Agnes Carpenter (Louise Fletcher), an imposing woman who found it almost impossible to show her love to her troubled daughter, even after her illness had been diagnosed and the threat to her life was clear.

The mother also is seen giving her own prescription drugs to Richard to help him sleep and, later, refusing to accept her son's addiction to the drugs, even after Karen tells her about it.

Mrs. Carpenter dominates her placid husband, Harold (Peter Michael Goetz), and shows the force of her personality in an early scene in which a recording contract is offered to Karen but not to her older brother. She comes close to killing the deal outright but ends up making sure Karen knows she's only half of a team that she won't allow to be separated.

The film shows Richard as protective of his sister but not above jealousy. Though it's clear that Richard's keen musical sense developed the trademark sound of the Carpenters, it's also clear Karen was the star. Yet when she hints at going out as a solo [act] while he's hospitalized, Richard is stunned and hurt. He bullies her out of it, convincing her that she, too, needs rest. She does, but his motives may not be completely unself-ish in talking her into it.

After a while, it becomes clear that Karen carried an enormous psy-chological burden. An apparently sweet, naive and good-natured young woman is transformed into a self-destructive neurotic by her failure to reconcile her inability to find love while being loved by millions.

The film is buttressed by two superb performances in the lead-ing roles. Cynthia Gibb, a graduate of TV's *Fame* and one of the most capable young actresses in Hollywood, makes the tortured Karen into a personal triumph. Gibb is a terrific musical performer herself, but mostly lip-syncs Karen's original recordings in a series of nicely staged musical sequences. Richard is played engagingly by newcomer Mitchell Anderson.

The movie picks up Carpenter's story in 1963 when the family moved from Connecticut to Downey, in Southern California, partly to be near the entertainment industry, where they hoped that the talented Richard could "become a superstar."

At 13, Karen makes her debut singing "End of the World" with her brother's trio and doubling on drums. After Richard's group wins a Hol-lywood "battle of the bands," they get a studio audition, but the label is really interested only in the magnetic vocals by young Karen.

The story carries them through their meteoric rise on the pop charts after a boost from band leader Herb Alpert, who gave them Burt Bacha-rach's "Close to You" to record, their first mega-hit.

Later, the film recounts the moment when Richard saw a Crocker Bank commercial on TV at 2 a.m. and was inspired to adapt the tune for the Carpenters. It became "We've Only Just Begun," another million-seller.

Also depicted is Karen's reluctance to get up and stand in front of the band to sing. Richard and their managers had to conspire to pry her away from her drums and get her out front where she belonged.

Her shyness obviously was a part of Karen's problem. After reading a [fabricated] review in *Billboard* that refers to her as Richard's "chubby sister," she launches herself on an obsessive weight-loss program.

Through the film, director Joseph Sargent neatly uses the Carpen-ters' lyrics to accentuate the psychological climate of Karen's life.

In one inspired sequence, Sargent offers a montage showing the breakdown of Karen's marriage while she sings "[This] Masquerade" on the soundtrack with its doubly meaningful lyrics ("We tried to talk it over, but the words got in the way . . .").

Though the film strives to avoid pessimism and remain entertaining, it still carries an emotional wallop, particularly in the closing sequence when the family shares a holiday dinner and Karen's mother tries to make up for lost time with her troubled daughter.

The Karen Carpenter Story is an above-average TV drama about a seemingly normal person who somehow went off the tracks on her way to the top of the world. It reminds us how little we really know about the dark side of the gifted people we admire so much.

"KAREN WAS WASTING AWAY . . . I HAD A DRUG PROBLEM . . . AND WE COULDN'T HELP EACH OTHER"

Richard Carpenter

TV Guide, 1988

I called her K.C., and she called me R.C. It seems as if we did everything together. We loved cars and went bowling and listened to Spike Jones, Nat "King" Cole and Elvis, among many others. More than brother and sister, we were best friends. Karen and I still lived with our parents when we recorded "Close to You," We've Only Just Begun" and quite a few of the subsequent hits. In 1974, we bought a house together and it seemed we couldn't miss. Yet it wasn't too long after we hit the peak of success that we were both careening down separate paths of destruction—me on sleeping pills and Karen starving herself. Our career was over long before I thought it would end.

Karen's death is still a mystery to me. If she had died in a more tangible way—if she had been hit by a car—it would have been equally tragic but something I could comprehend. The eating disorder that killed her, anorexia nervosa, was little understood then and only a little more now.

What would possess a woman like her to starve herself? Some people blame it on career pressures or a need to take more control over her life. I don't think so. I think she would have suffered from the same problem even if she had been a homemaker. She was not always a slave to her self-image. Sure, she had been concerned about her weight since she was a teenager and had dieted to lose her childhood chubbiness. Karen lost 25 pounds on a water diet when she was 17. Her weight remained stable, and she continued to eat sensibly.

By 1975, it was clear something was seriously wrong with her. We canceled part of our world tour that year because Karen was frail and tiring easily. She spent weeks in bed while my parents and I tried to coax her into eating. That was when we first learned about anorexia. Much has been written about the disorder since Karen's death. But back then, we had little to go on.

It wasn't much later that I realized I also was ruining my life through behavior I couldn't control. I had become addicted to Quaaludes, which I had begun taking to help me sleep after our first European tour. I continued taking the pills at night for several years without any problems, but my body was building up a tolerance to them and I found myself taking more than the prescribed dosage to achieve the desired effect. As a result, the drug would take longer to wear off the following day. My speech would become slurred and my hands would start trembling. I couldn't write anymore and had trouble performing. One side of me was saying, "You fool. You're killing yourself, you can't function, and you're letting your sister and parents down." But the other side convinced me I couldn't get by without those pills.

While I was trying to prevent Karen from withering away, she was trying to help me kick my drug dependency. I tried a couple of detox programs, but even if you get the stuff out of your system, it's hard to lick the problem. By 1978, I was in trouble, no two ways about it. We were playing at the MGM Grand in Las Vegas and I had reached the point where I couldn't stop slurring until about 5 P.M., and then all I could think about was going back to bed. Each night, all I wanted to do was get off that stage. We canceled halfway through the engagement, sent all the musicians home and left the room dark. I made up some excuse—like I was exhausted or something—and didn't think twice about it. This is totally unlike me, before and since.

At Christmas that year, Karen and I were going to do a benefit concert for the Carpenters Choral Scholarship Fund at our alma mater, California State University at Long Beach. We were set to play with the school's symphony and choir. As the day of the show drew closer, I started removing songs from the program because I couldn't perform them. My hands were shaking too much. I told Karen I was dropping "It's Christmas Time" because I didn't think it would go over well. And I told her I was dropping "The Nutcracker" because I didn't think the university orchestra could cut it. I pared that damn program down to almost nothing because I couldn't play most of it.

Poor Karen. She was buying all of this, even though she knew I had a problem. I always had excuses for everything. You get pretty devious—the same way anorexics do. But it finally got so bad that I couldn't get out of bed and I had to say, "Karen, I've got a problem here." So I checked into the chemical-dependency unit at the Menninger Clinic in Topeka, Kan. That was in early 1979.

It wasn't until her brief marriage ended in 1981 that Karen decided she needed help. She moved to New York to start daily sessions with a therapist who specialized in anorexia. But the treatment didn't take. When she came home around Thanksgiving 1982, she was heavier. But it wasn't the sign of a cure—she had been fed intravenously. Even with the added weight, she always appeared fatigued.

I remember so clearly the morning she died. She had called me the day before from her condominium. She was going to buy a new VCR and wanted to know what I recommended. Then we talked for a while. I guess she decided later to drive down and spend the night at our folks' house. My mother called me the next morning and, of course, she was hysterical. She had found Karen unconscious on the closet floor in her room. I remember driving over to the house, hoping against hope that it was just a collapse. I even thought that maybe it would be something serious enough to move her to seek treatment again. I got there just as they were bringing her out of the house on a gurney.

Making a movie about all this has been an emotional roller coaster. I've had to stir up a lot of memories—joyous ones as well as painful. But I realized soon after Karen's death that if I didn't make the movie, someone else would, and I wanted to make sure it was done as accurately as possible. I also gave long and hard thought to whether Karen would have wanted her story told. I think she would have. She was an honest person and not afraid to show her down side. She might also have seen this as a way to help others suffering from anorexia. And besides, it was in her makeup. I guess this goes for both of us.

CARPENTERS TELEPIC BOOSTS RECORD SALES

Variety, 1989

One month after *The Karen Carpenter Story* aired on CBS to high ratings, the Carpenters' catalog of hit albums is still selling at roughly two times its normal rate, after surging some 400% in the two weeks immediately following the January 1st telecast.

"It's almost like she died all over again," said Kathy Dosdall, a national buyer for the 630-store Musicland/Sam Goody chain. "We rarely see sales like this just from a TV show."

Dosdall said the operation was not prepared for the overwhelming response from the movie, which told of Karen Carpenter's losing battle with anorexia nervosa. "We ran out pretty quickly, so there's no telling how much we would have sold had we had the stuff on hand."

In some cities, the sales surge is being sustained by another film treatment of Karen Carpenter's life, *Superstar [The Karen Carpenter Story]*. Director Todd Haynes' underground documentary which uses Barbie and Ken dolls to portray Karen and her brother Richard, is playing to sold-out crowds at arthouses in San Francisco and Washington, D.C.

David Steffen, Senior V.P. of Sales and Distribution at A&M, the Carpenters' label and scene of some of the TV film's action, is hoping CBS reruns the show soon. "Sales on the entire catalog have more than doubled since it was broadcast," he said, though he would not reveal just how many units have moved as a result of the TV pic.

Unfortunately for Steffen and the rest of the folks at A&M, the popularity of the program did little to boost sales of Richard Carpenter's recent solo album for the label, *Time*.

BECOMING KAREN
AND RICHARD

AN INTERVIEW WITH CYNTHIA GIBB
AND MITCHELL ANDERSON

Randy L. Schmidt

2008

EDITOR'S NOTE: More than two decades after its premiere, *The Karen Carpenter Story* remains a campy favorite among fans of the TV-movie /biopic genre. In 2008, while completing research and interviews for *Little Girl Blue: The Life of Karen Carpenter*, I had the pleasure of interviewing the two lead actors from this infamous "Movie of the Week." The following interview excerpts didn't make it into *Little Girl Blue*, but I feel they are still quite relevant and even entertaining.

How did the two of you come to be cast?

Cynthia Gibb: My agency sent me on a meeting with Richard Carpenter, who was doing the casting. It was not the typical casting call where you're one of many actors sitting in a waiting room. It was more like a business meeting. This was very close to the time they were going to start shooting the film, and it was unusual to be called so late for this kind of film. I was cast about ten days before we started shooting.

Mitchell Anderson: I had worked with the director, Joe Sargent, in *Jaws: The Revenge*, which was a terrible movie! Joe went and fought for me at the network. Cindy and I worked together on the script, went in for our network audition, and had the right chemistry. They'd auditioned a lot of people, but I think we were the only two that they took to the network.

Did you know the Carpenters' music or story before then?

CG: Not at all. I was coming into this knowing very little except the broad, general facts. I knew that she and her brother were a music team and that they were enormously successful around the world. Also, I knew most of their hit singles. I knew that Karen had had an eating disorder and that she'd died because of it. Beyond that, I knew nothing.

MA: I knew of their music from the early 1970s because my parents listened to the Carpenters on eight-track tapes. I remember "We've Only Just Begun" was my sister's senior class song in high school. That was 1976.

What research and preparation did you do for the roles?

MA: I was able to do my preparation in the same way I did for any role. I looked at the arc of the character as it related to the story and to the relationship with Karen. It was important for both Cynthia and me to stay grounded in the moments of each scene. The hardest thing was not "playing the end" before we got there.

CG: Any role involves a great deal of character research, whether it's fiction or the truth. You have to figure out the character—their background, their strengths and weaknesses. You have to figure out who the person is in a three-dimensional way. On top of trying to create a character, I began researching the clinical aspects of anorexia. I tried to connect the dots between what happens in clinical cases of anorexia or bulimia and the aspects of Karen's life.

What went into preparing for the musical aspects of this movie?

MA: They knew they were going to cast us, but they didn't make the deals until a week before. We only had one week to prepare and do all of the things we needed to do, like taking piano lessons and so on. I also played a little piano and was comfortable with the singing, so faking the posture and hand position was something that came pretty easily. The rest of it was done with tricks. In one scene, Richard literally put his hands under my arms so he could play the keys. The camera panned from my face to his hands. It was pretty low-tech, but it worked given the intense shooting schedule. We didn't have much time for anything elaborate.

CG: As far as the singing was concerned, I was trying to learn about twenty songs well enough to lip-synch. I am a singer and had been on *Fame* for three years, so I was familiar with lip-synching. Every week, we had at least one or two songs on that show that were recorded and then lip-synched. I knew I could do it, but that doesn't mean it was a fast and easy thing to do. You can't do it quickly. You must really memorize the songs in absolutely every way—every breath, where the vibrato is, the nuances of the performance and so on. You have to really absorb and memorize until it becomes a part of you.

MA: Yes, the hardest thing for me was getting the lyrics to the songs down enough to be believable. Fortunately, I had a lot of "oohs" and "ahs," so it wasn't as hard as what she had to do.

What about the physical transformations?

CG: The script contained scenes showing Karen becoming thinner and thinner and I knew there wouldn't be a body double. When I found out I would be wearing her real clothes, I knew I would have to get as small as she was. We weren't going to shoot in sequence, so I needed to get down to the thinnest I could right away and then they could pad me up. I had two sets of padding so that I could be different sizes throughout the shoot. In real life, I was the smallest I could be but still in good health when I showed up to the set.

I recall there was some criticism from people when they learned you had to lose weight to play Karen. To them, it seemed like that expectation for you was similar to the pressures to be thin that Karen had faced. Did you see it that way?

CG: The weight loss was just a normal part of the preparation I have to do as an actor in any and every role I play. Sometimes I have to learn a language or learn a new skill. Sometimes I learn about a political situation in a foreign country. It's just part of an actor's research and preparation. In this case, Karen and I were approximately the same height. I am quite petite, so for me to fit into her clothes—even the very small ones—I just had to get thin but not sick. I ate well while preparing for this role. I just cut out the sugar and most carbs to get down to 103 pounds. At that weight, I fit into most all of her clothes. Although, I do recall a white lacy dress that she wore. I couldn't zip it up over my rib cage, even at that weight.

Tell me about the wardrobe. There were so many recognizable outfits in the movie.

CG: I had a fitting with the costume designer right away. She brought me into a room with racks and racks of Karen's real clothes, and we went through to find the wardrobe for the entire movie. There were many changes that spanned twenty years. At one point, when the designer and her assistant left, I started to put my hands through the clothes the way you would turn the pages of a book. I got a strong sense that Karen was in the room. I had an overwhelming feeling that I wasn't alone. A bunch of people walked through the room with a bustle, and the sensation left me immediately. It was almost like she was there and, when people came in, she went away. I felt that throughout the shoot, too. I had never really considered ghosts or spirits or anything like that—that was not part of my belief system at the time—but I must say that I felt some kind of energy that could have been her in a few moments throughout the shoot.

Another instance was the day we were shooting at A&M Studios in the same recording booth where Karen and Richard had recorded a lot of their music. Herb Alpert had come in to say hello and pay his regards. Richard was there in the engineering booth. It felt like Karen was there with us.

MA: We were in the studio where she recorded her last song, and I just lost it—not as an actor but as a human being. I was hearing her voice and thinking of this horribly sad story. Hearing Karen's voice and seeing Cynthia sing was emotionally draining and very moving to me. It was an incredibly sad story.

CG: It happened in her home as well, that feeling that Karen was with us. We filmed in her parents' home in Downey, where her room was still intact and still decorated the same way it was the day she died. Her parents had preserved everything, even the stuffed animals on the bed. In the opening scene, where Karen is taken from the house on the stretcher, the paramedics who had actually taken her away were the same paramedics used in the movie.

What were some of the characteristics you noticed about Karen and tried to emulate?

CG: I attempted to learn to play the drums. Ten days to learn any instrument and actually look convincing to somebody who has played before is really tough. Learning to play the drums in a matter of weeks is really a joke. I am not a percussionist, so I can't imagine the suffering that our poor editor must have gone through to find pieces that actually looked correct. In addition to synching the drums and lip-synching the music, Karen had a very distinct way of holding the microphone, so I practiced holding the mic that way.

What about Richard?

MA: Richard is a take-charge kind of guy. He really managed every aspect of their careers—the look, sound, press, schedules, and so on. He is definitely a type-A overachiever. I felt that was important to emulate since, in part, this was one of the causes of Karen's illness. Still, I intentionally softened him a little. In a TV movie, you don't have much time to fill in the nuances of personality, but I wanted to make sure he was a sympathetic person. I remember talking to the producer a few days into shooting and saying I thought I was getting it wrong. I felt that I was playing him much more emotionally accessible than he actually is. The producer told me he was glad I was adding the warmth, even though that may not be so apparent in Richard himself.

What was the production schedule like?

MA: We shot the whole movie in 19 days. Cynthia and I were working 16-hour days. Sometimes, when an actor says they're working 16-hour days it means they're sitting in their trailer most of the time. I know that part, too, but we were *exhausted!* At one point, I completely lost my voice. But that's a TV movie for you. There's no budget.

CG: And that is considered an extraordinarily *long* shoot schedule for a TV movie now. Most are made in less than thirteen shooting days. We shot a minimum of eight pages a day, and we did not shoot in chronological order. We jumped from scene to scene throughout the day, which meant year-to-year and age-to-age. I actually drew a map of Karen's life for myself as part of my homework on the script. That way, I could keep track of where I was in her journey while shooting out of sequence.

What insight did you gain into the Carpenter family and Karen's story as a result of this closeness to its subjects?

CG: In the Carpenters' home, Richard was recognized as a musical prodigy from the youngest age. Karen was very young when Richard started to be described by the family and others as a prodigy. [Karen] hadn't found what she was good at yet. She grew up feeling that Richard was the brilliant one and that Richard was the talented one and that Richard was the musician—which he was—but in some ways, this was discounting whatever value she had. Even though they were a performing team, Karen was out front. Karen was the one who was getting more attention. Karen was the one who was getting more praise. There was a tremendous amount of guilt for her because she was the one out in front getting that attention, when it should be Richard. She felt uncomfortable receiving that kind of praise because she felt that it usurped the praise from Richard.

MA: She was also looking for a place to control her life because everybody took over for her. They wanted her skinny. They wanted her to stop playing the drums. Everybody else made the decisions for her, and I think that was the only way that she was able to feel like she had some control. What I learned about Richard's personality is that he had a some-what closed-off, WASPy, unemotional approach to life—things happen, we deal, we move on. I think it's a weird trait for an artist. Because Karen didn't have that trait, I feel she internalized all those feelings and it mani-fested itself in a self-destructive disease. In other people, it might have manifested as a drug addiction or anger problems.

In his research for the teleplay, Barry Morrow interviewed the Carpenter parents and was shocked when Mrs. Carpenter introduced herself, so to speak, by saying, "I just want you to know I did not kill my daughter." What would cause her to do such a thing? Do either of you have any insights you'd share?

CG: The family was more old-fashioned in their beliefs that "normal" families don't need psychiatrists, only crazy people do. They really took offense to any implication of her upbringing being anything but per-fect. As we evolve as a society, I think most people are willing to admit there's no such thing as a perfect household. For their family, there was a tremendous amount of shame, as if they "killed" their daughter by not being perfect. But that's the perfectionism right there! Maybe Karen's issues with perfectionism were just that she was brought up with parents who thought they were supposed to be perfect.

Let's end on a lighter note. What was with those wigs?

MA: They were horrible!

CG: The wigs were really a nightmare. They were absolutely awful!

MA: The hairstylist had totally underbid to get the job. She was trying to put me in cut-up old-lady wigs and make them look like men's wigs.

CG: These things were like helmets. They were just enormous and had so much hair. I'm a pretty small person [and was] especially after losing all that weight. They put it on my little head, and I just looked ridicu-lous! There was room for *two* of me in there.

MA: My grandmother used to have plastic wigs for dress-up. They were like plastic helmets. That's what we felt like we were wearing.

CG: I would sit there in the chair, near tears, thinking that I can't let anybody watch this. I cannot let anybody see me like this. I am not going to tell anybody that I did this job or when it's on the air.

MA: At one point, I was sitting in the makeup trailer looking at myself in the mirror going, "I look like a complete fool," knowing that I'm going to be on screen. This is going to be preserved forever! I had a meltdown.

So you "wigged out" on them?

MA: Yeah, and I'm a totally even-keeled actor. I never created a fuss, but at one point, I just had a meltdown. Finally, the director said, "Okay, look. We have got to fix this. This is ridiculous." They gave them more money, and they got slightly better wigs.

CG: I was actually so embarrassed about people seeing the movie that I left town when it aired. I went to my grandparents' farm in Vermont and hid from the world. When I came home, I found out that it had broken ratings records. We got 30-something-million viewers, which is like Super Bowl numbers. Nobody gets those kinds of numbers anymore. TV movies don't.

The movie aired twice on CBS and has since found a home on the Lifetime network, where it is shown periodically. It may never be released on DVD since Richard is no longer pleased with having participated in its making. Still, it lives on. Did you ever imagine people would be talking about this movie twenty years later?

MA: It's funny to know that it's become somewhat iconic in terms of cheesy biopics. But Cynthia and I have this amazing bond now after having done this movie.

CG: I cannot believe there are still so many people who remember it. I get asked all the time, "When is it going to be out on DVD?" I think that is a testament to how important the Carpenters were—and still are—to so many people. Looking back now, I am so grateful to have been a part of this movie. Playing Karen Carpenter was a gift and an honor.

GETTING TO THE BARE BONES OF TODD HAYNES' *SUPERSTAR: THE KAREN CARPENTER STORY*

Sheryl Farber

Film Threat, 1989

EDITOR'S NOTE: Shown primarily at film festivals and small theaters throughout the United States, Todd Haynes' *Superstar: The Karen Carpenter Story* (commonly referred to in Carpenters circles as "the Barbie doll movie") garnered a huge underground following after its release in 1987. Haynes attempted to license a number of original Carpenters recordings and other music for the production, but his requests were denied. When he proceeded to use the material for which he was denied permission, legal injunctions from Richard Carpenter ensued, and the film was withdrawn from distribution in 1990. By 2000, *Superstar* had earned a place at number 45 on *Entertainment Weekly*'s list of "Top 50 Cult Films of All Time."

◆

On a New York oldies station tonight, the Carpenters are the featured recording artists. The DJ notes the *smooth as silk* voice of
Karen Carpenter before he plays one of their hits—"Rainy Days and
Mondays." The first few strains of the harmonica begin, heralding the
melancholy voice of Karen singing. [. . .]

I can't stop listening. The DJ plays all of my Carpenter favorites and I
am catapulted into memories of the seventies. "For All We Know" comes
on and I am in a music class full of pubescent pimply faced junior high
school kids, reluctantly waving plastic batons, learning how to conduct
to Karen's soothing voice and her brother Richard's elaborate arrangements. Actually this is the late seventies and I am wondering why my
teacher has chosen a song that I remember from my early childhood—a
song that is now only played on the annoying Muzak station that my
mother listens to in the car on the way to the supermarket and piped
into the speakers above the aisle of Lemon Fresh Joy and Bounty. None-
theless, I am, unlike most of my baton slinging peers, captivated by the
voice of the songstress of the seventies.

The hits just keep coming out of my radio. "We've Only Just Begun,"
written by that diminutive troubadour Paul Williams. "Close to You,"
written by Burt Bacharach, who called Karen, at the time of her tragic
death at 32, "a magical person with a magical voice." I fall asleep with
"Superstar" ringing in my ears.

My reawakened interest in the Carpenters' music began after I sat
through a slew of bad films at the New York Film Festival Downtown.
The evening seemed like it was going to be representative of the bleak
state of underground filmmaking in New York. The last movie to be
shown, however, was Todd Haynes' *Superstar: The Karen Carpenter
Story*, a 16mm, 43-minute film made in 1987 that has been receiving critical acclaim for over a year now. Along with strong recommendations to
see the film from friends, I was usually given a brief description—"It's
made with Barbie dolls." Like most American women (and even some
men) I was no stranger to the Barbie netherworld, and like most women
(but unlike many men), I had been forced to reconcile myself with the
fact that I would never be built like a Barbie. I was interested to see what
director Haynes would do with the issue of anorexia, the disease that

eventually led to Karen Carpenter's demise and wondered if the use of Barbie dolls would be purely comic.

The film opens with Karen's mother's point of view in February 1983. She discovers the collapsed, silk-shrouded body of Karen in their Downey, California home. Then we are shown the outside of a middle-class suburban house (which incidentally was the actual Carpenter digs in Downey) and the question "What happened?" is posed by the narrator. "Let's go back," he says as we are about to enter a journey, first, through the streets of sunny Southern California, providing a backdrop for fancy seventies stylized credits, and then through the simulated doll life of Karen Carpenter. With a straightforward narrative we are hooked into the story of Karen Carpenter's life, her rise to stardom and her problem with anorexia that accompanied it. Haynes has also managed to capture the period brilliantly with detailed sets, music that includes the Captain & Tennille, and Gilbert O'Sullivan, clips from television such as *The Brady Bunch* and *The Partridge Family*. There are clips of Richard Nixon, bombs over Cambodia. This seems to counter the clean-cut, close-knit youthful wholesomeness that the media tried to bolster with such teen stars as the Brady Bunch, Osmonds and the Carpenters.

I spoke with Todd Haynes at a restaurant that serves healthy, non-fattening foods.

Which came first: the idea to make a movie about Karen Carpenter, or the idea to make a TV docudrama-type of film with dolls?

Well, the idea to do a film with dolls actually came before anything. I saw this promotional black and white little trailer on television—a vintage piece of TV from the fifties, that introduced the Barbie to the American public. And it had a little miniature interior scene with the doll sitting around the living room, and then Barbie came in and showed Midge her new dress and it also intercut with live action—a little girl opened up a mailbox, shot from inside the mailbox, getting her Barbie fan club mail. And I was really intrigued with the idea of doing a fairly straight-forward narrative drawing on pre-existing popular forms, but simply replacing real actors with inanimate objects, with dolls. And being very careful with it and detailed in such a way that it would provoke the same kind of identification and investment in the narrative as any real movie would. But in watching it, this emotional involvement in dolls or something completely artificial that would possibly make us think. Maybe that's what happens when we see movies, it's more the forms and the structures that they take that provoke emotional responses; more than the fact that there was, at one point, a real actress or actor in front of the camera. We were watching shadows on a wall carefully fitting into pre-existing forms that we know very well that we still cry and laugh as if it were a real person.

So you are using the star story docudrama form to grip the viewer but at the same time you're being critical of that very form?

Yeah, I think so. The form I used definitely comes from probably the most tabloid form of narrative filmmaking, which is always telling the rise and fall of the fated star and revealing all the inside dirt in careful pre-determined ways. I juxtapose it with other kinds of styles sort of faux documentary style.

The anorexia films we saw in high school—

Exactly. Instructional kinds of films. And also montages which begin fairly like the typical image montage that [accompanies] a song number in a movie, but begin to get a little more abstract and more experimental as the film progresses. The film is basically held together by the narrative. And that's what makes people move from being cynical, critically engaged or laughing; to being implicated and emotionally attached to the character. And in a sense, I like it better when the narrative works than when it fails because since it's with dolls it hooks you in, and you have to admit to your implication by realizing you've been lured into a trap.

This movie seems to appeal primarily to people between the ages of 20–30, particularly I think because of your images of popular culture from the seventies.

The film supposes a kind of turning in popular culture from the sixties and the seventies that caught all of us in a certain generation at a vulnerable point because we were just starting to think of ourselves autonomously in the early seventies because of our being 8, 9, 10, 11. And when the music came out, it was such a strong kind of suggestion that everything was fine. The turmoil of the late sixties was over in a second and Nixon was in the White House and things were going to be just great. The family gained new value, of a new pertinence that had been questioned for the previous decade.

It was also the taming of the youth culture.

Yeah, completely. Although at the same time the Vietnam War was raging, Kent State, there was a continued explosion of social protests and causes but . . . I responded much more to the images of safety and tranquility that were on television and the radio—the Carpenters represent that to such a complete extent. What seemed to happen then is that everything started to fall through like Watergate pulled the rug out from under the Nixon administration. The Carpenters dropped in popularity and disco happened and we just began this really self-absorbed generation of hedonistic pleasures. I think we got cynical and the eighties celebrate that cynicism in a way that we never really anticipated. So when I look back at that period and when I heard the music, after not really hearing it for a long time, it was almost for me, like the last time I believed in popular culture and that it worked for me. It manipulated my view of the world and it also united me with my family and their values. Like this friend of mine said to me, "It was pre-irony." It was the last moment for our generation that was one of the last earnest sentimental times. The music gained all its resonance that probably, at the time, you would never have thought it carried.

How long did the movie take to make?

The whole film took about a year and half from writing to completion while carrying on other jobs. I shot it in upstate (New York) at Bard College. I began an MFA program there, a three-summer-long program, and I basically utilized the first summer—I haven't gone back since—to build all the sets and make all the props and by the end of the summer we shot it. I worked on it with three close friends. Cynthia Schneider co-wrote it with me and co-produced it as well. Barry Ellsworth, who is part of Apperatus, helped me shoot and write it and is really responsible for how beautiful the film looks. Bob Manenti worked on it laboriously as well. So it was a very small core group of maniacs working insane hours. I mean the film was fun but it was really hard. I underestimated how long everything would take.

The film has a strong feminist viewpoint and I know you had a female co-writer. I was wondering how you became sensitive to such issues?

Well I think the film couldn't have been conceived without Cynthia's participation. Neither of us have experienced anorexia personally but through the process of researching it and involving ourselves I think we both found connections to it that I may never had considered otherwise. I think the pressures and the kinds of neurotic motivations that would result in eating disorders are the same pressures and neurotic feelings that I've experienced but taken out in other ways. But definitely, the roots and causes [of anorexia that I began to see] were all things I knew really well. I found the whole story interesting and intriguing, the whole story, but I don't think I found it personally comprehendible in the way that I did after researching it. But the response basically has been extremely supportive from the feminist community. There had been a couple of incidents of what I would call a more narrow and dogmatic side of feminism which recoils with the idea of humor being engaged in any way in a film or a work about anorexia—that humor does not have a place in it. And the film does not at any point make fun of anorexia but I do think humor is a tool. It can even be a weapon and it's been a part of cultural production, a really interesting part of it, for a really long time. And it can be an incredible political tool and to just simply say, "That's not allowed!" I find to be the worst side of feminism or any other kind of political critique of our culture—when it takes on the same dogma that the culture imposes. That's wrong to me.

Did you use those high school–type health films that you imitated to help research anorexia?

No but we found general material that's available to the public that has the whole tone. And which is just as limited in the whole view of the problem.

You really managed to physically transform Karen's doll to show the effects of her anorexia. How did you get that emaciated effect on her face?

We carved down the plastic cheeks of the doll head. I found dolls at flea markets. . . . [They] were extremely thin already, but the faces were kind of round so I wanted to carve down the cheeks and then cover it over with pancake makeup and it had very creepy effects.

I saw a picture of Karen Carpenter from that time and the doll really looks like her. Are the dolls actual Barbie dolls from Mattel?

No, in fact none of them are literally Barbie dolls. The doll that portrays Karen is the Tracy doll, a Mattel product [who's] the dark-haired current Barbie friend on the market. A Ken doll does portray Richard but he has various wigs and hairpieces throughout the film and by the end of the film we changed his face a lot so it's no longer a Ken doll.

More like some strange mutant.

Exactly. I love the part in *Superstar* where Karen turns around and she says, "I am sick Richard," and he says, "What do you mean sick, mentally?" And he looks so much sicker than she does.

Did you know about Richard's quaalude addiction and choose not to explore it?

I didn't know about it, although my film's reference to his private life could be interpreted as referring to his drug habit.

Or his homosexuality.

Yes. But I don't have any solid evidence to what his private life entails so I guess I could leave it open.

So what did you think about the TV movie?

I enjoyed every second of it but I also found it disturbing. I thought it was interesting how it both very carefully revealed and concealed information about them.

Yeah, especially the way they treated her eating disorder. I charted scene by scene their showing of her voracious appetite like when the Carpenter family goes bowling, Karen yells eagerly, "Pizza, yeah!!" Then "Hot dogs, sure!!" They always had her stealing from the cookie jar.

And then "all of a sudden" sort of reverse [tack]. There were things I didn't know. That they lived together during that period. That was really interesting to learn. I didn't know that Karen's first recording contract was a solo contract. That was really extraordinary. . . . I heard the solo album and it's really an exciting collection of songs that don't sound like Richard Carpenter productions.

They weren't his arrangements?

No. It was during the time that he was detoxing apparently, that's what the movie tells us, and she went to New York. They bring it up in the TV movie. She tells him and he immediately gets mad [at] her but then it switches to the anorexia as the issue. She went to New York during that time and cut an album with Phil Ramone, who's a producer of Billy Joel and some classics and some disco classics. And it was '79/'80 so it was very disco influenced. It's really interesting because it's her voice up against stronger percussion and none of that saturated vocal background bullshit which I hate which is the Richard Carpenter trademark. This is really cool because it's so sad. I don't think people think of Karen Carpenter [as] diversely as she could have been considered as an artist. She never really got a chance to be anything but Richard Carpenter's product. She never got to experiment with sounds and playing with her voice in different ways. I think maybe if she had, and thought of herself more autonomously, she might have been able to live longer and give herself incentive to not think of herself solely in context of the family and Richard's world. What's really sad is the solo album may never get released because of Richard Carpenter even today. Karen Carpenter's image is still being controlled and manipulated by Richard and the family. That's so sad.

I know that this is getting into the private family stuff that you may not know about. But do you know what Richard's relationship to his parents is? I know he had control over this TV movie and the content is real derogatory to his parents.

His mother gave it her approval. And most people find the mother's depiction extremely critical and harsh. But it makes you think if the mother okayed this version you could only imagine what it was like in real life.

Parts of the TV movie seemed to overlap yours, for example, the use of the song "[This] Masquerade" when Karen meets her husband Tom Burris. What was your reaction?

I knew that there would be parallels. Partly because I was drawing on the TV movie form to begin with and obviously when you're doing a TV movie genre about an anorexic pop singer there's going to be similar dialogue. I'm also from California so the whole colloquialism of that world is familiar to me. People tell me, "They must have seen your movie and stolen from it," but I really think it was coincidental. [. . .]

Have they shown your films on cable yet?

No they haven't. Unresolved music rights really prohibit that. I can't and they can't take that risk. The festival showings of *Superstar* have generated a lot of response—not just for that film but for films of its kind. So I think that's really hopeful, I don't think we're seeing the revolution yet . . . it really surprises me that the big professionals of the industry have also found it inspiring. To me that means that everyone is eager for something different.

What is the fascination with pop culture?

I think it's inevitable that we're in such an information ridden society and we appropriate the past so quickly, that you can barely call it the past. Things get taken up so quickly, and become retro in this sort of hyper-accelerated speed that I sometimes think that the context gets lost and this massive attempt to re-examine the past kind of equates and collapses meaning or, I guess, purpose. It also comes out of Hollywood. . . . I just think sometimes the style precedes the purpose and content. We need to know why we're looking at the past and, what we're trying to learn from it and ultimately how it's informing the present. It gets really fun to do sometimes. It may be more fun than valuable and I think there's a danger there in just collapsing the reasons behind it, the motivations behind it. One thing that is evident with *Superstar* is that it's all contrasted examples of artifice. It's all fake. It's a doll world that's made to look like a real world. Or it's sort of a pseudo-documentary [collage] that [is] also scripted and completely constructed. So it's different examples of so-called truth that you, as a viewer, have to weigh against each other. I also think I was lucky in subject matter because the Carpenters provided a perfect dialectic, almost a before and after. The before being this one image of purity and wholesomeness and good-naturedness, and the after being this despair and anorexia. So you could very easily read one against the other. [. . .] At first [the Carpenters'] songs seem banal and manipulative and overly sentimental. They gain a new kind of depth as we've learned how Karen Carpenter has suffered. There's a real sadness and the voice gets all the more beautiful as you find out. You listen to it and you can't stop.

Part V

A SONG FOR YOU

YESTERDAY, ONCE MORE

Stephen Whitty

San Jose Mercury News, 1990

Sonic Youth recorded a tribute, "Tunic (Song for Karen)." A new greatest-hits package, *Only Yesterday*, went to No. 1 in Britain. And there's a definitive, four-CD set due next year from A&M. Seven years after her death, decades after her greatest success, Karen Carpenter is a pop star.

Why the sudden interest? Well, there was that three-Kleenex TV-bio last year. And "When you die so young," one record exec told *Entertainment Weekly*, "there's a sympathy factor." But the Carpenter cult is stronger than that.

Maybe it's just an overdue appreciation of a singer who, despite some terrible material, always had a pure pop voice. Or maybe it's simply a twinge of '70s nostalgia—for baby boomers in their 30s, "Close to You" was part of their AM-radio childhoods. But the Carpenters are back.

And it's only just begun. Again.

HE'S ONLY JUST BEGUN

LOYAL BROTHER BRINGS THE CARPENTERS' LEGACY INTO THE '90S

Janet Wiscombe

Long Beach Press-Telegram, 1994

Wearing a relentlessly colorful Hawaiian shirt splashed with red hibiscus, white cotton pants with white boat shoes and socks, Richard Carpenter's cheerful Beach Boys image is oddly unsettling.

The Dutch-boy haircut is shorter now, and he's lost 20 pounds, but the eyes are still doleful, the posture a little stiff. Hard as he tries to be affable and accommodating, it's clear the pianist/composer would rather be anywhere else.

He's come to the Richard and Karen Carpenter Performing Arts Center on the California State University/Long Beach campus today to talk about the Carpenters phenomenon and to reflect on his own life. Introspection does not come easy.

Saturday night he will be on stage with such friends as Herb Alpert, Marilyn McCoo and Rita Coolidge to perform at the center's gala premier. Last year he gave the university more than $1 million to help maintain the 1,162-seat multiuse theater.

The building is far more than a handsome gift to his alma mater. It symbolizes a stunning new era propelling the squeaky-clean Carpenters into the unlikely world of alternative rock.

"The worldwide focus is now on our music rather than on Karen's personality problems," he says, referring to his sister's death after an eight-year battle with anorexia nervosa. "It's very nice for a change. Now people are talking about the music."

ENDURING POPULARITY

Since Karen's death at age 32 on Feb. 4, 1983, he has spent much of his time at his palatial 7,500-square-foot home/studio in Downey making albums and preparing compilations of Carpenters songs for release throughout the world. Even if he wanted to do something else, the public has almost demanded he remain loyal Brother Carpenter.

Affection for the brother/sister duo has never dimmed, particularly in the United Kingdom and Japan. With the publication of a biography earlier this year and the release this month of an all-star tribute album, the Carpenters once again have risen to rarefied heights.

What's weird for all of those who remember them as bubbly all-American suburban kids is that the new album features 14 alternative-rock groups singing their versions of Carpenter oldies like "(They Long to Be) Close to You" and "Top of the World." And the album is not campy or sarcastic. It is a respectful tribute to the Carpenters by rock acts—from Sonic Youth to the Cranberries—who genuinely love their subtle sound.

Carpenter, now a 47-year-old father of four, is clearly pleased.

"I'm the Perry Como of my generation," he offers with a sweetly fragile smile.

Although the media had a field day psychoanalyzing the Carpenter family, using the name as a metaphor for the darker side of the American Dream, the Richard Carpenter Story has never been told.

By his own description, he is a somewhat reclusive, nocturnal man with the metabolism of a hummingbird. He says he prefers being at home to traveling, and would rather play "It's a Small World . . ." at his daughter's preschool than be on stage.

STRAIGHT OUTTA DOWNEY

"I've always been a homebody," he says. "I've lived in Downey for 31 years. It has a small town feeling. I'm furniture here. I like to do ordinary stuff. I go to the grocery store. I go to PTA meetings."

At the height of their career in the '70s, the Carpenters were releasing albums by the dozen, holding news conferences in Tokyo, singing at the White House, banking millions.

It was only after Karen's death that Richard married his wife, Mary, and began a family. He is the very proud father of three young girls and a 2-month-old son.

If asked what he does for a living, Carpenter jokingly says his kids would say he is a housekeeper or that he works on cars. And they would be right.

"I usually have a sponge in my hand," he says. "I'm very fastidious, and we have a lot of glass coffee tables."

When not sequestered in the music room or tinkering in the warehouse he owns to store his fleet of classic cars, he usually can be found organizing, painstakingly organizing everything in sight.

"I'm a bit persnickety," says the musician known for his obsessive attention to detail. "I am the tender of the family photographs and history. I keep track of all the dates and the family books. . . . All the music is ordered, labeled and put in alphabetical order."

In the new biography of the Carpenters, author Ray Coleman writes about how shocked and angered Richard was years ago when he was introduced as "Richard Carpenter, piano player with the Carpenters." Over the years there have been those who've identified Karen as the standout, Richard the backup.

Nothing could be further from the truth, a close friend comments in the book. "As much as she was the voice, he was the genius."

With characteristic humility, Carpenter makes this observation: "Karen has a timeless voice. The combination of our voices was quite appealing.

"I MISS HER"

"Karen's death was and is a tragedy," he adds. "There's really only so much that can be said. I miss her. I think about her every day. I have posters of her in the music room. She loved kids. She would have loved our kids."

He gazes at the dazzling windows at the entrance to the Richard and Karen Carpenter Performing Arts Center. "To be here in this building, to hear all of the new songs coming out . . . she would have loved it."

At the time he and Karen were students at Cal State in the '60s, they were far more interested in recording music than in reading books. He says he's just a few units shy of graduation.

"One of these days I'd like to get my degree," he says. "And once the gala is wrapped up, I'm going to start writing music again. What's important to me is raising my family and writing music." [. . .]

Editor's Note: On May 26, 2000, Richard Carpenter was presented with an honorary doctorate from the College of the Arts at California State University–Long Beach. The Richard and Karen Carpenter Performing Arts Center is now home to the Carpenters Exhibit, a museum-quality display showcasing Richard's Wurlitzer 140-B electronic piano, Karen's 1965 Ludwig Super Classic drum set, and a sample of the many awards received by the Carpenters over the years.

YESTERDAY ONCE MORE

AN EXCLUSIVE *HITS* INTERVIEW WITH RICHARD CARPENTER

David Konjoyan

HITS, 1994

Who would've thought that when highly regarded producer Matt Wallace [who produced albums for Faith No More, the Replacements, and John Hiatt] (by the way, a close, personal friend) and I conceived *If I Were a Carpenter* (A&M), our alterna-spin on the Carpenters, it would strike more than just the two of us as a fun, inspired idea for an intriguing record. We were simply fans, and knew the artists who took part were as well. The story going around that has Matt and I meeting in high school singing Carpenter songs in the boys' locker room has some basis in fact (though we categorically deny the nagging rumors we had Richard Nixon photos hanging in our lockers—Elvis Presley was as conservative as we got). Since then, our musical tastes have expanded from the Carps to the Clash to Kurt Cobain and this seemed like a great chance to marry them all in an unlikely and surprising package that was inspired by pro-Carpenter comments in the music press from artists like Sonic Youth and Babes in Toyland. A&M responded to it as a hip way to celebrate the Carpenters' 25th anniversary, and *If I Were a Carpenter* was born.

By the time we were done, such cool artists ranging from Sonic Youth, Redd Kross and Bettie Serveert to Grant Lee Buffalo, Shonen Knife and American Music Club, had joined the festivities. Of course, none of us knew as we embarked on the project what the Man himself— Richard Carpenter—would think. Would he like this quirky appreciation, or would he simply ignore or even disown it? We were gratified to discover that Richard enjoyed the record nearly track for track and truly appreciated its spirit and intent. He's been a gracious participant at a time when a quiet home life and a new baby are his biggest priorities, and he even granted this interview to *HITS*. [. . .]

What was your initial reaction when the idea for If I Were a Carpenter *was explained to you?*

I didn't have any trouble with it. I have to be honest, I didn't think it was going to happen. As you know, there were two proposals—one for a so-called "mainstream" record and one for an alternative. And of course, just about everyone thought the one that was gonna fly would be the mainstream one.

Were you nervous at all about how the record might sound or what the intentions were?

After the initial meeting, I didn't think about it at all. Then a couple of months went by and I got a phone call from Diana [Baron], and then from David [Anderle], saying this thing had really been coming along. Then a couple of articles came out saying this was being done so they could make fun [of us], "tongue firmly planted in cheek," and so forth. Diana wanted me to talk to a few people and I said, "Look, if this whole thing's a send-up, I don't want to be involved." But she assured me, "Don't believe everything you read." Then I heard a couple of rough mixes and they struck me as honest. Then I got a call from [VP A&R] Larry Hamby about guesting on Matthew Sweet's track.

Since the Carpenters always took flack from critics, is it a vindication to have artists who are sort of the pillars of cool today pay tribute to you?

I don't know that I feel vindicated. On the whole, I don't have much to complain about. I think what this might do is at least show to some people that our music has a little more appeal to varying tastes than might have been thought.

One of the things that struck Matt and me as the tapes came in is that the bands managed to stay true to themselves, yet didn't stray too far from your arrangements.

They all stayed true to themselves from what I could figure, but some of them actually did follow my road map on the tunes: [Grant Lee Buffalo's] "We've Only Just Begun," of course, and [Sonic Youth's] "Superstar," in its own way. [4 Non Blondes'] "Bless the Beasts" was quite a bit different from my arrangement. And I suppose I was expecting to hear more of that, but all of it seems from the heart.

I heard you might like Dishwalla's "It's Going to Take Some Time" better than your own.

I do enjoy their interpretation every bit as much as ours, if not more. I really think they not only took a fresh and inspired approach to it, they sound like a bunch of talented people to me.

And Sonic Youth.

Again, it pretty much follows the original, but of course the vocal interpretation is quite different, but in its way, it works. It's a haunting song and lyric and Thurston [Moore]'s half-sung, half-whispered vocal to me actually works very well. On some of the songs, I do hear some Beatles influence, particularly the *White Album*. If anyone was listening to the radio at all growing up—and these bands certainly did—you were going to hear the Beatles and the Carpenters. Consciously or not, this stuff is assimilated.

These artists were fans already, but I sensed they came out of the studio with a new respect for the music and especially Karen's voice.

Whether one likes it or not, Karen and I performed this stuff well, and a lot of times that makes things seem easy. Some Carpenters songs sound simple. Well, they're not. Even a song like "Top of the World" is not simple. Of course, Karen sang effortlessly. But once these artists started taking the songs apart, I can see how their appreciation might have grown.

When you think of bands influenced by the Carpenters, Babes in Toyland and Sonic Youth don't come immediately to mind. What's your take on how you might have influenced these artists?

It could be they just heard the songs on the radio and liked 'em. If you look back at the early '70s, you had Led Zeppelin and the Carpenters and the audience said, "I like both." That's something that tends to be forgotten today.

A lot of these artists seemed to relate to what they see as the "dark side" of the Carpenters—the sadder songs, the melancholy in Karen's voice.

The songs were selected first on the melody. If that got me, then I'd listen to the lyric. Karen's voice did have a built-in melancholia to it. It had a warmth, an intimacy, but also a sense of longing that really went beyond her years. You listen to Karen sing "Superstar" or "Rainy Days and Mondays" when she was maybe 21—she just sounds much older than that.

How did you like working with Matthew Sweet?

Oh, very much. Immediately simpatico. Very nice fellow. Talented, down-to-earth, and easy to talk with. Of course, we have a common interest in automobiles.

Matthew made a great comment regarding the atmosphere in the studio that day. He said it was like one of the Beatles came in.

Oh my. I can't imagine anyone feeling that way about me. I think most of us tend to think of ourselves as pretty average people. But I've met fans who actually shake in your presence and I think, "My God, it's just us. I mean, please settle down!" When Paul McCartney asked us to come by the studio in Manchester, we were world-famous and yet I took along my *Band on the Run* album to have him sign.

The idea for this record came from reading appreciative comments by k.d. lang, Chrissie Hynde and others in the press. Were you aware of this new generation of fans?

Oh yeah, through the years people would mention to me that they read an article, maybe k. d. lang—of course, I'm a big fan of k.d., and it doesn't surprise me she'd be a fan of Karen's—and Gloria Estefan, Michael Jackson, Chrissie Hynde.

What would Karen have thought of If I Were a Carpenter?

She'd like it for the same reasons I like it—that the people involved thought enough of our music or her talent to take time out of their schedules to contribute, and that there continues to be, after all these years, so much interest in our music.

Back at the peak of your popularity in the '70s, what did you think the Carpenters' legacy would be 20 years later?

We didn't think about it—there was no time to think about it. But now that I've been asked that a couple of times, I can say I'm not surprised at the length of time the music has remained popular. It was never really trendy music and Karen has a timeless voice. What surprises me now, as maybe it did then, is the degree of the interest. Especially in the UK. I hear from people just how big we still are there. There's a sound-alike act that sold out the London Palladium.

So there are Carpenter imitators?

Yeah, this one outfit—a guy and a girl—sent me a DAT, and they're very good. The lady is in Karen's vocal register, and the chap has the arrangements down. I mean I've heard some sound-alike things through the years, like this one from Japan called the "Car-Painters," and it's all off; the inversion on the intro to "Close to You," "Goodbye to Love," forget it! But these two, it's nuts on, right down to Tony Peluso's guitar solo. I was quite impressed. But I guess the whole thing continues to be a phenomenon over there.

I was told by someone at A&M that the label does three to four new Carpenter collections each year.

And I end up putting them together! We're down there right now doing a six-volume set for Japan. Six CDs! And I think, "What more could anyone want?" It's the same stuff! And I just got a note from a fellow at Rondor Music wanting me to know that for the year ending 1993, the Carpenters were still Rondor's biggest selling act in Southeast Asia. I guess, in a sense, I have to feel a little vindicated. I'm not saying everybody should like this stuff; I just think early on we were a little unfairly treated in dismissing us as bubblegum and lightweight. I remember one British article saying, "It's middle-America hokum, and I say to hell with it!" [*Laughs*] Could you make yourself a little more clear?

Will the die-hard, card-carrying Carpenter fan club member like this record?

Probably not. I could be all wrong, but I tend to be, maybe because I'm a musician, open to a lot of different sounds if they're done well and honestly. I hope the "card-carrying" fan opens up their mind and appreciates the intent behind this, and the work that went into it. But I know some of the mail I get, if I just remix something, they'll say, "How could you remix this? It's classic stuff!" Well, it's *my* classic stuff!

How does it feel to be doing all these press interviews again?

I can do without it. I've said all I have to say about Karen's personal problems. There's nothing new I can add. And I want Karen to be remembered for a little more than having died of anorexia. So the only reason I've agreed to do what I've done for this is because it's more about the music.

This record was truly a labor of love for both Matt and me. Do you think it makes a fitting 25th anniversary celebration for the Carpenters?

It's certainly different, fresh and inspired. And I wanted to thank both you and Matt for the idea and the work you've put in on this.

POP CHARTS

HOW RICHARD CARPENTER'S LUSH ARRANGEMENTS TURNED HIT SONGS INTO POP CLASSICS

Daniel J. Levitin

Electronic Musician, 1995

A distinguishing feature of pop tunes in the '60s was their lush horn and string arrangements. A good arrangement not only brings texture to a composition, it can also go a long way to setting the right mood and adding excitement to the tune. One of the most gifted arrangers to emerge in popular music is Richard Carpenter, one half of the Carpenters the duo he formed with his sister Karen.

While Karen drew most of the attention as the vocalist, Richard's behind-the-scenes contributions to the Carpenters' success are immeasurable. He acted as A&R man, selecting tunes, he wrote many of their hits (such as "Yesterday Once More" and "Top of the World"), and he played keyboards. In addition to these roles, he also arranged and orchestrated nearly all of their recorded output. It is these contributions as an arranger that have earned him a reputation among insiders as one of the best pop arrangers of all time. Five nominations for a "Best Arrangement" Grammy testify to this.

"The arrangement is *everything*," Richard explains. "No one could think more of Karen than I do, but you can have the best singer on the planet and the best song, but if you don't have the right arrangement for that song, the singer's going nowhere and neither is the song. The arrangement is everything that makes a hit record."

A good arrangement becomes inseparable from the song itself. Subsequent artists who cover such a tune find themselves keeping these arrangement ideas, because performing the song without them is unimaginable. Try to imagine the Rolling Stones' "Satisfaction" without the distorted guitar lead at the beginning, or U2's "New Year's Day" without the heavily reverbed piano intro.

What made Carpenter's arrangements so clever and musical, and how did he come up with them? One characteristic of his work is that he gives each instrument a unique place, not just in the frequency spectrum, but also in time. Featured instruments weave in and out of the spotlight, filling holes where necessary, but never stepping on each other. The different parts of his arrangements lock together to form a seamless whole.

A case in point is the Leon Russell/Bonnie Bramlett composition, "Superstar," one of Carpenter's most beautiful arrangements. The song was first recorded on Joe Cocker's *Mad Dogs and Englishmen* album with Rita Coolidge on vocals and Leon Russell on piano. But Richard first heard its potential as a Carpenters single when a then barely known Bette Midler sang it on the Johnny Carson show. Richard's arrangement introduced lots of new music that has become so identified with the song, so inseparable from the melody, that when people go back and hear the other versions, they're overwhelmed by the sense that something is missing from them.

Carpenter starts off with a harp glissando using the Eb (V) major scale (the song is in Ab). The gliss starts on F and ends on G a 9th above, as the strings come in on an F (vi) minor chord. Just as the harp reaches its G, Richard introduces an opening theme he wrote, played on the oboe. At first the theme anticipates the first few notes of the vocal melody which enters nine bars later, and then it evolves to an entirely new melody, a sort of variation of the main vocal line.

As the oboe decrescendos in bar 5, Richard brings in a three-part French horn line, which ends on an F minor (in second inversion) in bar

8. But you won't find this last chord anywhere but the old vinyl version of their third album; Richard recently added three more horn voices to the track using Kurzweil horns, putting the 10th on the bottom; and it is this version that was pressed onto all CD versions of the tune. "We'd play Vegas a couple of times a year," Richard explains, "and our conductor in Vegas, Dick Palombi, came up with this idea. He said, 'Have you ever tried filling out the arrangement?' And he played it for me on the piano and it was beautiful, so I said, 'Do it!' So he wrote that into the charts and from then on—this was '72 or '73—we did it that way. When we remixed the song for the *Yesterday Once More* album, I didn't want to hire a band just for that one chord on the remix, so I played the Kurzweil, adding it to the existing horns."

Notice next, in bar 9 [00:20 on the CD], how Richard sets up the main rhythmic theme for the song, a dotted quarter-eighth-half note rhythm on the kick drum and bass, doubled on the left hand of the piano for a really fat, and commanding, sound. Enhancing the fatness of the sound is the way the bass comes into bar 9 by dropping an octave—when Joe Osborn finally hits his low F from an octave above, it sounds like the lowest note you've ever heard.

This introduction to the tune is very carefully crafted to set the mood, and uses orchestral instruments to provide a lush texture. Richard's opening oboe theme is all most people need to hear to recognize the song. Two groups recently covered the song—Sonic Youth (on the *If I Were a Carpenter* tribute album) and Chrissie Hynde (under the pseudo-band name "Superfan," from the *Wayne's World* [2] soundtrack album)—and they left Richard's intro line untouched.

Richard's use of "call and response" lines is also classic, and typical of his approach to creating cohesion between different instrumental parts. At the top of the second verse [00:52] Karen sings the lyric "your guitar" on the notes G-F-C (recognize this from the oboe intro?), and this line is then immediately echoed by the violins.

For the chorus, Richard pulls out all the stops. Hal Blaine's drum fills coming into bar 26 ("B" on the chart) are accented by Richard's frenetic electric piano fills. A tambourine plays 16th notes throughout the chorus, adding to the rhythmic build. Karen sings the first line of the chorus, "Don't you remember you told me you loved me, baby," which is answered by the trumpets in bar 27 with a horn fill that is one of the most recognizable signature lines in all of pop music, filling the space between vocal lines with a bright, Tijuana Brass–type fanfare. To many, it would be unthinkable to perform the song without this line. Although Chrissie Hynde left it out, Sonic Youth kept it, transferring it to piano.

Coming out of the first chorus, a 10-bar interlude parallels the intro, complete with harp glissando [1:35] and the obbligato oboe. Notice that this second time through the theme, Richard's grand piano echoes the oboe line in octaves in "call and response" style.

Another interesting part of the track is Karen's vocal performance. Listen to the way she sings the words "far away" [from 00:34–00:37 on the CD]—while holding the word "away" she brings out a subtone in her voice that conveys deep and troublesome emotions. Richard knew her range incredibly well, and his choice of key made moments such as this possible. Karen was also a master at phrasing—in the subsequent words, "I fell in love with you," she sings just behind the beat—not unlike Sinatra—playing around with the time to impart more depth to the vocal.

Another of Richard's witty arrangements is the brass part for the Paul Williams/Roger Nichols tune "Let Me Be the One," also from their third album, *Carpenters*. Scored for three trumpets and two trombones, in bar 5 of the tune Richard writes horn hits on beat 2 and on the "and" of beat 3. These propel the song rhythmically into bar 6, where the usual thing to do would be to repeat the rhythm. But instead, Richard delays the bar 6 entrance by half a beat, putting the next hits on the "and" of beat 2 and straight on beat 4. This lack of symmetry takes the listener by surprise and spices up the rhythm of the arrangement. Note also how Richard voices the sus4 chord in bar 8 for a fat sound: the trombones take the root and 7th, while the trumpets cluster tightly with the sus4, seventh and octave.

Richard usually knew exactly what he wanted, and he was not afraid to be stubborn about getting it. For most of the tunes, Richard didn't just write out parts for orchestral instruments, but he wrote out all the drum beats, too—the kick, snare, hat and crash—in most cases leaving the fills for the drummer to improvise. On "Let Me Be the One," however, Richard knew exactly what he wanted. "To me, the fill [into bar 5] had to go 'tiba-dump, dump,' so I wrote it out that way."

Richard also wrote out the bass parts, and wrote out certain fills the way he wanted them, too. At first, this approach ruffled session bassist Joe Osborn. "At first, Joe wasn't a big fan of mine," Richard recalls. "He was hot on Karen and just put up with me—I don't think he really wanted me around. I wrote a fill for him, note-for-note for 'Crystal Lullaby' and he looked at it and he said, 'I can't do that. The bass won't go that high.' And I said, 'Of course it'll go that high!' Now when he was doing the Mamas and Papas and 'Never My Love' [the Association] and 'Travelin' Man' [Ricky Nelson] and all that, he could never read a note—he was just a natural musician. And the producers would put up with him learning the songs on the spot because he was so damn good. But a chart meant nothing to him. So they'd play him the demo or sing it to him—John Phillips would play him 'California Dreamin''—until he learned it. It finally got to him and so he taught himself—or had someone teach him—how to read. He was reading by the time he worked with us. And I'll tell you, once he learned how to read, he was among the best in the business. That 'Man Smart (Woman Smarter)' thing, where it starts on the downbeat and yet it sounds like a pick-up, 'ba-bomp'—when we counted that off, and it was a room full of good musicians—the only person who came in was Joe Osborn. You know, just like the theme from *The Apartment* sounds like it's starting on a pick-up, you can't tell where the downbeat is. So we'd written out this part and he played it and of course it worked fine. And as soon as that was done, he said 'You're a genius!' And I said, 'I'm not a genius, Joe. All I did was write what I pictured you doing!'"

This is one of Richard's arranging secrets: he loves certain players, and he'll write parts just the way he imagines they would play them. For the flugelhorn solo in "Close to You," for example, Richard tried to imagine how Herb Alpert would play a part written by Burt Bacharach. When it came time to do the session, though, Alpert wasn't available so they brought in Chuck Findley. But Richard had written out the way Herb would naturally bend notes at the end of phrases [see score in bars 38–40]. "Chuck didn't play it that way at first, but I worked with him and he nailed it. A lot of people thought it was Herb—Bacharach thought so, too. But it's the way Findley is playing it."

"Arranging the ending of that tune was a problem for me," Richard continues. "I hate fade-outs and try to avoid them. Now we had the background vocals doing the 'wah-ah-ah-ah-ah' part and then what should come next? Well, again, I thought, 'How would Bacharach do this?' He often had these kinds of trick endings, like at the end of "Raindrops Keep Fallin' on My Head" [*sings ending of "Raindrops"*]. Completely new music. Why is it there? Well, why shouldn't it be there? It makes it! It's a neat part. In fact, the best part of the record. And obviously, that's why we ended the song with the wahs—they're an important part of that record. Then in rehearsal, Karen came up with the idea to push [syncopate] the third one and *that* is great." Of course, the Cranberries' new version of the song retains the "wah" background vocals. How could they not?

"I never really learned how to technically orchestrate," Richard says. "There's a credit that says 'Special Thanks to Ron Gorow.' Ron is an actual orchestrator, and a hell of a nice guy, and he understands my idiosyncrasies and we've been working together for over twenty years. I would usually work out all the instrumental parts on a piano and then Ron would sit next to me and write down what I played! I write music, of course, but I never spent so much time at it that it became second nature the way it is for Ron. Plus, I always felt it was a bore to sit down to write out music!"

In general, Richard works from the general to the specific, sketching out some rough ideas and filling them in later. "When I'm just starting the arrangement, I'll listen to the song and I'll think, 'I want the strings to come in here.' I can't tell you at that point in time what exact notes they're going to be, but I know I want strings. I'll know also whether it's going to be a single line or a pad.

"To me, the best things are inspired things that just fall out. Of course, this goes for writing tunes, too. Nichols and Williams said they wrote 'We've Only Just Begun' in something like four minutes. And it didn't take much longer for me to write 'Yesterday Once More.' When I was arranging 'Superstar,' for example, that horn lick [*sings the horn part from bar 27*] was just there—I didn't have to stop and think about it. As soon as I heard 'don't you remember you told me you loved me, baby' I heard 'ba-da-da-dap-da-da-da-da' in my head."

Carpenter says another crucial aspect of arranging is to pay a great deal of attention to the key, optimizing it for the singer. This means getting to know your singer's capabilities and deficiencies intimately.

In the old days, when he arranged everything on the piano, he says he would "just picture it, and cross my fingers! Now, of course, with what I have in the other room [*his current home studio—see "Carpenter's Tool Box" on page 306*], I can take home a rough [mix], lay down a track and futz with strings and brass all I want.

"It's so much easier now, with modern technology, because I can get some semblance of what the string parts are with my synths, even though they certainly can't duplicate them. But back then, there was nothing—I just had to envision them. There's a setting on the [Roland] D50 I like called 'Arco Strings' and it's not as buzzy as some of the other ones. The buzzy ones really bug me. With the synths I can fine-tune an arrangement more. And I can get it so I know exactly what it is before we go into the studio with the real musicians. When you add MIDI and sequencers, you have a great tool. You can fiddle around with things at home before you get to the studio, and of course stuff's so good these days that if you get proficient with the equipment you can just dump it onto the multitrack when you get to the studio.

"For an arranger and a keyboardist, just having a different sound'll bring out a different emotion, maybe a different series of chord changes. I can go to a Rhodes and immediately start playing something different than I would on a Baldwin, or a Steinway, or a Wurlitzer electric—because the sound brings out something different.

"I don't like the idea of becoming [a] fossil, because I used to be up on all the new technology. It's scary how fast things have changed. It doesn't seem that long ago that the Arp Odyssey [analog synthesizer] came out. I kept mine; I figured I'd show it to my kids someday. It seems like all anybody got out of that thing was that one sound, you know, like at the end of Emerson, Lake and Palmer's 'Lucky Man': 'oo-wee-oo, wee-oo, wee-oo.' "

In summary, the key to good arranging, according to Richard, starts with these steps: (1) Find a song you really like. (2) Make sure the key is exactly right for the singer. (3) If the arrangement doesn't just "fall in your lap" through pure inspiration, build it up slowly, working from general ideas to more specific ones. (4) Weave instrumental and background vocal parts in and out of each other, and in and out of the lead vocal. Don't bury parts by having too many things going on at once. Let

the arrangement echo forward and backward to other parts of the song.
(5) Don't be afraid to stubbornly insist that players give you what you
really want to hear.

CARPENTER'S TOOL BOX

Richard's home studio is warm and comfortable, and is built into the
bottom floor of his Southern California home. Equipment includes a
Yamaha Upright Acoustic ("I love these because they have the dampers,
the 'apartment mode' so I can play after the kids are in bed"), Yamaha
electric piano, Soundtracs 32 x 8 x 8 console, Alesis ADAT, Roland R8M
and JB880 sound modules, Proteus II, Emax II, Peavy Bass module,
REV7, Quadraverb, SPX900, Mac Centrus 650, Performer, Finale, Tan-
noy SGM10-B speakers, Alesis 3630 compressor, SV3700 DAT, [and a]
Hafler power amp.

KAREN CARPENTER'S "LOST" LP

Jerry Crowe

Los Angeles Times, 1996

K aren Carpenter didn't live long enough to see her only solo album released, and it didn't look as if her fans around the world would live long enough either.

A&M Records has kept *Karen Carpenter,* a 12-song collection, locked away for [16] years.

But after a 1994 Carpenters tribute album—featuring versions of the group's hits by such acts as Sheryl Crow, Sonic Youth, Matthew Sweet and the Cranberries—sparked renewed interest for the duo's work, A&M will release the solo package on Oct. 8.

"Interest in the Carpenters has never waned; it has only varied in degree from one time to another," says Diana Baron, a senior vice president at A&M. "Since the release of *If I Were a Carpenter* two years ago, we've experienced a wave of renewed interest from fans. . . . This record is for them."

Recorded in 1979, four years before Carpenter died at age 32 of heart failure caused by anorexia, the solo album offers a rare glimpse at a looser side of a singer best known for her ultra-sweet romantic ballads and wholesome girl-next-door image.

The collection includes three disco tunes, a reworking of Paul Simon's "Still Crazy After All These Years," a duet with Chicago's Peter Cetera and even a country ballad.

"She was one of those amazing vocal talents—and a very interesting girl, a lot deeper than a lot of people gave her credit for," says eight-time Grammy winner Phil Ramone, who produced the record. "She was really at a phase in her life where I think she was facing womanhood and . . . needed to expand her horizons.

"Like anybody who comes out of a group, it was time for her to express herself as a vocalist, and also to show that . . . maturity was setting in. The goody-two-shoes thing, I think, was getting to be a problem for her. Not on a personal level, but career-wise."

The album concept came about when Richard Carpenter, Karen's older brother and musical partner, announced in 1979 that he wanted to take the year off after a hectic recording and performing pace that established the duo as the most successful US pop group of the '70s. [. . .]

Karen, though, couldn't imagine sitting around for a year.

"It was OK for a little bit," she told an interviewer in 1981, "but then, I was anxious to go back to work."

She denied rumors that the album was part of a plan to eventually sever ties with her brother.

Herb Alpert, the label co-founder who had signed the Carpenters to A&M, put her together with Ramone, whose work with Billy Joel, Kenny Loggins and Paul Simon had made him one of the hottest and most respected producers in the industry.

"I thought it was strange in a way [to be picked] because the collection of artists I was working with at the time [was] a little more tough and a little less middle of the road," Ramone says. "But it was her vocal ability that attracted me and made me feel that we could work together."

The producer and singer listened to hundreds of songs before selecting about 20 to record. Among the tunes that made the album were two by Rod Temperton.

"It was fun cutting it and seeing that I could do all that, sing a different type of tune and work with different people," Carpenter said in 1981. "I wasn't sure if I could do it myself."

She and Ramone were happy with the initial results, and A&M added the album to its 1980 release schedule. But when recording dragged on, Richard started getting itchy to return to work. The record was subsequently shelved because Karen had decided that her work with Richard should take precedence and that she didn't want her solo record to interfere with the Carpenters' projects.

"You obviously get disappointed," Ramone says of his reaction at the time. "Timing is important on a record release. I blame myself for some of the songs sounding a bit dated now, but it was recorded at the time of *Saturday Night Fever* and all those other disco hits. When it didn't come out, I thought, 'Oh, damn. This won't have a long shelf life.'"

Richard Carpenter, who has included alternate versions of six of the record's tracks on Carpenters retrospectives, has endorsed the album's release. And even though the disco-heavy tracks seem stuck in a time warp, Ramone also is pleased to see it finally come out.

"I hope her fans will excuse some of it," Ramone says, "but I don't apologize for any of it. I know how she felt about it, and I know how I feel. I still feel good about it. Some of the songs on there are definitely mature works—and worthy of Karen Carpenter."

ALBUM REVIEW

KAREN CARPENTER

Tierney Smith

Goldmine, 1997

When Karen Carpenter began recording her first solo record in the spring of 1979 with producer Phil Ramone, the aim was to broaden her musical appeal by trying for sounds not normally heard on a Carpenters album. (Though Ramone evidently did not want to stray too far from their signature sound; lush Carpenters-style vocals are all over the place here and the overall feel is distinctly mellow.) Less-than-enthusiastic reactions from brother Richard and some A&M execs, though, convinced Karen to shelve the project.

Now that the record has seen the light of day, one thing is certain— her best work was well behind her at that point. The record does, however, have its moments. Backed by Billy Joel's band, the record's saving grace is Carpenter's always warm and expressive vocals: She brings a sweetness to the buoyant, gently ringing pop of Peter Cetera's "Making Love in the Afternoon," shines on the lovely understated country ballad "All Because of You" and sounds right at home with the infectious mellow pop of "Guess I Just Lost My Head."

On the other hand, Ramone was obviously making a concerted attempt to steer Carpenter away from her established wholesome image (though the issue of whether the public was really clamoring to see Carpenter cast as sex siren is open to question). The results were awkward to say the least—"Still in Love with You," the only rock 'n' roll track here, is the worst offender ("I remember the first time I laid more than eyes on you" goes one line, replete with the singer's breathy little coos and tics—the effect is utterly false, as though Carpenter were forcing herself to play a very uncomfortable role). The perky pop of "Remember When Lovin' Took All Night" and the lame disco of "My Body Keeps Changing My Mind" continues these odd, unconvincing attempts at crafting Carpenter a new image. Clearly, her squeaky clean image preceded her, and rather than alter it, Ramone would have instead done well to honor it.

The real, unaffected Karen does manage to come through in the earnest tenderness she brings to "Make Believe It's Your First Time." Mostly though, she's saddled with bland, adult contemporary numbers including Rod Temperton's "Lovelines" and "If We Try." It didn't help that the fine body of work that preceded this solo effort made Carpenter a prime candidate for raised expectations.

AN INTERVIEW WITH RICHARD CARPENTER

Greg Rule

Keyboard, 1998

What was the inspiration behind [Richard Carpenter:] Pianist, Arranger, Composer, Conductor?

I was asked by our affiliate in Japan, Polydor, to put it together. They asked for an album with piano, orchestra, and some vocal arranging after the remarkable new success of the Carpenters starting in late 1995 through '96 and continuing as we speak. Since we'd sold well over two million copies of *Twenty-Two Hits of the Carpenters*, they wanted the bulk of it to be those songs. At first, I wasn't quite certain, then I got to thinking, "Well, Burt [Bacharach] is a producer and arranger. He produced records for a number of people—Dionne, Herb Alpert—and then every year or so he put out an album where he played the same songs, but reinterpreted them mostly as instruments."

Describe the steps you went through as you started to make the new arrangements. Was it in this room with sheet music?

It was in this room without sheet music. I figured out without spending very much time which songs I wanted. There are certain ones of ours that I didn't exactly care for as instrumentals. So I picked a number of ones I felt had a great deal of melodic sweep that would work for this approach, and a couple of album cuts such as "One Love." Then I mapped the whole thing before we ever set foot in the recording studio. Rather than record ten or 12 or however many and then say, "Well let's see how we're going to sequence them," the whole thing was designed almost to play as a suite. "Prelude" has the bridge of the ending track "Karen's Theme." Then each thing kind of flows into the next. It was all planned that way.

Planned by mentally visualizing the end result?

Yes. I can visualize mentally . . . especially working on my orchestral parts. Even though I have all this [synth and sequencing] stuff, I go right back to the piano. I guess I'm just an old dog. [*Laughs.*]

How did you save those ideas? Pen and paper or computer?

No. I wouldn't even know how to put it into a computer, even though I had good intentions when I got into all this stuff. But, as I've said, and as [Paul] McCartney says, "If you can't remember something that you came up with the night before, then it wasn't worth saving." And that's true! So I would store this stuff mentally and make some changes to be written later, but not the piano parts; I never bothered writing those down. I just went and played them. I wanted to record the piano first to keep everything leakage proof. Being that the music was rubato in places, I was picturing where the orchestra was going to come in, how much a ritard there was going to be, and playing the piano first that way.

Not too many people can do that.

It was a bit of a trick, I'll tell you. But it worked.

Where did you record?

Capitol [Studio] A. A few tracks have bassist Joe Osborn and drummer Harvey Mason. Well of course Joe goes direct into the booth and it didn't call for much drumming. The rest of it was just at the piano.

Some of them, like the medley, start and have to go all the way through. When it got to the one rhythm part in "Superstar," the hook, I cued, the click started, and Joe and Harvey played; there's no piano on that. I just waited for it to go by, and then when it got to [sings "dee-da-da-dee"], click off, and I started playing again.

I was going to ask you if you used clicks or not.

Well, yeah, you know Murphy—Murphy's Law. Even if you're doing your best out there, the click drags. [*Laughs*] I didn't want to take that chance. So we set it right where I wanted it. It was almost like recording sessions from many moons ago when artists were actually cutting records. If you made one mistake, you stopped and started all over again. And when you're dealing with digital of course, it's not so easy to splice. So [the medley] was the hardest obviously because it's so long [12:13]. But we ended up under budget, and came out all right.

When you showed up to do those piano tracks, were you very particular about what type of piano, mics, placements, and so on?

Yes. We used the AKG 414s. Capitol has a particularly good nine foot Yamaha. It's been there awhile. It's been played by a lot of people with heavier touches than I. It needed a little work at first. When we got there to record I said, "I can't use this." Certain parts of the action were rattling and it hadn't been evened out. Our engineer said, "This doesn't show up with much of what we usually do here." So Keith Albright [tuner] spent quite a bit of time with it and got it to sound pretty good, although, I hear one note still that sticks out on the album. So next time we'll be even more particular. It's tough, you know, to get any piano with 88 notes that are consistent. It's next to impossible no matter who builds it. Yamahas record well. I'm not wild about them live, but they do record well.

After the basic piano and rhythm tracks were done, what came next? The orchestra?

Yes. We did the strings separately in [Studio] A, a fairly good sized room. Then we brought in brass and wind and separated them. The percussion and the harp were done separately—all to make it as clean as could be.

Were you recording to analog or digital tape?

Digital, 32 track.

And everything went down pretty dry to tape in terms of effects?

Oh yeah! I am not one to put any effects on the actual tracks. Never have been.

What about room ambience?

[Studio] A has just the right amount of ambience for an orchestra. But I still like an in-your-face piano sound. If you listen to our mixes of the Carpenter stuff, the kick, vocal, everything, it's in your face. And I wanted the piano that way. If we wanted a little effect, well then we could work with that in the mix. You certainly don't want to marry it. It will come back to haunt you.

And the vocal tracks were the final elements you added?

Pretty much so. There were overdubs, and of course I sang with them. I got a big kick out of doing that.

In the A&E Biography *on the Carpenters, there was vintage footage of you and Karen recording overdubs for "Hurting Each Other." It made me wonder if you used a similar, ultra-thick layering technique this time around.*

Well, it's different from the Carpenter sound, of course, because that was just the two of us. All those Carpenter vocals were sung originally two parts at a time, then we doubled and tripled them later. This was an actual studio group. It's the same type of vocal approach that Karen and I used; not a great deal of vibrato on the backgrounds. But even though it's my very same arrangement on the chorus of "Top of the World," there's a world of difference in the sound. Both of them are perfectly in tune, but with Karen and me there's that overdubbed familial sound.

About the tour . . . was it only scheduled for Japan?

Yeah. For openers. We did Tokyo, Fukoka, Osaka and a number of other cities. It went very well. The crowds were great, the theaters are lovely, and the orchestras were damn good. They really delivered.

In the A&E special, they showed clips of the tour where you were playing along with a video of Karen—reminiscent of how Natalie Cole did "Unforgettable" with her father onscreen. Was that a technical pain to sync to Karen's video onstage?

No. I'm used to accompanying Karen. Of course I was also accompanying myself. . . . There was a slight flam every now and again. But no, on the whole it wasn't very difficult. I just played and sang along with the videos.

Will you bring this show to the States?

Well we're working on it. I think the audience will actually get a big kick out of it. It's a lot of good music. And Mitzie and Ken Welch did a great job of putting the show together.

Tell us about the inspiration and the creation of the song "Karen's Theme."

Originally "Karen's Theme" was a cue for *The Karen Carpenter Story.* Maybe 40 seconds long, and that was it. I always liked it. It was written in '88, and the show aired January 1, 1989. But then when the time came to put this new album together I thought, "I'd really like to finish 'Karen's Theme.'" I came up with the bridge and third verse, so it was finished. Then I got to the beginning of the album and thought, "I want to come up with something a little bit different." And I came up with the *F* minor opening ["Prelude"] and just happened to go through a *B* half diminished and *Bb* over *C.* And I thought, "Hey, I could put the bridge of 'Karen's Theme' here." That way, if someone listens from the start to the finish it bookends the whole thing.

We understand there's a big Carpenters box set in the works.

Oh yeah! Bernie Grundman and I, along with Barry Korkin, the archivist over at A&M, are working on it. A Japanese request again. Eleven CDs, all digitally remastered from the original master tapes. All these

CDs that are out of the original album, they're off the TCMs. It was "Sherlock Holmes" time finding the actual original quarter inch in some cases.

Did you have to bake any in the oven?

I think only two out of all of them needed to be baked. On the whole the stuff survived fine. I know oxide had fallen off a split second of the '73 single mix of "Top of the World," just in the beginning, but very early on you can hear it on the *Singles* album. Just a little chunk of oxide missing. So we fixed that. Every now and again we went to a different source and just put in one bar where the oxide was missing. But I'm so glad they asked me because I had no idea that some of our masters were decimated, having certain hits pulled to various compilations over the years.

And will the box set be for Japan only?

Well, at the moment it's Japan only. But again, with the Internet, websites, and people typing saying, "This is available, that's available," I don't know. I think it should come out here. But who knows?

It was ten years between your two solo records. What occupied most of your time between '87 and '97?

Was it ten years? Well, working on the [TV] movie, producing other artists [Scott Grimes, Akiko Kobayashi, Veronique Beliveau], working on the [Ray Coleman] book, raising a family, having this house built and [preparing] any number of compilations for any number of countries. And, boom, all the time went by. I couldn't believe it. There's that old saying: As you get older the time goes quicker, which I know is impossible, but I'll be damned if it doesn't feel that way. So it's been ten years, but it's not going to be ten years 'til the next one.

What has your relationship with the piano been like through this period of time? Are you still a devout player daily?

No. I'd like to be. Again, with this, that, and the other thing I don't. Thankfully, I have a good memory, and a technique that comes back with just a little brushing up.

Looking into the crystal ball, what do you see yourself doing in the future?

Well, recording-wise I haven't thought about it yet. I think [John] Bettis and I are more than capable of writing memorable main titles for movies, things like that certainly, and just songs. After that I would start thinking about another album, because I really enjoyed it after all that time—instead of just putting together compilations. And it's nice that the interest in the Carpenters has not subsided.

I'm curious to know what your impressions [are] of the state of records today in general when you listen to the radio or catch a video, as compared to, say, 20 years ago?

I'm not happy! I just miss hearing some real instruments. So much synthesizer, so much, and on the ballads too. As k. d. lang pointed out in *Biography*, and it can be said about Como and Cole and Bing and others as well: Karen just sang the tune. No fooling around. No vocal acrobatics.

She just delivered it.

Just delivered it. Because it was a song worth delivering and a voice worth delivering it. The same applies to k.d. I think she's terrific. So I'm hearing too much what I consider bombastic ballads. I think they're longer than they should be. I guess I'm just too old school for that. "We've Only Just Begun" is all of three minutes and three seconds long.

"Yesterday" by the Beatles at two minutes something.

There you go! And you know it said what it had to say, which was plenty. So I think they tend to be overly long, overly bombastic, and certainly not the caliber of song that you used to hear years ago. Granted, some greatness has been getting through: "Colors of the Wind," and there are some others that are very soft ballads. They put a little survey card in the Japanese CDs asking, "Why did you buy this? What is your age? What is it you like most about it?" And one of the things they found out was . . . kids! They liked Karen's voice, obviously, but they also pointed out that they liked the vocals and that real instruments were used. They liked the real violins. They liked the real brass, and the real electric bass, if you will. They called it "neo acoustic." They called the Beatles "neo acoustic." And I said, "How can you call the Beatles neo acoustic?" "Well because they're actually playing an electric bass, an electric guitar, and not a synthesizer trying to be an electric guitar and electric bass." And I'm thinking, "My God, I am getting old!"

RICHARD CARPENTER SHOWS WHY HE'S STILL ON TOP OF THE WORLD

John Woolard

Long Beach Press-Telegram, 1997

We always knew Richard Carpenter was a good musician. But a good comedian? That we didn't know.

Kicking off his first public tour in years, Carpenter kept a near-capacity crowd happy Friday night [February 14, 1997] with his versatile performance at the Cal State Long Beach facility that he helped build and that carries his name.

Those in attendance at the 1,065-seat Carpenter Performing Arts Center were treated to a show that was musically, verbally and visually pleasing.

Accompanied by a 60-piece orchestra, a children's choir and overhead photos of his family, Carpenter looked little like a man who has spent much of the past decade or so at home in Downey helping to raise a young family.

Instead, dressed in a casually chic bowtie-less tuxedo with a Valentine's Day red handkerchief in a front pocket, he looked in mid-tour form. He not only performed well, but also related well to his fans.

Musically, Carpenter showed his virtuosity on the piano with deft handling of the new arrangements he has created for his soon-to-be-released album, *Richard Carpenter: Pianist, Arranger, Composer, Conductor.*

Working in unison with the orchestra, he mixed in renditions of well-known Carpenters hits such as "Superstar," "Yesterday Once More," "For All We Know," "We've Only Just Begun" and "Rainy Days and Mondays" with classical pieces by Debussy and Paganini.

For good measure, he threw in some Dixieland, some show tunes and a touching musical tribute to his late sister, Karen, with whom Carpenter recorded hit song after hit song in the late 1960s and '70s, winning three Grammy awards, an Academy Award for Best Song and earning 18 gold and platinum records.

Verbally, Carpenter was at ease with the audience, and funny. He drew laughs throughout the evening, especially with commentary about his desire for a new Ferrari (he's a car collector) and—perhaps in deference to his upcoming March tour of Japan—a routine about sumo wrestling in which he reveals his legs.

Well, you had to be there.

Visually, overhead screens were put to good use, showing interesting close-ups of Carpenter's hands during such tunes as "Dizzy Fingers." They also offered up a well-produced montage of photographs of Richard, Karen and their parents, the late Harold and Agnes Carpenter.

The displays were touching reminders of Carpenter's past, but those in the crowd were not drawn into a sense of pathos. If anything, it gave the opposite impression—that Richard Carpenter is alive and well and happy to be back on stage.

The most impressive part of the evening was the end, when Carpenter paid tribute to his sister, who died of anorexia nervosa in 1983.

Carpenter closed with the audience participating in "Top of the World."

"It's great that I'm up here looking at you," Carpenter said. "And it's even better that you're out there looking at me."

Back at ya, Richard.

RAINY DAYS
FOR A SUNNY GIRL

NEW BOOK EXPLORES SINGERS'
PRIVATE TORMENT

Sara Jordan

Midwest Today, 2010

Karen Carpenter's rich contralto voice, self-taught drumming, and lush multi-vocal harmonies, characterized the Carpenters' sound. But a grueling touring schedule, controlling mother, and living in the shadow of her brother would contribute to her untimely death. In Randy Schmidt's new book, *Little Girl Blue: The Life of Karen Carpenter*, the full and shocking details of Karen's life and career are chronicled for the first time. [. . .]

In this interview with *Midwest Today*, Schmidt discusses the many facets of the Karen Carpenter we never knew.

How did you first become interested in writing an account of Karen Carpenter's life?

When I was a teenager, I happened to watch the CBS television movie *The Karen Carpenter Story*, which aired in 1989. From the opening strains of

"Rainy Days and Mondays" I was hooked on Karen's voice. I had never heard anything quite like that. I'd never heard a voice with which I had such a connection. Shortly after watching that movie, I began collecting their albums and researching their lives and music.

Dionne Warwick was a friend of Karen's and she wrote the foreword for your book. How did you go about asking Dionne to participate in your book?

Strangely enough, I just sent an email through her website and received a response back within a couple of days. She was willing to participate from the beginning and said she was excited for the opportunity.

The Carpenters always had a very straight-laced persona. How much of that image did they try to fight in their career?

In the early days, they were giving some pretty honest interviews. They would talk about their opinions on religion and politics and all the things they were quickly told they weren't supposed to get into. They were given an image from the record label—whether it was intentional or not, I'm not sure. I don't think that A&M Records really knew how to market the Carpenters and they ended up stuck with this "goody four shoes" image. Their efforts to fight the image just backfired on them, though.

The records sold, regardless, but the image did create buyer awareness. There were a lot of closeted Carpenters fans in the '70s. No one would admit to owning a Carpenters album, but somehow they were selling in the millions and millions. There was a bit of a stigma in buying or owning a Carpenters album, but most of the people who were making fun of them had one of their albums in their own collection, too!

There's been a petition to have the Carpenters inducted into the Rock and Roll Hall of Fame, yet it seems like no one on the induction committee is very interested in inducting them. What do you think that stems from?

I think they are definitely considered to be what most people would call "pop" or "pop rock." In the past, it has been said the Carpenters are "not rock enough" to be in the Rock and Roll Hall of Fame. But then, other groups were inducted, like ABBA [a 2010 inductee], and they aren't exactly "rock" either. The inductees are definitely of a wide enough range of musical genres that there is room for the Carpenters in there—if they would just consider them.

I did an interview with Mike Curb, the head of Curb Records in Nashville. A bit of trivia—he dated Karen Carpenter for a period of time in the mid-1970s. He is very supportive of the idea of the Carpenters being in the Rock and Roll Hall of Fame and said they were right there on the charts with all of these heavy, hard-rocking groups in the '70s. Their style of music had an edge to it, he says—like the fuzz guitar solo on "Goodbye to Love." They were keeping up with everyone else on Top 40 radio at the time and often eclipsing them.

For fans who are familiar with Ray Coleman's book on the Carpenters, what would you tell them is strikingly different about your book?

The fact that *Little Girl Blue* is unauthorized makes the book quite a bit different from Ray Coleman's. Some people might be hesitant to pick up an unauthorized biography because, a lot of times, they're associated with scandal or done with a tabloid sort of approach. But this book is quite the contrary; it was definitely approached with a foundation of love and respect for Karen's legacy and her music.

I think the biggest difference is that there was not any participation by the Carpenter family. I know that Ray Coleman had quite a bit of trouble in trying to tell the story because everything he was writing had to go through Richard Carpenter for editorial approval. So it was very frustrating for him at times to try and tell the story he was getting from the people he was interviewing. If the story didn't match what Richard remembered or how he saw it, oftentimes it wasn't included in the book.

You interviewed former classmates, boyfriends, friends and associates. Do you feel that there was a general consensus to protect the Carpenter family in previous years, even at the expense of Karen's legacy?

I think people were more hesitant to give their full opinion and to talk freely when Agnes Carpenter was still alive (she died in 1996). I think it was out of respect for her. Or perhaps they were scared to talk.

The main sources for my book were Karen's close circle of girlfriends who, for the most part, had not been interviewed for previous books or documentaries. On occasion, they would be asked and, unless they were all on board for it, they wouldn't submit to interviews. After I was able to get one of them to commit, they began calling the others and saying things like, "Hey, I think he is doing a really good job with this," or "I think you're going to like his approach. There's not an agenda and it's not being controlled by the family." I think they finally thought, "It's okay now. It's been almost 30 years since Karen's death. Enough time has passed." People who weren't ready to talk fifteen years ago when Coleman's book came out were ready at this point.

Which friend, in particular, did you find was the hardest to pursue?

There were several. Her best friend, and matron of honor in her wedding, was a lady named Frenda Franklin (former wife of the Carpenters' manager, Ed Leffler). I tried off and on for eight years to get in touch with Frenda. Because she never answered or responded, I kept after her. Finally, just a few months before my deadline, she emailed me and invited me to her home for tea. We connected right away and she was very open with me about things no one would talk about. After Frenda, I think Terry Ellis—her boyfriend and almost fiancé—was most difficult to convince. He and Karen were very close to being married in the mid-'70s. Terry was a very informative source and was great, but he was very hesitant to begin with. Before he would commit to an interview, he wanted to know what my intentions were, what I knew already, and how I was going to approach certain subjects that had been skirted around in the past. I felt like he was interviewing me, to begin with.

What role did Karen's mother play in her illness and general well-being?

From the time Karen was a little girl, she was schooled in Agnes Carpenter's family philosophy that seemed to say, "We're all here to support Richard. Richard's the one with all the talent." Of course I'm paraphrasing here, but the family's goal seemed to be that Richard was to become a superstar. Everybody had to do their part to make that happen. That meant the parents taking on an extra job of washing cars on the weekends or sometimes taking on two jobs at a time for extra income. They did that so they could support his career. Along the way, Karen took her own interest in music, but I feel her interests were only supported because she could play back-up for Richard. She could play drums for him and sing along with his music, but Richard was still the star in their mother's eyes. This began to take its toll on Karen over the years because, naturally, she was extremely talented and wanted that same recognition and approval from her mom. But Agnes was pretty fond of Richard and, at the same time, maybe even a little unimpressed with Karen. Over the years, that hurt her.

According to Karen's friends, there was a hole in Karen's heart that couldn't be filled by the love of friends. Still, they tried to love her extra. That void couldn't be filled by adoring fans around the world that loved her music. It couldn't be filled by the love of a husband. It could only be filled by the love of a mother and that just wasn't there—at least not in the way Karen desired. Her friends feel that it was the mother-daughter relationship that seemed to manifest itself in the form of the eating disorder years later.

One of the things that was interesting to me—and this was echoed by quite a few of the sources that I interviewed—is that even after Karen became the obvious superstar in the forefront of the Carpenters duo, within the family, Richard was still thought to be the superstar and Karen his back-up. To all these adoring fans around the world, Karen was the star, but she couldn't get that same recognition within the home.

Her father seemed very passive with the mother. He seemed to love Karen, but was utterly powerless against that struggle. Why do you think he was so passive?

I think it was just his personality. He was the type of man that only spoke when spoken to or when asked for his opinion. Many times, when he would begin to give his opinion, Agnes would override it or chime in with her own opinions. That was evident in interviews through the Carpenters' entire career. Agnes was the type of woman who "wore the pants in the family," as they say. Harold just followed her lead. I think he was still a strong and silent, loving force in Karen's life, but he wasn't one to speak up or one to argue with his wife.

Richard has asserted that he believes Karen would have developed anorexia regardless of her profession. Do you feel that's true or is that just a way of covering up the family's actions?

I do agree with him on that—because of the family influences. I used to think that the pressures of fame had more to do with Karen's disorder. That could have contributed on some level. I can't imagine Karen—or anyone dealing with body image issues—singing in front of an audience of thousands of people and it not bothering her. But after conducting all this research and having visited with Karen's friends, I feel that the core of what caused this eating disorder within Karen would have been there, regardless of the fame. She would have still had the same family dynamics. So I do agree with Richard in that way. But whenever he says that, I don't think he is pointing the finger at his mother, whatsoever.

How was Karen able to maintain her voice during those low periods in her weight?

That's a good question. With a lot of malnourished people, dehydration sets in and the voice really starts to suffer. A voice has to be hydrated and kept healthy. The only thing I can think of is that she sang in such a low, rich register that it didn't have as much affect as if she had been a soprano and having to support really high tones. I can't imagine the abuse could have gone on much longer without taking its toll. That said, there's definitely a marked difference in Karen's voice from the time most of their hits were recorded around 1970 to 1973 or 1974. From 1981 to '82, there was a weakness to her voice. It was still beautiful—still stunning, and still recorded amazingly—but there was definitely a slight weakening of her voice over the years.

Do you think A&M records had an agenda for not releasing Karen's solo album?

Herb Alpert, Jerry Moss and others—those guys known as "the A&M brass"—all seemed to be behind Karen in the very beginning and even got her in touch with Phil Ramone, who produced the album. I do feel, though, at some point during the project, they changed their minds. Everything seemed to change when Richard decided he was ready to go back to work. I think Herb and Jerry got on board with him in order to get Karen back into that Carpenters duo frame of mind.

During playbacks for the solo album, the initial response on the East Coast was one of celebration. The champagne flowed and the congratulations were abounding. When it was played back on the West Coast, with Richard present, the mood was completely different. It's been described by Phil Ramone as a "deafening silence." There was no celebration, no champagne, just song after song with little or no response. I think that was a very hurtful thing for Karen to endure. She had poured so much of her heart, soul, time, energy and money into this project, only to have it shot down. I think there was fear from A&M. They knew they could have a successful solo artist in Karen Carpenter, but was it worth the possibility of losing this duo that had made so much money and been so successful over the years? I think Richard was able to convince A&M that Karen "going solo" may not be the best thing for the future of the Carpenters.

So Richard felt threatened by this album?

Yes, I think, to some extent. One of their close friends said that Agnes didn't seem threatened by Karen's solo album because she felt Richard would always make a better album with her than she could ever make on her own. In many ways, that was probably true, but Karen needed to break free. I think the family saw there was potential for Karen to go off and do her own thing. If that were to happen, what would be left for Richard? I don't think Karen would have broken ties with him or gone *exclusively* solo, but I do think there was that fear within the family. What would become of Richard if Karen went solo?"

What does this album say about what was going on in Karen's life in 1979?

I think she was seeking independence. She desired recognition for herself as an individual and was starting to say, "I'm grown and I have something to say." It was really the first assertion by her to do something on her own and it was definitely representative of a lot of things in her life. She wanted to be a little more sophisticated and a little less "Downey"—a little less goody-goody. This was her chance to break out, do something different and let her hair down a little. According to Frenda, this project was Karen's "Emancipation Proclamation."

The fact that the album did not see release in 1980 was critical. You can't judge the success of an album recorded in 1979 and 1980 when it's not released until 1996. That's a totally different audience. I really wish Karen would've had the chance to find out—on her own—whether the album was commercially viable instead of being told by Richard and the label it wasn't good enough. To be told that an album is un-releasable by the people you love and trust most in your life had to be crushing to her. I feel this was the first of several defeats over the final years of her life that contributed to her worsening condition.

Karen married Tom Burris on August 31, 1980. In your book, you shed light on more of the intimate details about the marriage and what made it fall apart. Do you think that was another turning point in her life that contributed to her death?

Karen was at such a vulnerable state when she met Tom that it was a recipe for disaster. She had just experienced the rejection of the solo album. I view her relationship with Tom as a rebound romance. It's not that she had been in another romance immediately before, but she had been dedicating all of her time, energy and love to the solo project. That was shot down and then, the next thing you know, she meets this guy and they moved very quickly. It ended up furthering the condition she was in.

Did Karen ever realize just how sick she was?

There came a time when she couldn't deny it any longer. Near the end of 1981, the Carpenters had just finished an international promo tour of several countries. Karen was under 80 pounds. She knew she was in trouble and wanted a prescription for healing—a bit of a quick fix, you might say. She knew she was too thin. She was layering her clothing to hide what she had done to herself. I understand she did not like to use the words "anorexia nervosa." Even so, this was really the first time she started to take ownership of the problem.

She began to seek help around that time. She had heard of a self-styled "eating disorder therapist" by the name of Steven Levenkron in

New York. He'd written a book called *The Best Little Girl in the World*, which had been made into a TV movie. This caught Karen's attention. She had read the book many times over, seen the movie, and was fascinated knowing this guy knew and understood what she had been battling. She sought treatment, but wanted to do it her way. She told Levenkron, in so many words, "Fix me."

How much of the therapy do you think actually helped the condition?

She was talking about it and opening up. That had to be healthy and therapeutic in some ways. What was not ideal was the timing. This was a time when even the people who were considered to be the "experts" hadn't been "experts" for more than a couple of years. No one really knew what they were dealing with. If only there had been an inpatient program that could have addressed all of her needs—something along the lines of a Betty Ford Clinic, but for eating disorders. Karen was visiting Levenkron for an hour a day, but in between visits, she was back to her old habits—using laxatives, diuretics, and thyroid pills to speed up her metabolism.

Do you think that Agnes Carpenter ever came to terms with how her coldness towards her own daughter contributed so much to Karen's demise?

Based on the research and interviews I conducted, Agnes never owned up to the fact that her actions may have, in some ways, contributed to Karen's insecurities. It seems obvious she was very much in denial.

Do you expect to hear from Richard?

I don't anticipate a response from him, but I would be open to discussing the book. Some of it is probably "fiction" in his eyes, but we all see things from varying perspectives.

Even after all these years, there seem to be so many wounds in that family and a consensus that "We tried. We did everything we could and it didn't work." I think fans just didn't quite buy that.

The book has stirred up a lot of emotions among the fans. Some are really upset about the things they're reading and even wish they could seek revenge. That was never my intention. I just wanted to put the story out there, but not point fingers at any one person or any one cause. I wanted to let people draw their own conclusions.

Are there any additional misconceptions about Karen you would like to clarify?

Karen was a very deep individual. She was as multilayered as any Carpenters recording. The press releases and television specials never really captured her depth as a person. She was an old soul—perceptive and understanding. There was a lot to her and I don't think the public was privy to that. The watered-down accounts of her life have contributed to that and they made her seem very one-dimensional. In reality, she was so funny and quirky. There are a lot of aspects to Karen that people didn't previously know about. I think *Little Girl Blue* shows the many different sides of Karen.

As a singer, no one really can compare. In my eyes, Karen Carpenter is the greatest singer and communicator of songs over the last century. She sang so effortlessly and with such simplicity. Most of all, she communicated her songs in every tiny detail, from the intonation to the phrasing and all the subtle nuances. There will always be a place in music for a voice like that.

ACKNOWLEDGMENTS

Grateful thanks to Yuval Taylor, senior editor at Chicago Review Press, and Cynthia Sherry, publisher, for saying yes to another Carpenters-related book. Thanks also to Kelly Wilson and Mary Kravenas.

Thanks to Jeff Bleiel for taking a chance on this idea the first time around and for your guidance all through the years. I am grateful to Daniel Levitin for agreeing to pen the foreword to this new edition and Peter Desmond Dawe for photo research assistance.

Much appreciation to my partner, Jaime Rodriguez, for the patience, dedication, and character voices supplied during the many hours spent poring over the manuscript—I couldn't have done this without you.

Thanks also to: Amanda Abbett, Mitchell Anderson, Carolyn Arzac, Gregory Barber, Rona Barrett, Frank Bonito, Ron Bunt, Donnie Demers, Downey City Library, Downey Historical Society, Bob Finholm, Cynthia Gibb, Sue Gustin, Jon Konjoyan, Joshua Mahn, Chris May, Andy McKaie, Jim O'Grady, Camryn Schmidt, Kaylee Schmidt, Linda Schmidt, Norma Segarra, Chris Tassin, Universal Music Group, Evelyn Wallace, and all those whose entertaining and insightful writings are contained herein.

CONTRIBUTORS

Dan Armstrong was a staff writer for the *Southeast News* in Downey, California.

Lester Bangs was an American music journalist, author, and musician. He wrote for *Rolling Stone*, *Creem*, and the *Village Voice* until his death in 1982.

Johnny Black is the author of *Jimi Hendrix: The Ultimate Experience* and a regular contributor to *Q*, *Mojo*, and *Hi-Fi News*. He lives in London.

Marcello Carlin has written extensively about music, both in print and online, since 2001 and also contributes to *Time Out*, *Uncut*, *The Wire* and other publications. His book, *The Blue in the Air*, was published in 2011. He lives in London.

Ray Coleman, former editor of the British pop music weekly *Melody Maker*, authored *The Carpenters: The Untold Story*, published in 1994. He also penned biographies on John Lennon and Eric Clapton. Coleman died in 1996 at the age of fifty-nine.

Jerry Crowe served as staff writer and sports critic for the *Los Angeles Times* for more than twenty years.

Digby Diehl is a Los Angeles–based arts critic and the founding book editor of the *Los Angeles Times Book Review*. He has been a literary correspondent for *Good Morning America* and written several nonfiction books. Diehl also wrote the liner notes for the Carpenters' *Singles* and *Passage* albums.

Sheryl Farber is a three-time Grammy-nominated entertainment archivist, writer, and editor. She coproduced the Rhino box set *One Kiss Can Lead to Another: Girl Group Sounds, Lost & Found*; has worked on hundreds of Rhino releases as editorial supervisor; and has written liner notes for several.

Rod Fogarty is a musician and writer based in the Toronto area. As a percussionist, he has recorded and toured with artists including Dizzy Gillespie, Ruth Brown, Jackie Wilson, Vince Guaraldi, the Coasters, and Chuck Berry.

Dean Gautschy was a staff writer for the *Los Angeles Herald-Examiner* and also wrote for a number of entertainment-oriented publications.

Ed Harrison was a writer and a reviews editor for *Billboard*.

Robert Hilburn was the pop music editor and a critic for the *Los Angeles Times* from 1970 to 2005. His memoir, *Corn Flakes with John Lennon and Other Tales from a Rock 'n' Roll Life*, was published in 2009.

Sara Jordan is a features writer for *Midwest Today*, a regional magazine published in Iowa.

David Konjoyan is the editor of *GRAMMY* magazine, the official publication of the National Academy of Recording Arts and Sciences. He was co–executive producer of the 1994 *If I Were a Carpenter* tribute album.

Daniel J. Levitin is a professor of psychology and music at McGill University in Montreal. He is the author of *This Is Your Brain on Music* and *The World in Six Songs*.

Frank H. Lieberman was commissioned to write a special Carpenters tribute supplement for the November 17, 1973, issue of *Billboard*. Following a long career as a publicist and journalist, Lieberman died in 2011 at the age of sixty-eight.

Fiona MacDougall interviewed numerous musicians and celebrities during her time as a staff writer for *'Teen* in the early 1970s.

Pat McGreevy was a staff writer for the *Southeast News* and *Downey Herald-American* before joining the *Los Angeles Times*.

Joel McNally was a columnist for the former *Milwaukee Journal*. At present, his opinion column can be read in the *Shepherd Express*, Milwaukee's alternative newspaper.

Dave McQuay was a music enthusiast who began his writing career in the Baltimore, Maryland, area. He was a columnist for the *Orange County Register* at the time of his death in 1993.

Ken Michaels was a staff writer for the *Chicago Tribune* in the 1960s and 1970s.

Ron Miller was a syndicated columnist and TV editor for the *San Jose Mercury News* for twenty-one years. He is also the author of *Mystery!: A Celebration*, the companion book to PBS's *Mystery!* TV series.

Bill Moran's career in radio spans more than thirty years on leading Los Angeles radio stations including KABC, KFI, KISS-FM and AM, and KGIL.

Nancy Naglin is a New York–based author and freelance writer.

Ted Naron is a musician and writer. He has won numerous creative awards in advertising with television work for United Airlines, Sony, General Motors, Kellogg's, and other clients. Additionally, he makes documentary films.

Tom Nolan is the author of *Ross Macdonald: A Biography* and *Artie Shaw, King of the Clarinet: His Life and Times*. His features and reviews appeared regularly in *Rolling Stone*, *Phonograph Record*, and many other publications. He lives in Los Angeles.

Frank Pooler is a professor emeritus at California State University–Long Beach. He is respected in both academic and professional music circles as a leading authority on choral music. His association with the Carpenters dates back to 1964, when Richard became accompanist for Pooler's CSULB University Choir. As orchestral director for the Carpenters, Pooler traveled with the group to Australia, Japan, Hong Kong, and England, as well as Lake Tahoe, Reno, and the White House.

Greg Rule is an audio programmer who has toured the world with the Eagles, Christina Aguilera, Jennifer Lopez, Don Henley, and others. His writing has appeared in *EQ* and *Keyboard* magazines.

Tierney Smith is a freelance music writer whose work has appeared in *Relix*, *Goldmine*, and other magazines.

Tom Smucker has been writing about pop culture and politics since the 1960s. His work has appeared in publications including *Fusion*, *Creem*, and the *Village Voice*.

John Tobler is a British rock music journalist, record company executive, and author of *The Complete Guide to the Music of the Carpenters*.

Charlie Tuna has worked as morning-drive personality for more stations and formats than anyone in Los Angeles radio history. He has been honored with a star on the Hollywood Walk of Fame and inducted into the National Radio Hall of Fame.

Stephen Whitty is a columnist and film critic who has contributed to *Entertainment Weekly*, *Cosmopolitan*, and other magazines.

Janet Wiscombe was a staff writer at the *Denver Post* and *Long Beach Press-Telegram*. She has also been a regular contributor to the *Los Angeles Times* and the *Los Angeles Times Magazine*.

John Woolard was a staff writer for the *Long Beach Press-Telegram*.

SELECTED DISCOGRAPHY

The Carpenters released ten traditional studio albums between the years 1969 and 1981. This selected discography refers to each original conception as first released on A&M Records in the United States. Singles from each album are noted, as are peak US chart positions for both albums and singles. Only the most significant posthumous releases and compilations (notably those containing previously unreleased material) are included. Also listed are Karen's and Richard's solo releases and other various issues.

CARPENTERS

Offering / Ticket to Ride   (A&M 4205)   1969 (#150)

Invocation / Your Wonderful Parade / Someday / Get Together / All of My Life / Turn Away / Ticket to Ride / Don't Be Afraid / What's the Use / All I Can Do / Eve / Nowadays Clancy Can't Even Sing / Benediction

SINGLES:

Ticket to Ride / Your Wonderful Parade (#54)

Close to You   (A&M 4271)   1970 (#2)

We've Only Just Begun / Love Is Surrender / Maybe It's You / Reason to Believe / Help / (They Long to Be) Close to You / Baby It's You / I'll Never Fall in Love Again / Crescent Noon / Mr. Guder / I Kept On Loving You / Another Song

SINGLES:

(They Long to Be) Close to You / I Kept On Loving You (#1)
We've Only Just Begun / All of My Life (#2)

339

Carpenters   (A&M 3502)   1971 (#2)

Rainy Days and Mondays / Saturday / Let Me Be the One / (A Place to) Hide-away / For All We Know / Superstar / Druscilla Penny / One Love / Bacharach-David Medley: Knowing When to Leave, Make It Easy on Yourself, (There's) Always Something There to Remind Me, I'll Never Fall in Love Again, Walk On By, Do You Know the Way to San Jose? / Sometimes

SINGLES:

> For All We Know / Don't Be Afraid (#3)
> Rainy Days and Mondays / Saturday (#2)
> Superstar / Bless the Beasts and Children (#2 / 67)

A Song for You   (A&M 3511)   1972 (#4)

A Song for You / Top of the World / Hurting Each Other / It's Going to Take Some Time / Goodbye to Love / Intermission / Bless the Beasts and Children / Flat Baroque / Piano Picker / I Won't Last a Day Without You / Crystal Lullaby / Road Ode / A Song for You—Reprise

SINGLES:

> Hurting Each Other / Maybe It's You (#2)
> It's Going to Take Some Time / Flat Baroque (#12)
> Goodbye to Love / Crystal Lullaby (#7)
> I Won't Last a Day Without You / One Love (#11)

Now & Then   (A&M 3519)   1973 (#2)

Sing / This Masquerade / Heather / Jambalaya (On the Bayou) / I Can't Make Music / Yesterday Once More / Oldies Medley: Fun, Fun, Fun; The End of the World; Da Doo Ron Ron; Deadman's Curve; Johnny Angel; The Night Has a Thousand Eyes; Our Day Will Come; One Fine Day / Yesterday Once More—Reprise

SINGLES:

> Sing / Druscilla Penny (#3)
> Yesterday Once More / Road Ode (#2)

The Singles 1969–1973 (A&M 3601) 1973 (#1)

We've Only Just Begun / Top of the World / Ticket to Ride / Superstar / Rainy Days and Mondays / Goodbye to Love / Yesterday Once More / It's Going to Take Some Time / Sing / For All We Know / Hurting Each Other / (They Long to Be) Close to You

SINGLES:

Top of the World / Heather (#1)

Horizon (A&M 4530) 1975 (#13)

Aurora / Only Yesterday / Desperado / Please Mr. Postman / I Can Dream, Can't I? / Solitaire / Happy / (I'm Caught Between) Goodbye and I Love You / Love Me for What I Am / Eventide

SINGLES:

Please Mr. Postman / This Masquerade (#1)
Only Yesterday / Happy (#4)
Solitaire / Love Me for What I Am (#17)

A Kind of Hush (A&M 4581) 1976 (#33)

There's a Kind of Hush (All Over the World) / You / Sandy / Goofus / Can't Smile Without You / I Need to Be in Love / One More Time / Boat to Sail / I Have You / Breaking Up Is Hard to Do

SINGLES:

There's a Kind of Hush (All Over the World) / (I'm Caught Between) Goodbye and I Love You (#12)
I Need to Be in Love / Sandy (#25)
Goofus / Boat to Sail (#56)

Passage (A&M 4703) 1977 (#49)

B'wana She No Home / All You Get from Love Is a Love Song / I Just Fall in Love Again / On the Balcony of Casa Rosada / Don't Cry for Me Argentina / Sweet, Sweet Smile / Two Sides / Man Smart (Woman Smarter) / Calling Occupants of Interplanetary Craft (The Recognized Anthem of World Contact Day)

SINGLES:

All You Get from Love Is a Love Song / I Have You (#35)

Calling Occupants of Interplanetary Craft / Can't Smile Without You (#32)

Sweet, Sweet Smile / I Have You (#44)

Christmas Portrait   **(A&M 4726)**   1978 (#145)

O Come, O Come Emmanuel / Overture: Deck the Halls, I Saw Three Ships, Have Yourself a Merry Little Christmas, God Rest Ye Merry Gentlemen, Away in a Manger, What Child Is This (Greensleeves), Carol of the Bells, O Come All Ye Faithful / The Christmas Waltz / Sleigh Ride / It's Christmas Time / Sleep Well, Little Children / Have Yourself a Merry Little Christmas / Santa Claus Is Coming to Town / The Christmas Song / Silent Night / Jingle Bells / The First Snowfall / Let It Snow / Carol of the Bells / Merry Christmas, Darling / I'll Be Home for Christmas / Christ Is Born / Medley: Winter Wonderland, Silver Bells, White Christmas / Ave Maria

SINGLES:

The Christmas Song / Merry Christmas, Darling

Made in America   **(A&M 3723)**   1981 (#52)

Those Good Old Dreams / Strength of a Woman / (Want You) Back in My Life Again / When You've Got What It Takes / Somebody's Been Lyin' / I Believe You / Touch Me When We're Dancing / When It's Gone (It's Just Gone) / Beechwood 4-5789 / Because We Are in Love (The Wedding Song)

SINGLES:

I Believe You / B'wana She No Home (#68)

Touch Me When We're Dancing / Because We Are in Love (#16)

(Want You) Back in My Life Again / Somebody's Been Lyin' (#72)

Those Good Old Dreams / When It's Gone (It's Just Gone) (#63)

Beechwood 4-5789 / Two Sides (#74)

Voice of the Heart   (A&M 4954)   1983 (#46)

Now / Sailing on the Tide / You're Enough / Make Believe It's Your First Time / Two Lives / At the End of a Song / Ordinary Fool / Prime Time Love / Your Baby Doesn't Love You Anymore / Look to Your Dreams

SINGLES:

Make Believe It's Your First Time / Look to Your Dreams
Your Baby Doesn't Love You Anymore / Sailing on the Tide

An Old-Fashioned Christmas   (A&M 3270)   1984 (#190)

It Came Upon a Midnight Clear / Overture: Happy Holiday, The First Noel, March of the Toys, Little Jesus, I Saw Mommy Kissing Santa Claus, O Little Town of Bethlehem, In Dulci Jubilo, Gesu Bambino, Angels We Have Heard on High / An Old-Fashioned Christmas / O Holy Night / (There's No Place Like) Home for the Holidays / Medley: Here Comes Santa Claus, Frosty the Snowman, Rudolph the Red-Nosed Reindeer, Good King Wenceslas / Little Altar Boy / Do You Hear What I Hear? / My Favorite Things / He Came Here for Me / Santa Claus Is Comin' to Town / What Are You Doing New Year's Eve? / Selections from "The Nutcracker" / I Heard the Bells on Christmas Day

SINGLES:

Little Altar Boy / Do You Hear What I Hear? (promo)

Lovelines   (A&M 3931)   1989

Lovelines / Where Do I Go from Here? / The Uninvited Guest / If We Try / When I Fall in Love / Kiss Me the Way You Did Last Night / Remember When Lovin' Took All Night / You're the One / Honolulu City Lights / Slow Dance / If I Had You / Little Girl Blue

SINGLES:

Honolulu City Lights / I Just Fall in Love Again
If I Had You / The Uninvited Guest (promo)

Interpretations: A 25th
Anniversary Celebration   (A&M 31454 0312 2)   1994

Without a Song (a cappella version) / Superstar / Rainy Days and Mondays / Bless the Beasts and Children / This Masquerade / Solitaire / When I Fall in Love / From This Moment On / Tryin' to Get the Feeling Again / When It's Gone / I Believe You / Reason to Believe / (They Long to Be) Close to You / Calling Occupants of Interplanetary Craft / Little Girl Blue / We've Only Just Begun

The Essential Collection:
1965–1997   (A&M 069 493 416-2)   2002

Disc 1: Caravan / The Parting of Our Ways / Looking for Love / I'll Be Yours / Iced Tea / You'll Love Me / All I Can Do / Don't Be Afraid / Invocation / Your Wonderful Parade / All of My Life / Eve / Ticket to Ride / Get Together / Interview / Love Is Surrender / Maybe It's You / (They Long to Be) Close to You / Mr. Guder / We've Only Just Begun / Merry Christmas, Darling / For All We Know

Disc 2: Rainy Days and Mondays / Superstar / Let Me Be the One / Bless the Beasts and Children / Hurting Each Other / It's Going to Take Some Time / I Won't Last a Day Without You / A Song for You / Top of the World / Goodbye to Love / This Masquerade / Sing / Jambalaya (On the Bayou) / Yesterday Once More / Oldies Medley: Fun, Fun, Fun; The End of the World; Da Doo Ron Ron; Deadman's Curve; Johnny Angel; The Night Has a Thousand Eyes; Our Day Will Come; One Fine Day / Yesterday Once More—Reprise / Radio Contest Outtakes

Disc 3: Morinaga Hi-Crown Chocolate Commercial / Please Mr. Postman / Santa Claus Is Coming to Town / Only Yesterday / Solitaire / Tryin' to Get the Feeling Again / Good Friends Are for Keeps / Ordinary Fool / Sandy / There's a Kind of Hush (All Over the World) / I Need to Be in Love / From This Moment On / Suntory Pop Jingle #1 / Suntory Pop Jingle #2 / All You Get from Love Is a Love Song / Calling Occupants of Interplanetary Craft / Sweet, Sweet Smile / Christ Is Born / White Christmas / Little Altar Boy / Ave Maria

Disc 4: Where Do I Go From Here? / Little Girl Blue / I Believe You / If I Had You / Karen-Ella Medley: This Masquerade, My Funny Valentine, I'll Be Seeing You, Someone to Watch Over Me, As Time Goes By, Don't Get

Around Much Anymore, I Let a Song Go Out of My Heart / 1980 Medley: Sing, Knowing When to Leave, Make It Easy on Yourself, Someday, We've Only Just Begun / Make Believe It's Your First Time / Touch Me When We're Dancing / When It's Gone (It's Just Gone) / Because We Are in Love (The Wedding Song) / Those Good Old Dreams / Now / Karen's Theme

As Time Goes By   (A&M 069 493 112-2)   2004

Without a Song / Medley: Superstar, Rainy Days and Mondays / Nowhere Man / I Got Rhythm Medley / Dancing in the Street / Dizzy Fingers / You're Just in Love / Karen-Ella Fitzgerald Medley: This Masquerade, My Funny Valentine, I'll Be Seeing You, Someone to Watch Over Me, As Time Goes By, Don't Get Around Much Anymore, I Let a Song Go Out of My Heart / Medley: Close Encounters, Star Wars / Leave Yesterday Behind / Carpenters–Perry Como Medley: Yesterday Once More, Magic Moments, Sing, Catch a Falling Star, Close to You, It's Impossible, We've Only Just Begun, And I Love You So, Don't Let the Stars Get in Your Eyes, Till the End of Time, No Other Love Have I / California Dreamin' / The Rainbow Connection / '76 Hits Medley: Sing, Close to You, For All We Know, Ticket to Ride, Only Yesterday, I Won't Last a Day Without You, Goodbye to Love / And When He Smiles

KAREN CARPENTER

Looking for Love
/ I'll Be Yours (single)   (Magic Lamp ML704)   1966

Karen Carpenter   (A&M 31454-0588-2)   1996

Lovelines / All Because of You / If I Had You / Making Love in the Afternoon / If We Try / Remember When Lovin' Took All Night / Still in Love with You / My Body Keeps Changing My Mind / Make Believe It's Your First Time / Guess I Just Lost My Head / Still Crazy After All These Years / Last One Singin' the Blues

RICHARD CARPENTER

Time (A&M 5117) 1987

Say Yeah! / Who Do You Love? / Something in Your Eyes / When Time Was
All We Had / Time / Calling Your Name Again / In Love Alone / Remind Me
to Tell You / That's What I Believe / I'm Still Not Over You

SINGLES:

Something in Your Eyes / Time

Richard Carpenter:
Pianist, Arranger,
Composer, Conductor (A&M 31454-0703-2) 1997

Prelude / Yesterday Once More / Medley: Sing, Goodbye to Love, Eve, Rainy
Days and Mondays, Look to Your Dreams, Superstar, Someday / I Need to
Be in Love / Sandy / Time / For All We Know / One Love / Bless the Beasts
and Children / Flat Baroque / All Those Years Ago / Top of the World / We've
Only Just Begun / Karen's Theme

SINGLES:

Karen's Theme / Bless the Beasts and Children (promo)

RICHARD CARPENTER TRIO

Battle of the Bands (Custom Fidelity 1533) 1966

Includes: The Girl from Ipanema / Iced Tea

SELECTED TELEVISION
APPEARANCES

This list includes all known appearances by the Carpenters on American television from 1966 through 1983. Since many of the programs were syndicated, occasional discrepancies between air dates exist. Other inconsistencies have been found in past publications (notably the Carpenters Fan Club's Decade publication from 1979), which have not always distinguished between the taping and broadcast dates. Whenever possible, corrections have been made here to reflect the earliest-known air dates.

1966

07/03   *Battle of the Bands!* (Richard Carpenter Trio, KNBC-TV, Los Angeles)

1968

06/22   *Your All-American College Show* (Richard Carpenter Trio)
06/29   *Your All-American College Show* (Richard Carpenter Trio)

1969

09/09   *Your All-American College Show* (Karen Carpenter)
11/23   *Your All-American College Show* (Karen Carpenter)
12/01   *Your All-American College Show* (Carpenters)
12/04   *The Della Reese Show*

1970

01/18   *Lohman & Barkley's Name Droppers*
06/24   *The Virginia Graham Show*
07/20   *The Dating Game*
09/15   *The Don Knotts Show*
09/18   *The Tonight Show*

10/02   *The David Frost Show*
10/18   *The Ed Sullivan Show*
11/08   *The Ed Sullivan Show*
11/13   *The Tonight Show*
11/14   *American Bandstand*

1971

01/24   *Peggy Fleming at Sun Valley*
02/13   *The Andy Williams Show*
02/18   *This Is Your Life*
03/16   *The Grammy Awards*
03/24   *The Johnny Cash Show*
06/30   *The Tonight Show*
07/13   *Make Your Own Kind of Music*
07/20   *Make Your Own Kind of Music*
07/27   *Make Your Own Kind of Music*
07/29   *The Mike Douglas Show*
08/03   *Make Your Own Kind of Music*
08/10   *Make Your Own Kind of Music*
08/18   *The 5th Dimension Traveling Sunshine Show*
08/24   *Make Your Own Kind of Music*
08/31   *Make Your Own Kind of Music*
09/22   *The Carol Burnett Show*
11/05   *The Tonight Show*

1972

01/14   *The Ed Sullivan Show*
01/19   *The Carol Burnett Show*
02/21   *Jerry Visits* (Jerry Dunphy)
03/14   *The Grammy Awards*
04/10   *The Academy Awards*
05/07   *The Special London Bridge Special*
10/05   *The Bob Hope Special*

1973

06/01   *Robert Young with the Young*
11/05   *The Tonight Show*
11/13   *The Bob Hope Special*

1974

03/02 *The Grammy Awards*
08/04 *Evening at Pops*
12/17 *The Perry Como Christmas Show*

1975

02/18 *The American Music Awards*

1976

05/22 *The Midnight Special*
12/08 *The Carpenters' Very First Television Special*

1977

01/27 *The Tonight Show* (Steve Martin, host)
03/02 *The Dorothy Hamill Winter Carnival Special*
12/09 *The Carpenters at Christmas*

1978

02/05 *The ABC Silver Anniversary Celebration*
03/16 *Thank You, Rock and Roll*
05/17 *The Carpenters: Space Encounters*
06/27 *The Tonight Show* (John Davidson, host)
11/19 *Wonderful World of Disney: Mickey's 50*
12/19 *The Carpenters: A Christmas Portrait*

1980

03/13 *20/20*
04/14 *Olivia Newton-John: Hollywood Nights*
05/16 *The Carpenters: Music, Music, Music*

1981

07/11 *America's Top Ten*
10/02 *The Merv Griffin Show*
10/12 *Good Morning America*

1983

01/11 *Entertainment Tonight*

CREDITS

E very effort has been made to identify the sources of publication for the contents of this book and make full acknowledgment of their use. If an error or omission has occurred, it will be corrected in future editions, provided the appropriate notification is submitted in writing to the publisher.

"The Carpenters: They've Only Just Begun" by Dean Gautschy. From *TV Radio Mirror*, August 1971. Reprinted by permission of the author.

"Moondust and Starlight: The *Close to You* Album" by John Tobler. © 2000 John Tobler. Reprinted by permission of the author.

"The Carpenters and the Creeps" by Lester Bangs. From *Rolling Stone* issue dated March 4, 1971. © Rolling Stone LLC 1971. All Rights Reserved. Reprinted by Permission.

"Karen in the Kitchen: Who Says a Young Female Superstar Can't Be a Top-Notch Cook?" A&M Records Press Release, 1971.

"They Put Romance into Rock" by Digby Diehl. From *TV Guide*, August 14, 1971. Reprinted with permission from TV Guide, © 2000 TV Guide Magazine Group, Inc. TV GUIDE is a registered trademark of TV Guide Magazine Group, Inc.

"The Carpenters: Nailing Down Success" by Fiona MacDougall. From *'Teen*, October 1971. Reprinted with permission from 'Teen, © 1971.

Concert Review: Sands, Las Vegas, March 24, 1971. From *Variety*, April 7, 1971. Reprinted by permission of Variety, Inc., © 2012.

"'Superstar': The Carpenters' Surprisingly Dirty Ditty" by Johnny Black. From *Blender*, October 2002. Reprinted by permission of the author.

"Rainy Days and Carpenters Always Get Me Down" by Ken Michaels. From *Chicago Tribune Magazine*, November 21, 1971. Reprinted by permission of the author.

"Why They're on Top?" by Dan Armstrong. From *Southeast News*, a Herald Community Newspaper, December 9, 1971.

Concert Review: Riviera, Las Vegas, September 22, 1972. From *Variety*, October 4, 1972. Reprinted by permission of Variety, Inc., © 2012.

"Karen Carpenter: A Drummer Who Sang" by Rod Fogarty. From *Modern Drummer*, April 2001. © 2001 Modern Drummer Publications, Inc. Used by permission.

"The Choral Sound of the Carpenters" by Frank Pooler. From *The Choral Journal*, April 1973. Reprinted by permission of the author and the American Choral Directors Association.

"It Happens in the Middle of the Road: Confessions of a Carpenters Fan" by John Tobler. Originally printed in 1974. Reprinted by permission of the author.

Concert Review: Sahara, Tahoe, August 24, 1973. From *Variety*, August 29, 1973. Reprinted by permission of Variety, Inc., © 2012.

"The Carpenters: Soft Rock and 14 Gold Records" by Frank H. Lieberman. From *Saturday Evening Post*, October 1974. © SEPS licensed by Curtis Licensing, Indianapolis, IN. All rights reserved.

"*The Carpenters: The Singles 1969–1973*" by Marcello Carlin. From Then Play Long, October 11, 2011. Reprinted by permission of the author.

"The Carpenters: Forbidden Fruit" by Tom Smucker. From *Village Voice*, June 2, 1975. Reprinted by permission of the author.

"Up from Downey" by Tom Nolan. From *Rolling Stone* issue dated July 4, 1974. © Rolling Stone LLC 1974. All Rights Reserved. Reprinted by Permission.

"The Carpenters: An Interview." From A&M Compendium, July 1975. Reprinted by permission of Universal Music Group.

"The Carpenters: An Appraisal" by Tom Nolan. From A&M Compendium, July 1975. Reprinted by permission of Universal Music Group.

Concert Review: Riviera, Las Vegas, August 24, 1975. From *Variety*, September 3, 1975. Reprinted by permission of Variety, Inc. © 2012.

"Like TV Dinner for the Ears" by Dave McQuay. From *Columbia Flier*, August 1975. Reprinted by permission of the David McQuay Estate.

"The Carpenters 'Nail' Neil Sedaka." From *Rona Barrett's Hollywood*, January 1976.

"Carpenters—Good, Clean, All-American Aggro!" by Ray Coleman. From *Melody Maker*, November 8, 1975. © Melody Maker / IPC+ Syndication. Reprinted by permission.

"It's an Overdose of Pretty" by Joel McNally. From *Milwaukee Journal*, 1976. Reprinted by permission of the author.

"Karen Carpenter: Nothing to Hide Behind" by Charlie Tuna. Interview Transcript, 1976. Transcribed by permission of Charlie Tuna.

INDEX